D1241373

PLACE IN RETURN BOX to remove this checkout from your record.
TO AVOID FINES return on or before date due.

DATE DUE	DATE DUE	DATE DUE
MAY 3 1991		

MSU Is An Affirmative Action/Equal Opportunity Institution

ORCHIDS

OF THE

WESTERN GREAT LAKES

REGION

Frontispiece: Pink Lady's-slipper (*Cypripedium acaule*)

ORCHIDS

OF THE
WESTERN GREAT LAKES
REGION

Revised Edition

by

FREDERICK W. CASE JR.

CRANBROOK INSTITUTE OF SCIENCE
BULLETIN 48
1987

Copyright © 1987 Cranbrook Institute of Science

Library of Congress Catalog Card No. 86-70869

ISBN 87737–036–2

BULLETIN 48
Revised Edition

Edited by Christine E. Bartz
Base maps by William Brudon
Line drawings by Ruth Powell Brede and Betty E. Odle
after originals prepared by the author
Composition by Edwards Brothers, Inc.
Color printing by White Pines
Printed and bound by Edwards Brothers, Inc.

To my wife Roberta and son David, with love and much gratitude, and to all our friends and companions with whom we have shared adventures along the orchid trails, I dedicate this book.

PREFACE TO THE FIRST EDITION

THIS BOOK, intended for the amateur field botanist, has been prepared as a field guide, with identification keys, diagrams, descriptions, and ecological notes. Photographs taken in the field illustrate each species; for, whatever their shortcomings, such photographs, showing the plant in its natural setting, have values lost in a studio photograph or a drawing. To differentiate among similar and easily confused species, line drawings of flower parts are used in the keys.

The nomenclature and treatment of species follow those of Donovan S. Correll in *Native Orchids of North America North of Mexico*. In a few instances where my field experience differs from his, I have added my interpretation.

Over the past 20 years I have searched out in the wild all the orchid species native to the Great Lakes region. Except for Michigan stations for *Triphora trianthophora*, *Epipactis helleborine*, and *Spiranthes lucida*, my stations are new ones independently discovered. The search for these orchids has been both exciting and rewarding. Since many species have a wide range, I have observed most of them at various points in the course of botanical field work across America.

Two excellent field books on orchids of our area, now unfortunately out of print, have greatly influenced the style of this book. They are *Our Wild Orchids*, by Frank Morris and Edward A. Eames, and *Orchids of Wisconsin*, by Albert M. Fuller.

Except for the photograph in black and white of *Corallorhiza maculata*, taken by Robert T. Hatt, and the color photograph of *Calypso bulbosa* made in Utah by Warren Stoutamire, all photographs are the work of the author. All were taken at various points in Michigan, except for those of the following species, which were taken at the places specified: *Corallorhiza maculata* var. *flavida*, Duluth, Minnesota, July, 1957; *Malaxis paludosa*, Sibley Peninsula, Ontario, August, 1962; *Orchis rotundifolia*, Anchorage, Alaska, June, 1946; *Tipularia discolor*, near Leavenworth, Indiana, August, 1963; and *Triphora trianthophora*, Turkey Run State Park, Indiana, August, 1963.

Searching for and acquiring the information that led to the

preparation of this book involved many years of field work and botanical study, during the course of which many persons have given me aid. To all those whose help, encouragement, information, and advice have contributed in some manner to this book I express my gratitude.

At Cranbrook Institute of Science I am especially indebted to Robert T. Hatt, Director, for his help and many fine suggestions; to Warren P. Stoutamire, botanist, for his aid, companionship in the field, and critical reading of the manuscript; and to Dale J. Hagenah, Research Associate, for many ideas and for suggesting the scope of this book. Margaret Fletcher and Elizabeth Nissler of the staff gave valuable help with correspondence and the herbarium specimens.

For help in the field and for their scholarly botanical knowledge I am indebted to several persons. Among them are Edward Voss, University of Michigan, who gave me much helpful information from his wealth of knowledge of Great Lakes botany; William S. Benninghoff, who read critically the ecology material and gave me valued suggestions concerning it; Donovan S. Correll, author of *Native Orchids of North America North of Mexico*, to whom I am indebted for his kindness in examining certain questionable *Spiranthes*; the Bernard Hornes and Mrs. C. R. Hanes, who informed me of a Michigan station for *Triphora*, and the late Mr. Hanes, who gave me valuable information on orchid stations in southwestern Lower Michigan; Clayton Bauzin, to whom I am indebted for his wealth of information on orchid distribution, and who aided me in my search for *Spiranthes lucida*; W. H. Wagner, Jr. and Edward Brigham, Jr. who gave me information concerning the occurrence of stations for *Cypripedium* hybrids other than my own; and to Sandy Burnett, then Naturalist at Sibley Provincial Park, Ontario, who gave me aid and field guidance at the Thunder Cape stations for *Malaxis paludosa*.

To the American Orchid Society and the editor of its *Bulletin* I am grateful for permission to use in the section on "Growing Native Orchids" an adaptation of the article on that subject published in the *Bulletin* for June, 1962.

Christine Webb gave me generous help in preparing the manuscript.

To my wife, Roberta Burckhardt Case, I am deeply grateful, not only for help in compiling the distribution maps, but especially for sharing the chores, joys, and satisfactions of the work.

No words can adequately express my gratitude to the many field companions of the 20 years of "bogtrotting" that paved the way to this book. The friendships thus gained and shared were not merely means to an end, but rather my greatest reward. For this comradeship in the field I wish especially to thank George L. Burrows IV, Elizabeth Stearns, the Roy A. Winchells, Herbert Veltman, and O. H. Clark.

F. W. C. Jr.

Saginaw, Michigan
January, 1964

PREFACE TO THE SECOND EDITION

THIS BOOK is intended primarily for the amateur field botanist or naturalist. As with the first edition, this one is generally in the style of a field guide, with identification keys revised and updated to accomodate new discoveries and changes in nomenclature, diagrams where I deemed them useful, descriptions of the plants, distribution information, and ecological notes based primarily on my own field observations and experiences.

Twenty years have passed since the first edition. I have learned much more about the occurrence and cultivation of the species. I have tried to incorporate this information into this book.

Experience in my own education, in the comments of others concerning the first edition of this book, and in teaching courses on native plants and wildflowers to amateur field naturalists over the past 32 years, continues to convince me that for the beginning field student, at least, habit photographs taken in the field have values and convey information which is lost in studio portraits and drawings. I have, therefore, again emphasized field photographs.

In this edition, all photographs are in color. Most of them are my own, although a few, particularly a few close-up photographs of flower detail, are those of the late Erich DeLin of Fort Montgomery, New York. One excellent habit portrait of *Corallorhiza striata* is that of James Wells. If the photograph is not my own, the photographer's name appears with the photograph.

My wife and I have continued to explore the wild and to observe native orchid populations across the entire United States and Canada. We feel strongly that one cannot adequately understand a species from too local an observation. We have made a concerted effort, therefore, to observe our species at as many different points in their continental ranges as we could. Our efforts have taken us to Newfoundland, Alaska, the Rocky Mountains, the Cascade Mountains, the Great Smoky Mountains, the Blue Ridge Mountains, the northern Appalachians, the Gaspé Peninsula, the North American prairies, the eastern coastal plain, and, of course, the entire Great Lakes region. Recently, we had the opportunity to see certain circumboreal species in the wild in Sweden, and to observe several European species, now adventive in Ontario and Michigan, growing natively in Sweden and Switzerland.

In the course of our field work, we have discovered our own stations for every native species of orchid covered in this book.

Our experiences in exploring and bogtrotting for our orchids have been rich and rewarding. I have sought out the native orchids for over 40 years. During this time, the fascination and excitement I feel for this group of plants has not dimmed.

For the beginning orchid hunter, three outstanding books, long out of print, convey more of the excitement and joy of exploration and discovery than any recent volume. Reading them is a must! They are: *Our Wild Orchids*, by Frank Morris and Edward A. Eames; *Orchids of Wisconsin*, by Albert M. Fuller; and *Bogtrotting for Orchids*, by Grace G. Niles. These books were an inspiration and education to me and have greatly influenced both editions of this book.

NOMENCLATURAL CHANGES

In the first edition, I followed Correll's (1950) broad, conservative approach to orchid nomenclature. Recent works on North American orchids by Luer (1975), Catling (various), and others follow Dressler's classification system (1960), sometimes with modifications.

Luer's *The Native Orchids of the United States and Canada Excluding Florida* (1975) is the most recent complete treatment of North American orchids. I have been urged by many botanists and naturalists to follow his nomenclature in this edition and I have done so, except for one or two instances where I disagree with him. To facilitate cross-referencing between this edition and the first, or between this book and Voss's *Michigan Flora*, Part I (1972), the old name appears with the notation "1st ed." below the new one when Luer's usage differs from that of the first edition.

The order of the genera remains the same as in the first edition, with the species listed alphabetically under each genus.

ACKNOWLEDGMENTS

After 40 years of exploring for our native orchids, the number of persons to whom I owe thanks for guidance, companionship in the field, information given, or botanical advice is immense. If, in the following paragraphs, I have omitted thanks to any person, I apologize here and claim only memory failure. No omissions are intended!

For guidance and criticism in preparing this book, I am grateful to T. L. Mellichamp, who read the entire manuscript and gave valued criticism; to A. A. Reznicek who read selected sections and offered sound advice, I am grateful. To John Freudenstein, student and friend, Roberta and I extend our thanks for many suggestions and help with the manuscript, much companionship in the field, and special thanks for checking many references and botanical formalities so necessary to this work and so difficult for us to check in Saginaw where botanical library resources are limited.

My thanks to the Board of Directors of the Michigan Orchid Society for permission to quote or use material from my article, "Notes Concerning Changes in Great Lakes Orchid Populations," and the article by Charles Sheviak, "United States Terrestrial Orchids, — Patterns and Problems," from their *North American Terrestrial Orchids Symposium II: Proceedings and Lectures*, October 1981.

At Cranbrook Institute of Science, I am much indebted to its Director, Dr. Dennis M. Wint, for encouragement and the decision to go ahead with a second edition. To James Wells, Botanist, our special thanks for many kindnesses, for much advice on the production of this book, and for arranging for the herbarium loans and visits.

To Ms. Christine Bartz, Editor, our thanks for her patient and careful work and advice.

Checking the herbarium records for the distribution maps proved to be one of the most time consuming and difficult preparations for this book. The number of orchid specimens in herbaria has greatly increased. It was necessary for us to visit most of the herbaria utilized. At all of them we were treated with utmost courtesy and kindness. To all of their directors and staff members we extend our grateful thanks. We are especially grateful to Hugh Iltis for his hospitality and cooking skills, and to J. Eckenwalder and his herbarium assistant, Deborah Metzger, for arranging access to the University of Toronto Herbarium at a difficult time and for their helpfulness to us.

Charles Sheviak, researching *Platanthera leucophaea* and thus temporarily in possession of all herbarium records for that species necessary to our mapping, kindly checked all of the records and provided us with map information. All map dots new to this edition for *P. leucophaea* are based upon information furnished by him and for which we are grateful.

Claude Garton, curator of the Garton Herbarium, Lakehead University, graciously provided access to that herbarium and gave freely of his time to accompany us in the field.

Richard Pippen, Western Michigan University, graciously guided us to his Michigan discovery of *Spiranthes ovalis*, as did his student Bill Stice.

Kim Chapman exchanged important information with us concerning each other's stations for *P. leucophaea* and spent much time in the field with us.

Joyce Reddoch kindly discussed with me her views on habitat terminology, some of which I incorporated into this volume.

John Van Arsdale shared his information and discovery of *Triphora trianthophora* in northern Lower Michigan with us, as did Coni and Sam Maisano when they discovered *Spiranthes tuberosa* in Midland County, Michigan.

Victor Soukup gave us information of a hybrid *Platanthera* station new to us in southwestern Lower Michigan. The late Ruth Gruitch of Grayling guided us to an unusual station for exceptionally dark-colored *and* white-flowered *Cypripedium acaule*.

Edward G. Voss, through the years, has given much advice and assistance, as well as field companionship.

W. H. Wagner, Jr. has given valued advice both as teacher and friend. He has also given us valued information on plant locations.

Don Henson generously guided us to several of his orchid discoveries in the Upper Peninsula.

Paul Catling shared much information from his research in the genus *Spiranthes*.

William Schwab guided us to his discovery sites for *Isotria medeoloides* and *Tipularia discolor*.

J. Ross Brown kindly guided us to his Ontario station for *Spiranthes ovalis* and shared his observations and data with us.

For field companionship on the orchid trails, Roberta and I thank all of those mentioned in the preface to the first edition and the following persons: George L. Burrows, IV; David and Sharon Case; Kim Chapman; Ruth and Hugh Cocker; Erich and Mary DeLin; Marvin Dembinsky; Harry and Irene Elkins, John and Tom Freudenstein; Karl and Birgitta Flinck; Tom Gibson; Ethelda Hagenah; Dave and Jeff Littell; Sam and Coni Maisano; Max Medley; Larry and Audry Mellichamp; Charles F. and Mary Lee Moore; Skip Mott; Ken and Ann Nitschke; A. A. and Susan Reznicek; William Schwab; Molly O. Smith; Vic and Shirley Soukup; H. S. Veltman; Edward G. Voss; Jim and Jan Wells; and Emerson Whiting.

Without the help, understanding, and enthusiasm of my wife, Roberta B. Case, neither edition of this book could ever have been completed. She helped and shared in the burdens of the entire work; field studies, much of the painstaking detailed record keeping for the distribution maps, helping to check and record information, and as thoughtful critic and listener as the book was put together. For her assistance, forbearance, and companionship there are no adequate words of thanks. The adventures of the past 32 years will have to serve.

F. W. C. Jr.

Saginaw, Michigan
March 1985

CONTENTS

THE ORCHID FAMILY

F EW PLANTS have so fascinated man as have the orchids, though others have been more important to him for their economic use or some specific quality. What accounts for this fascination? One of the largest of all flowering plant families, orchids are surpassed in numbers only by the Asteraceae, the daisy family. But neither their numbers nor wide ranges are responsible for the interest evoked by orchids. Rather, it is their extreme variation in flower shape, color, size, and adaptation. Moreover, tropical orchids became the darlings of the greenhouses of wealthy Europeans and a veritable status symbol in the nineteenth century—a reputation sustained to the present day. Finally, the rarity of some species, the exciting nature of the bogs and deep forests many inhabit, and their sporadic occurrence all lend a charm and interest no other plants can equal.

Orchids are Anthophytes, Monocotyledons

Orchids belong to the division of seed plants, Anthophyta (the flowering plants). Within this division occur two classes, Monocotyledones (monocots) and Dicotyledones (dicots) (Raven et al. 1981). These two classes differ in the arrangement of their internal structure, in the number of floral parts, and in the number of seed leaves possessed by the embryo. Orchids are monocotyledons.

Botanists recognize orchids as the most highly evolved family of monocotyledons. Some 10,000 to 15,000 species in many genera comprise the family. Nevertheless, a basic flower plan appears in all orchids. To understand better the structure of the orchid flower, it may be compared with that of the lily, a more familiar flower. (See Fig. 1)

In the lily, the flower, borne at the end of a specialized branch, the peduncle, consists of several whorls or circles of specialized organs inserted upon the relatively enlarged end of the peduncle, the receptacle. The outer whorl of organs consists of three sepal's, which in color and texture resemble the petals. The next inner whorl is of three petals. These organs together are commonly called the floral envelope.

Inside the floral envelope are two whorls of three male structures, the pollen-bearing stamens, so arranged that they appear

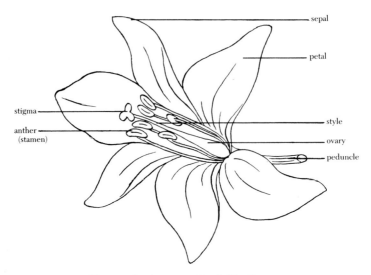

FIGURE 1. A generalized lily flower

as·a single circle of six. In the center of the flower stands a three-chambered (or modified three-chambered) female structure, the pistil. This organ consists of a seed chamber or ovary, an elongated stalk or style above it, and at the apex a three-part structure, the pollen-receiving stigma. The floral segments are essentially free and separate, except for the chambers of the ovary. From this basic plan the amaryllis, iris, and orchid families are derived essentially by the reduction or fusion of parts.

Structure of the Orchid Flower

Keeping the basic lily flower in mind, let us compare it with an orchid blossom. In all orchids the floral parts are attached to and extend beyond the ovary (an inferior ovary), and the reproductive organs are reduced in numbers and fused into a common central organ, the column. As in the lily, orchids have three sepals and three petals. Unlike the lily, these flower parts are dissimilar in shape and function. (Fig. 2)

An outstanding feature of all orchid blossoms is the modification of one petal. This structure, called the labellum or lip, nearly always differs in size, shape, or color from the other two petals, and often becomes the most conspicuous feature of the flower. Technically uppermost in the flower, the labellum typically becomes lowermost by a twisting of the ovary or pedicel. This change in position usually takes place before the flower opens. The labellum serves as a landing platform for insects.

Specialization of the orchid flower has proceeded along two distinct lines. In one group, the cypripediums, the labellum is pouch- or slipper-shaped, the two lateral sepals are variously fused (except in *C. arietinum*), and the dorsal sepal is usually quite large. The column consists of three fused anthers, the upper one sterile and forming a shieldlike structure called the staminode. Three stigmas are present, and the pollen is free and granular. Lack of complete reduction of parts in the cypripediums leads botanists to regard the group as primitive. Some even argue that the lady's-slippers may actually comprise a separate family.

In all orchids outside the cypripedium alliance, the sepals are free or fused only at their bases, the lip is variously shaped, and there is but one fertile anther. The stigmatic surface is made up of two of the three stigmas. The third stigma, which is sterile, has developed into a sticky structure, the rostellum. The rostellum serves to glue the pollen to insects to aid in its transportation to another flower. The pollen, formed into masses called pollinia, may be connected to the rostellum by threads and travel

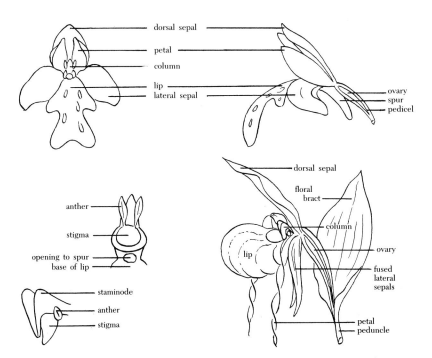

FIGURE 2. A typical amerorchis (above) and a typical cypripedium flower (below), showing the variations in structure in the two main lines of orchid flower development

with it, or there may be various mechanisms which eject the pollen masses and rostellum glue onto an insect. Beyond these basic flower features almost endless variation exists. Botanists do not agree as to the actual relationships of the genera in the orchid family.[1]

The Evolution of Orchid Species and Their Pollination

The evolution of orchid species has paralleled the evolution of certain insects which pollinate them. Nearly all species of orchids have developed complex floral structures which encourage insect cross-pollination, and depend upon specific species of insects to effect pollination. These insects, in turn, have evolved structurally to increase their efficiency in obtaining food from the flower. Some surprising examples of interdependence have developed.

The exacting nature of pollination in orchids, one of the outstanding features of the family, is truly remarkable. Insects are lured to the bloom by sweet, sour, or fetid odors. In most orchid species the lip, lowermost in position, serves as a landing platform. Since many day-flying insects will not enter dark places, many orchids depending on diurnal species of insects for pollination have patches of light color deep in the lip, creating the optical illusion of brightness. Often guidelines of color or fleshy ridges guide the insect in definite directions or into exact positions. Following these guidelines and the lure of the flower's scent, the insect enters the heart of the blossom. Its path takes it along the undersurface of the column. It is noteworthy that the pollen is not dislodged by any pressure of the insect's body while it enters the flower. When it reaches the nectar, the insect feeds.

When the insect backs out of the flower, its back passes against the sticky surface of the stigma or against a comblike projection of the tissue surrounding the stigma. Pollen, if present on the insect, adheres to the stigmatic surface or is scraped from its back onto the stigma. When the insect withdraws further, any outward pressure upon the rostellum causes that sticky structure to adhere firmly to the insect's back in the proper position to contact the stigma of the next blossom visited. A few orchids, such as the tropical genera *Mormodes* and *Catasetum*, actually

[1]The technical considerations of morphology and developmental anatomy, the bases of classification, do not fall within the scope of this book. An excellent starting point for the reader who wishes to pursue such studies are papers by Leslie A. Garay (1960), *On the Origin of the Orchidaceae*, published by the Botanical Museum of Harvard University; or by R. L. Dressler and C. H. Dodson (1960), *Classification and Phylogeny in the Orchidaceae*, published in the Annals of the Missouri Botanical Gardens no. 47, or by L. A. Garay (1972), *On the Origin of the Orchidaceae, II*, published in the Journal of the Arnold Arboretum vol. 53.

shoot the pollen masses and the rostellum to the insect target with some force.

So precise are the devices for pollination in the orchids that the element of chance scarcely exists.[2] But despite the tremendous role played by insects in the pollination of most orchids, some species, including a number of *Platanthera* and *Corallorhiza* species of the Great Lakes region, appear to be self-pollinating, the pollen germinating in place. It is not known whether such species are always self-fertilizing, or whether occasional cross-pollination occurs.

Orchids, like other plants, expend only as much energy during flowering as is necessary to accomplish reproduction. Few orchids, even those with strong fragrance, produce fragrance at all times. If the species depends upon a dusk-flying moth for pollination, the flower produces fragrance only at dusk. If the pollinator flies at midday, the fragrance is produced at that time.

If not pollinated, many orchid blossoms last for long periods of time. However, once pollination occurs, most plants waste no energy maintaining needless cells. The presence of hormones from the pollen on the stigma causes the blossom segments to collapse within hours. Thus, in some lady's-slippers, the dorsal sepal drops soon after pollination, sealing off access to the pouch through which insects must pass to reach the nectar.

The Practical Uses and the Legend of the Orchids

Orchids grow in most climates where flowering plants can exist, yet this vast, nearly worldwide family contains only a few species which furnish food or medicine to man. Some pseudo-bulbous tropical types yield a sweet, candylike confection to the natives of Central America, and some cypripediums yield a nerve drug of some value. However, only *Vanilla* produces a product of major use. The fermented pods of this climbing tropical vine yield crystals of vanillin, a most popular flavoring.

Despite such limited use as food or medicine, orchids are known to nearly everyone, primarily for their bizarre or lovely flowers. Whether as cut flowers or as plants for the hobbyist grower, the raising of tropical orchids is today a multi-million-dollar business.

The almost sacred popular regard for orchids began in England in the nineteenth century. Long a land of avid gardeners, the English constantly searched for new and spectacular plants. As tropical lands were developed, the orchids of these lands were

[2]Charles Darwin (1862) was so fascinated by the subject of orchids and insect pollination that he wrote one of the classical works of orchid literature on the subject. Dodson (1961) has worked out studies of the elaborate companion evolution of certain tropical orchids and the insects that pollinate them.

shipped back to England. Poor shipping conditions, slow freight, and inadequate care en route severely limited successful orchid importation. The blooming of those few that survived created a sensation. Since orchids could not then be reliably grown from seed, vigorous competition for the existing plants kept the demand high. Wealthy rival gardeners forced prices to fantastic heights at plant auctions, thus spreading the fame of orchids as a luxury of the nobility. Albino forms and other unusual types sold for the equivalent of thousands of dollars. High market values led plant importers to send out more and more collectors. Some collectors purposely misidentified areas to safeguard their prized stations. The resulting confusion gave rise to stories of "lost orchids." Some collectors died at the hands of competitors. Thus began the orchid legend.

The ability of many orchids to interbreed across species and even generic lines has resulted in the creation of many new and spectacular flowers. These flowers often display bizarre or lovely color patterns, and the plants frequently possess the ability to grow in climates where their progenitors could not survive. These hybrids have created much hobbyist interest as well as commercial demand.

Many of our native terrestrial orchids are small and relatively inconspicuous plants. However, the fact that they *are* orchids and frequently grow in bogs, deep forests, and other interesting habitats, creates much appeal. The fact that known colonies of many are rare, widely separate, and very difficult to locate produces in many naturalists, amateur and professional alike, a desire to find and photograph orchids out of all proportion to the interest in other native wildflowers. The modern, man-created orchid hybrids, and the widespread interest in seeking out and conserving our rare native species continues the lure of the orchid today.

ORCHID ECOLOGY

Sᴏᴍᴇ ᴏꜰ the complex requirements and narrow tolerances that restrict the occurrence of orchids within a given region are considered in this section.

Seed Germination and Development

As mature plants most orchids bear chlorophyll and carry out photosynthesis, and so are classed as independent organisms. A few orchids live as saprophytes, deriving their nourishment almost entirely from organic matter in the soil through an association with fungi. Some, such as *Triphora*, appear to be intermediate. That is, plants from a given colony may have well developed green leaves one year, but in another season may have only tiny, bractlike leaves nearly devoid of green color. Whether dependent or independent, nearly all wild orchids live in association with a soil fungus.

Orchid seeds, so dustlike as to be nearly microscopic, are produced in very large numbers. The actual number within one capsule varies with both the species and the vigor of the individual plant. Estimates of as many as a million seeds per pod have been made for some orchids (Withner 1959). The tiny seeds, usually waterproof at the time of distribution, are carried by air or water.

Orchid seeds lack the differentiation into embryo, endosperm (stored food tissue), and protective seed coat of most flowering plant seeds. Instead, an orchid seed consists of an outer, lacy, netlike testa and an inner, morphologically undifferentiated mass of cells. Lacking a well-formed embryo, the seed must reach an environment where suitable conditions make germination possible. After initial germination and growth, it must organize a plant body. Having no special food supply within itself, the germinated seed must then obtain food before much development can take place.

In nature, epiphytic tropical orchids depend upon a symbiotic association of the seed with a fungus for germination and development. As outlined by Knudsen (1925) and others, fungi of certain genera invade and digest the seed coat and outer cell layers of the embryo. Digestion of these outer cells produces sugars which the inner cells utilize to grow and develop. If the fungus does not engulf and destroy the seed, the undifferentiated cells then form a mass of tissue, the protocorm, which develops green

7

coloring, manufactures food, and begins the process of development into the orchid plant. The associated fungus remains throughout the life of the orchid as an invader within the roots, an arrangement generally regarded as symbiotic and beneficial to both organisms. However, many epiphytic orchids can be germinated asymbiotically with sugars and other nutrients in a suitably sterile situation.

In terrestrial orchids, the situation is not as clearly understood. As mature plants, nearly all live in symbiosis with soil fungi of the class Phycomycetes, the majority with those of the genus *Rhizoctonia* (Burgeff, in Withner 1959), although Sheviak (1983), suggests that many soil fungi may be involved. The association is mainly through the roots. The term "mycorrhiza" is applied to the combined orchid plant-fungus structure. In most species the association of fungus and orchid is believed to start at germination, and to continue throughout the life of the orchid plant. However, for many species it has not been demonstrated that the fungus that initiates germination is the one that remains associated with the plant when it matures. Nor has it been shown conclusively that a specific fungus is required by a specific orchid for germination or growth (Burgeff, in Withner 1959; Curtis 1937, 1939; Downie 1940). Sheviak (*op.cit.*) states that many orchids, especially northern terrestrial ones, establish mycorrhizae with "any number of fungi." Those involved include "ubiquitous soil aerobes, and facultative pathogens" and some "important crop pests."

According to Burgeff (*op.cit.*), two mycorrhizal conditions occur in orchids, namely, tolypophagy and ptyophagy. In tolypophagy the fungus mycelium (fungus body) invades the cells of the roots and rhizomes of the orchid, where the invaded cells deactivate and at least partially digest the mycelium, deriving nourishment from the process. In ptyophagy special hyphae of the fungus penetrate root cells, where "fungal plasma is injected into the absorbing cells."

Burgeff reports the occurrence of both conditions in European terrestrial species. That the fungus-orchid relationship is beneficial to the orchid, rather than one of the orchid host's being attacked by the fungus, is shown by the occurrence of occasional chlorophyll-lacking, flowering individuals among normally photosynthetic plants.[1] Were it not for nutrients supplied by the fungus, such individual plants could not exist. The benefit to the orchid of the fungus associate is also shown under experimental conditions, when normally photosynthetic orchids can be grown

[1]We have observed such chlorophyll-free albinos in the introduced European orchid *Epipactis helleborine* in Michigan and Canada.

with nutrients in darkness for long periods of time, provided the mycorrhizal relationship is established (Burgeff, *op. cit.*). Little is reported regarding the conditions present in American species, but it would be surprising if several different types of fungus-orchid-soil relationships had not evolved in our flora, which has so many species with widely differing habitat requirements. Some of our orchids are regularly saprophytic when immature. They spend several years in a dependent, subterranean condition before sufficient growth occurs and stored food accrues for the production of leaves. Then, for the first time, the plant appears above ground. Growth is then rapid, and within a season or two flowering commences (Curtis 1943).[2] Some of our native orchids, namely, *Calopogon, Pogonia, Spiranthes,* (*fide* Stoutamire), develop chlorophyll in the earliest protocorm stages in experimental cultures and may do so in the wild as well. Permanently saprophytic orchids, such as our coral-roots, do not appear above ground until their first flowering.

It should be clearly stated that no one has yet, under controlled conditions, consistently grown our native American terrestrial orchids from seed to flowering.[3] Researchers report some germination of certain species, especially those such as *Calopogon* or *Spiranthes* which tend to be rapid colonizers in the wild. Some workers accept the swelling of the protocorm and the bursting of the seed coat as proof of germination, but carry the experiment no farther. Withner worked with immature *Cypripedium acaule* seed, which produced protocorms and leaves, but he reports nothing of their development beyond that stage. Roberta Case can germinate *C. acaule* using green seed, and can maintain the plants in asymbiotic flask culture until the plants produce good rhizomes, roots, and green leaves. However, we have failed to transfer these several year old seedlings to a natural environment. Several persons have grown seeds of *Calopogon*

[2]I have found large numbers of developing plants of *Platanthera ciliaris* and *Platanthera blephariglottis* in sphagnum bogs in Van Buren, Allegan, and Montmorency counties, Michigan. Only seedlings with tubers 1–2 cm long or longer produce photosynthetic leaves that appear above ground. Smaller seedlings appear as tiny, white, spindle-shaped tissue masses, the larger ones with a leaf or stem bud differentiated at one end. The seedlings appear in all size gradations and occur mostly in the brown, dead sphagnum below the living moss layers. Each year I find full-sized rhizomes of *Epipactis helleborine* in my flower beds where no leaves have ever appeared previously. Large flowering plants also appear on my mowed lawns where no plant was ever allowed to develop. Such plants have obviously developed underground, saprophytically or symbiotically, until producing the normal, mature, flowering green plant.

[3]In the 20 years since the first edition of this publication, many workers have attacked the problem, but the situation remains relatively unchanged.

tuberosus to the green, leaf-producing stage on agar and nutrients. In Germany, Burgeff grew a number of European species to flowering by various methods, mostly involving symbiotic culture. Vermeulen has done the same in Holland. Developmental data on our terrestrial orchids have been obtained mainly from these few experiments; by inference from incomplete studies; or by examination of developing seedlings found in soil near parent stock.

Estimates on the length of time necessary for development of native species from seed to flowering vary considerably. Morris and Eames (1929) report the appearance of blooming *Spiranthes* on "filled in" soils in the third season following the filling. Curtis (1943) worked out an approximate time scale for growth and development of some *Cypripedium* species of Wisconsin, determining that length of time till first flowering there varies between eight and sixteen years. Summerhayes (1951) reports preflowering development of seven to fourteen years for various British orchids. Some of these same species grow in our region.

So long a period of development is undoubtedly true under certain conditions. However, field observations of numerous orchid population build-ups in ditches, in borrow pits, and on developing bog mats convince me that, under ideal conditions, at least some species attain flowering in a much shorter time.[4]

Summerhayes (*op. cit.*) asserts that in an unfavorable environment many orchids can revert to a saprophytic state, remaining entirely underground for many years, and reappearing when conditions again are favorable. I have seen no evidence to indicate such a history for our species, although various authors report a long dormant period for *Isotria verticillata* or *I. medeoloides*.

I am inclined to ascribe to recent changes in environment the reappearance of an orchid at a spot where it had disappeared. These changes might, in effect, push back habitat conditions to a stage more favorable to the species which then reseeds into the area. Such an explanation seems more reasonable than to assume that the same individual plants persisted underground for so many years. There is virtually *no documented evidence* that normally photosynthetic, mature native orchids ever *revert* to a dependent, underground state, and certainly none for plants under cultivation, even under very unfavorable growing conditions.[5]

[4]I have raised *Goodyera pubescens* from seed to flowering in just under three years from the time I scattered fresh seed in a marked, suitable soil. Seedlings of *Spiranthes lucida* bloomed in a pot of *Sarracenia* in my greenhouse in the second season after flowering plants discharged seeds there.

[5]Our native orchids, like many trilliums, lilies, and many other Monocotyledones from temperate and northern climates, develop their yearly growth from buds on an underground rhizome or corm. These buds require a dormant period

Soil and Habitat Relationships

Like other living organisms, orchid species have through time become adapted to specific environmental conditions. Each species has developed definite requirements and tolerances for soil acidity, texture, moisture, available minerals, oxygen content, and temperature. A species occurs within its geographic range only where these requirements are met. A few of our orchid species are restricted to one type of habitat. However, most species occur in several types. In general, orchids, like most plants, show greater tolerance for varied habitats in the heart of their geographic range, but become more selective and exacting near the periphery.

The factors that determine an orchid's presence in a given habitat may not be manifest. Seeing an orchid growing in a bog, one is likely to conclude that the plant requires a very wet soil. Some species may require such conditions, but for many species that inhabit bogs other factors may be equally important. Most so-called bog orchids actually grow as well in other situations. Often it is not the water, but rather a condition indicated by the high acidity of the bog soil, which satisfies the orchid's requirements. Such species occur not only in bogs, but also in dry, sterile sands of old fields, on dunes, or even on rock ledges, if these situations supply the necessary acidic condition.

Surprisingly, some species may occur in both strongly acid bogs and strongly basic bogs, but do not occur under conditions of neutral or midrange pH. This seems paradoxical at first, but Sheviak (1983, *op. cit.*) reports that certain soil components, particularly the metals phosphorous, boron, copper, and zinc, may, for a variety of complicated chemical reasons, become more available to plants and soil fungi in the circumneutral ranges. The absence of many orchid species on circumneutral soils (other requirements being met) may be due to the inhibition of orchid growth or seed germination at that pH by these metallic elements acting as toxins. These metallic elements may also inhibit

---

with suitably cold temperatures before they initiate new growth. Most native orchids develop only one bud or a very few buds from a number of dormant buds each year. Once a bud or group of buds commences growth, the other buds revert to a dormant condition and cannot develop until another period of cold has occurred. Once an orchid plant has attained photosynthetic maturity, the absence of above ground growth for a season is almost certainly due to damage to the season's growth from frost, grazing, trampling, or insects, rather than to a "reversion to a saprophytic, underground state." Although some authors aver that such reversions occur, I am not aware of any studies which demonstrate conclusively that our native orchids behave in this manner, except for the reasons of bud damage I have described above.

the growth of the mycorrhizal fungus or may render the symbiont pathogenic.[6] Different elements may affect the orchid or its mycorrhizal fungus associate in different ways. Thus it may be *the balance* between those elements present and certain other environmental factors such as soil pH, organic matter present, aeration of the soil, soil temperature, and rate of drainage working in concert which determines whether a particular orchid species can grow or germinate in a given soil.[7]

Uniformity of soil temperature, at least during the growing season, may be a factor. In seed germination experiments, Case and Stoutamire found rather limited temperature fluctuations at a six-inch soil depth near orchid roots during the spring to late fall season.

Soil temperatures both during the growing season and during the dormant season appear to be critical to the growth and distribution of our terrestrial orchids. Species primarily confined to the transcontinental boreal forest regions (*Listera cordata, Corallorhiza trifida, Calypso bulbosa, Platanthera obtusata*) grow almost exclusively in heavily wooded, cold, mossy, coniferous bogs at the south of their ranges, but occur as well in open upland forests, clearings, or even on exposed sunny ridges and in meadows farther north. Species which grow ubiquitously in wet or dry acidic habitats in the South (*Platanthera blephariglottis, P. ciliaris, P. clavellata, Calopogon tuberosus*), occur only in wet sands or, more frequently, in sphagnous bogs in the North. Yet, in parts of the Great Lakes region, these northern and southern orchids grow together in the same bog. It is clear that none of these species is confined to a single set of environmental conditions, but still it is surprising to find northern and southern species sharing the same habitat.

To understand this phenomenon, one must look at the conditions present in the bog itself. The bogs develop either on springy hillsides and stream headwaters or in a peat-filled lake basin. In either case, cool ground water percolates slowly through the soil. During the summer, the surface coating of live mosses

[6]It is well known that cultivation of orchids, sarracenias, and some other bog plants in metal containers, or the use of mineral fertilizers on cultivated wild orchids often proves fatal.

[7]Many gardeners, unaware of these complexities, have brought orchids from wild habitats to home garden soils only to see them quickly succumb, or at best subsist on stored food until the following spring, when they appear, bloom, wither, and die. The typical garden soil is fairly heavy loam, rich in nutrients or added fertilizers, and has a circumneutral pH. The behavior of the plants is exactly what one would expect. The very minerals which enhance garden fertility are those suspected of inhibiting or poisoning orchid growth, or of turning its fungal associates into facultative pathogens which consume the orchid partner.

acts as a wick to draw some of the water to the surface where it evaporates. The evaporation further cools the soil and acts to keep the summer temperatures at the orchid's roots below that of surrounding drier sites. During the winter, when nearby upland soils may freeze deeply, the slowly moving ground water of the bog, coupled with heat from bacterial decay of the peat and the insulating effect of snow cover moderates bog soil temperatures. Observations by Stoutamire (pers. comm.) and Case and Case (unpublished) on some northern Lower Michigan bogs showed that bog soil temperatures a few inches below the surface seldom dropped far below freezing.

In short, it appears that some of the bogs in the Great Lakes region meet the the soil and competition requirements of both southern and northern orchids. These bogs have soil temperatures low enough to fall within the tolerances of the northern species in summer, and maintain soil temperatures high enough in winter to support the hardier southern species.

In nearby upland habitats, the southern species might not survive the more deeply frozen soils while the northern species might succumb to the heat of the soil in summer. Hence, for different reasons, these species could not coexist in these habitats.

It is also possible for two orchid species of very different soil requirements to grow in proximity to each other. Fuller (1933a), Wherry (in Correll 1950), and others have pointed out that in many situations, and especially in bogs and deep, cool forests, different soil horizons at a given spot may display very different chemical characteristics. Surface layers may be mainly accumulations of peat or humus, strongly acid if wetness limits oxidation. Drier peats may decay more quickly, producing less acid conditions. A few inches below the peat layers organic matter may give way to mineral soil, the content and chemistry of which differ greatly from those of the layers above. Thus the orchid species rooting in surface layers may live in a far different situation from a deeply rooted species a few feet away.

Some orchids grow almost exclusively in close association with stands of certain other plants. *Triphora trianthophora*, for instance, is usually reported growing in beech leaf mold or in mixed beech-white oak stands. Generally, however, it is not the meeting of one exact condition or the presence of one or two dominant plants which determines the appearance of the orchid, but rather the existence there of an ensemble of favorable environmental factors.

Despite the intricate ecological relationships of orchids, each species is a part of a community of plant and animal species. Needing or tolerating the same basic conditions, such a community occurs where these suitable environmental conditions prevail. Thus whole groups of orchid species typically grow in black spruce-tamarack bogs, others in beech-sugar maple or mixed deciduous forests. Some associate with white cedar-balsam fir cover, while others colonize moist meadows or wet prairies.

The presence of certain species in a plant community often indicates conditions favorable to the presence of other, less common species. Ecologists long ago recognized the value of using these "indicator species" and "indicator habitats" in hunting rare plants. The searcher for orchids should learn to recognize these typical orchid indicators. Reliable indicator habitats are listed in Table 1, together with names of orchid species likely to be encountered in such habitats. The species accounts also give the names of reliable indicator plants.

Conditions Which May Affect Wild Orchid Populations

It is commonly reported that known colonies of orchids persist for a period of years, and then dwindle or disappear. Much has been written about this phenomenon in conservation literature. Such plant disappearances are generally ascribed to man's depredations. It is true, of course, that excessive collecting, pasturing, draining, burning, destructive erosion, construction, and other human activities alter existing conditions, often sufficiently to make life impossible for existing plants and animals. These activities have, at times, depleted orchid populations worldwide. But, natural phenomena and mild disturbances by man and animals can also affect native plants in various ways. In this section I consider *some* of the conditions and events which can influence our native orchid populations.

Disturbance of the Habitat

Any disturbance of a habitat is soon reflected in a change in the balance between the species present. If the disturbance, whatever its cause, is sufficient, nearly all existing plants including orchids may perish because they cannot cope with the changed conditions. In such a situation, a new assemblage of species, better adapted to the new habitat, appears and becomes established. Except for massive disturbances caused by great natural catastrophes or man and his machinery, most disturbances do not destroy *all* existing vegetation, but merely alter it.

We are accustomed to hear of specific orchid populations which have disappeared through the destruction of their habitat. However, it is seldom noted that the disturbance which destroys one orchid species may enable another species to thrive or a new species to colonize the area. The effect of habitat disturbance on the orchids present depends upon the nature of the disturbance, the type of habitat, and the species of orchids present. Some of the types of disturbance which *can* affect native orchid populations are considered in the following sections.

Disturbance by Animal Actions

The pasturing of wet meadows, if intensive, can be very destructive to cypripediums and certain platantheras. However, such pasturing may also reduce herb competition and favor the development of extensive colonies of *Spiranthes* species. Indeed, *Spiranthes lucida*, the shining ladies'-tresses, seems to occur in central Michigan largely upon intensively pastured sites. In Gratiot and Montcalm counties, I have found several colonies of *S. lucida*. The plants grow in areas where the boggy turf has been rather severly broken up by cattle hooves and where cattle have closely cropped the surrounding vegetation. In one such area under observation, the owners fenced a part of the pasture and excluded the domestic animals from it. Here, tall sedges and willows grew and *S. lucida* soon disappeared. Within the active pasture the orchid continued to bloom for many years. The tall leafy green bog-orchid (*Platanthera hyperborea*) was absent within the pasture, but grew in the unpastured area.

It is not possible to make broad generalizations about the effects of pasturing on orchid populations. Mild pasturing may permit the increase or maintenance of cypripediums by admitting more sunlight and by reducing competition with other plants. In one lumbered northern Michigan cedar bog-pasture, the owners have carefully developed and maintained a large colony of showy lady's-slippers by regulating pasturing to control competition from shrubs and young trees. The owners have used this method to increase the cypripedium population over two human generations!

Similarly, certain platantheras seem to tolerate pasturing (unlike *P. hyperborea* which commonly shuns pasturing) and survive and even increase in numbers. On a riverbank near Saginaw, a local man pastures horses intensively. The grasses are cropped as short as if they were cut by a lawn mower. Yet, for over 20 years, several plants of the very rare eastern prairie fringed-orchid, *Platanthera leucophaea*, have persisted and bloomed each year.

Overpasturing by wild animals also has its effect upon orchid populations, as was clearly shown by the behavior of a colony of the showy lady's-slipper in Montmorency County, Michigan, between the years 1946 and 1961. The plants grew in an extensive balsam fir-cedar bog. At the outset of observation, deer had overbrowsed the cedar for several years, creating a condition of open, lightly shaded or sunny glades. In these openings, well over 2,000 showy lady's-slippers grew luxuriantly, with most plants producing two or even three flowers per stem. In the years 1950 to 1953, the number of deer greatly exceeded the carrying capacity of the land, and the herd decreased sharply through starvation. At the same time further reduction of the herd was accomplished in the general area with special hunting regulations. With fewer deer, many balsam fir and cedar seedlings appeared in the glades of the bog. By 1957 the former glades were well shaded. The *Cypripedium reginae* plants became weak and spindly, and many ceased to flower; those that did flower had only a single bloom per stalk. By 1960 most of the original plants had disappeared or were so small as to appear like seedlings. In the winter of 1959–1960 a small section of the area was lumbered for cedar posts, thus improving light conditions. By 1962 a few plants in this section of the swamp had started to bloom again. The late Professor Warren Waterman felt that the relationship between the showy lady's-slipper and deer populations was a vital one, favorable to the orchid. His observations and conclusions are discussed under the species treatment.

Liparis lilifolia, the lily-leaved twayblade, typically occurs as scattered plants in a variety of woodland and brushy habitats across its extensive range. Occasionally, unusually large populations occur. In Michigan, where the plant had not been reported between the early 1900's and the 1960's, observers discovered several colonies numbering hundreds or even thousands of plants. Each of these enormous colonies developed in man-made plantations of Norway spruce (*Picea abies*) or Scots pine (*Pinus sylvestris*). A colony in the Saginaw Forest of the University of Michigan had thousands of plants when I first visited it. Several years later only a few plants could be located. No evidence was found to explain the plant's demise at this location.

In a brushy, aspen-red maple thicket on my property, I found some scattered plants and a few robust clumps of this twayblade. In the years since its discovery, the plants have persisted with occasional "seedlings" developing in new locations, although I have never seen seed pods set on these plants. Most of the larger plants of this species produce offset corms and develop into small clumps. These clumps were carefully marked. Often a marked clump disappeared over the winter, leaving only a few tiny offsets. Upon examination it was found that the larger corms (which sit above the ground) had been gnawed away by mice. This pattern has been repeated over several winters.

Liparis loeselii also grows on my property. Like its cogenitor, *L. lilifolia*, the plant apparently suffers from the depredations of mice which eat the tiny, succulent, vanilla-scented corms. It is not unusual to find the gnawed-off remains of the overwintering corms beside the persistent remains of the previous season's seed stalk.

Effects of Human Disturbance

Massive and rapid change in the environment, wrought by nature or by human activity, obviously destroys vast amounts of wildlife including orchids. The effects of less severe disturbances depend upon the nature of these changes. Such disturbances are not necessarily destructive to all orchids.

Road construction, sand excavation, and similar activities may actually create orchid habitat. An early raw-soil or wet-shore condition is the preferred habitat for many species. Ditch cleaning, road building or grading, draining or flooding—any activity which creates wet, exposed, sparsely vegetated, sandy soils—can create new orchid habitat. Very large populations of orchids sometimes develop in such areas. Highway rights-of-way and recently cleaned ditches in suitable soils become lined with ladies'-tresses. These orchids grow abundantly along freeways in central and northern Michigan and in adjacent borrow pits. In Tuscola, Midland, and Saginaw counties, Michigan, Loesel's twayblade abounds in the damp sands at the bottom of core-sand excavations. Many orchid species line the banks of roadside ditches along U.S. 2 west of St. Ignace, Michigan. Often the plants are more common in the ditches than on the surrounding, less disturbed, land. The yellow lady's-slipper is found by the hundreds on lightly graded roadsides in the limestone areas near northern Lakes Huron and Michigan.

In June 1983, A. A. Reznicek took us to a Canadian station for *Spiranthes lucida*. The natural area, a limey, cobbly, interdunal swamp, had grown up considerably and no flowering *S. lucida* could be found. While searching roadside ditches slightly inland in hopes of locating a few *S. lucida* to photograph, we came upon a homesite where the resident had recently filled a swampy, limestone-cobble lot with a few inches of yellow sand. The site was still rather damp and raw; grass growth was poor. In this highly disturbed, rather artificial, habitat grew literally thousands of shining ladies'-tresses, far more than I have ever seen in a "natural" habitat.

A similar situation developed some years earlier on a lake shore lot in Allegan County, Michigan. The owner, desiring to raise his land a bit higher above lake level, filled the swampy shoreline with sand. As in the Canadian illustration, the damp sand soon supported hundreds of shining ladies'-tresses. As more vigorous grass cover developed the orchids dwindled and eventually disappeared completely.

Human influence upon native orchid populations is not re-

17

stricted to highway construction or land filling. Other human activities can also affect these plants. In 1949 an opening for a high tension power-line was cut through a bog forest in Montmorency County, Michigan. The area had been populated with what appeared to be young seedlings of the showy lady's-slipper (*Cypripedium reginae*). After two years nearly all the plants in the power-line cut were blooming, while those in the heavily shaded areas remained in their "seedling" state. The plants in this power-line cut remained vigorous and abundant until the advent of herbicides. A massive spraying in 1965 destroyed almost all vegetation, even mosses, within the power-line right-of-way.

In Roscommon County, Michigan, a similar power-line cut favored a vigorous increase of *Cypripedium reginae* and *C. calceolus*, but a large colony of small round-leafed orchis (*Amerorchis rotundifolia*) disappeared before the end of the first season. In the following years, no plants appeared in the power-line cut, although the orchid grew nearby in undisturbed wooded sections of the bog until the forest cover was destroyed by spruce budworm.

I am aware of two instances where habitats containing *Amerorchis rotundifolia* were lumbered and opened up. In both instances this rare orchid immediately disappeared from the exposed areas. Similarly, when two wooded areas harboring calypso were cut, the plants disappeared from the open areas immediately. In each of these instances, both species failed to reappear in the lumbered areas of the bog, even after 10–20 years. Both of these species are of primarily far northern distribution and in the instances mentioned occurred at the southern edge of their range. I suspect that forest shading was necessary to keep soil temperatures within the species' range of tolerance, since both species grow in fully exposed, sunny sites much farther north.

A different effect of timber cutting can be reported for the common whorled pogonia (*Isotria verticillata*) in Saginaw County, Michigan. Three colonies of this *Isotria* grow in a state-owned woodlot of oak and red maple. Plants were not uniformly present throughout the 60-acre woodlot. Rather, they grew in three compact colonies of 15–40 stems, each colony occupying a three to four square yard plot. In each colony, 9–18 plants bloomed annually. For several years after we discovered these plants there was little variation in numbers or flowering.

When very moderate cutting of some of the larger oaks was allowed, there was only mild disturbance to the woodlot. Logs were dragged out directly over one colony disturbing the soils (and probably the orchid's roots). Plants within the drag track failed to reappear. Cutting of the larger trees removed some of the heavy shade from the other two colonies, but their roots were undisturbed. With increased light, these plants showed an immediate increase in vigor. Five years following the cutting one colony had grown to over 150 stems with 90 flowering in one season. The other colony was slightly more shaded and it doubled in numbers of plants and flowers produced. With increased vigor, numerous seed pods are set each year. Thus far, however, we have not been able to locate new seedlings or new colonies in the woodlot.[8]

Effects of Water Table Fluctuations

Natural cycles of rainfall within the Great Lakes drainage system produce both short range and long range changes in water levels, not only in the Great Lakes, but also in marshes, meadows, and inland lakes. These changes significantly affect native orchid populations. In the Bruce Peninsula, Ontario, and in northern Lower Michigan, Upper Michigan, and Wisconsin, numerous "beach bogs", interdunal swales, or low, sandy, moist beach flats occur. During years of lowered lake levels, these flats and bogs are exposed as mud or damp sand beds, open or sparsely grassed. Where these areas remain in a natural state large stands of orchids and other unusual vegetation soon appear. Such plants as bird's-eye primrose (*Primula mistassinica*), pitcher-plant (*Sarracenia purpurea*), butterwort (*Pinguicula vulgaris*), bladderworts (*Utricularia* spp.), sundews (*Drosera* spp.), and various orchids, form one of the most unique and picturesque native plant assemblages. The orchids which may grow in these beach bogs include rose pogonia (*Pogonia ophioglossoides*), arethusa (*Arethusa bulbosa*), grass pink (*Calopogon tuberosus*), *Cypripedium reginae*, *C. calceolus*, *Liparis loeselii*, *Platanthera hyperborea*, *P. dilatata*, *P. psycodes*, and *Spiranthes* species.

During high water years, many of these colonies are inundated and destroyed. Simultaneously, the raised water table causes sufficient disturbance to more inland sites to destroy competing grasses, sedges, and shrubs. This allows new colonies of these orchids and their companion plants to develop.[9] When the water

[8]One must be careful, however, not to overgeneralize or take this one experience as a model. Various species occupying the same forest cover might react differently to the effects of disturbance. Before any orchid management is undertaken, we need a series of carefully developed experimental studies in order to understand the orchid species' behavioral tolerances and needs.

[9]Unfortunately, this beach vegetation, while favored by slow, natural disturbances, is, in reality, very fragile at any given moment and especially vulnerable to man-created disturbance. Severe damage results when off-the-road vehicles traverse these habitats. Real estate development, vacation homes, drainage projects, and campgrounds all take heavy toll of this unique environment and in many areas unspoiled natural "beach bogs" have become very rare.

table drops, seeds from these colonies spread to newly exposed habitats closer to the shore. Similar changes in water level occur in smaller inland lakes, in meadows and marshes. These changes also destroy some orchid stands while creating new habitats elsewhere.

A similar pattern of relationships between water table levels and orchid colony development once existed along Saginaw Bay. Forty years ago, numerous colonies of eastern prairie fringed-orchid (*Platanthera leucophaea*) grew in wet prairie and marsh borders. Today, *P. leucophaea* has become exceedingly rare with most of its best habitats occupied by industry, marinas, oil tank farms, sewage disposal plants, or cottages. A few battered colonies of the orchid still survive. I do not feel, however, that the developments mentioned above are solely responsible for the orchid's problems. Outside the urban areas some suitable habitat survives, often lacking the orchid. Another factor, too, has contributed to the orchid's decline. In earlier times, as lakeshore levels changed, colonies of prairie fringed-orchid were able to seed inland or move shoreward as the lake levels responded to rainfall cycles. Some wet prairie which contained the orchid when I was a boy has become standing water cattail marsh with present higher lake levels, where the orchid cannot grow today.

At the end of World War II, the use of heavier equipment for draining and farming the land appeared, and many of the wet prairies along Saginaw Bay fell to the plough. Inland prairies and marshes, where *P. leucophaea* formerly seeded when shoreline prairies were inundated, are today ditched, diked, pumped, and planted to potatoes, cabbages, and sugar beets. Even the ditch-bank habitats, where the prairie fringed-orchid previously survived, have been destroyed by herbicides or buried in drain dredgings. It appears that the only hope for this lovely orchid in this region is the establishment of a natural shoreline prairie preserve sufficiently deep to provide for the orchid's nature of moving inland or shoreward as the water table fluctuates.

While long range changes in the water table through flooding or exposure create suitable habitats for some species, short range

---

Quite possibly, the attempt to artifically maintain high Great Lakes water levels may also present a great threat to this unique series of habitats, for it would remove the fluctuations in water levels so necessary to maintain the open, competition-free conditions required to develop large populations of these rare plants.

The beach-flat-fen-old-shoreline-ridge habitats deserve much more research attention and greater efforts at their preservation and management than they have received. Although some of their denizens occur in other situations, nowhere else in our region do such large assemblages of certain rare and showy species develop.

changes such as exceptionally wet or dry seasons, seem to have little effect upon numbers or endurance of most orchid populations. It is true that in very dry seasons *P. leucophaea* may become stunted and flower poorly. This probably affects the long term seedling production, but I have not observed it. The only native orchid commonly reported to be directly affected by seasonal variations in rainfall is *Triphora trianthophora*, which produces vegetative offsets more abundantly in wetter seasons.

Effects of a Late Frost

It is my impression that, in some districts, late frosts can influence the abundance of early blooming species. At one northern Lower Michigan station, I have observed a population of *Arethusa bulbosa* annually for over 35 years. During this time there has been no disturbance to the population through picking, digging, draining, or grazing. Yet, the numbers of flowering plants in one season have varied from as many as 300 to as few as 16–20. In the same bog over this period of time, *Calopogon tuberosus* has bloomed quite uniformly, producing 75–125 flowering plants each year. I think there are several factors causing these two similarly-constructed, corm-producing, perennial orchids to behave so differently on the same site, one flowering rather uniformly and the other showing a wide variation in the number of flowering individuals from season to season.

Arethusa blooms early, from late May to mid-June, a time when late heavy frosts occur frequently in these small pot-hole bogs. When such late frosts occur, not only *Arethusa*, but also pink lady's-slipper and pitcher-plant flowers are cut down. *Calopogon*, however, flowers later in the year, late June and into July. It commences growth much later than *Arethusa*, is seldom frosted, and sets seed almost every year.

Both of these species produce small, succulent corms attractive to rodents. I suspect that both species suffer significant rodent damage during some seasons, since marked plants frequently fail to appear the following year. Both species, therefore, rely heavily upon seed production to maintain their numbers. Since *Arethusa* flowers early and is more subject to frost damage, it is successful in producing seed less often. This variability in seed production is reflected in greater variation in the numbers of flowering individuals seen for *Arethusa* from season to season than for *Calopogon* which remains more stable.

White fringed-orchid, *Platanthera blephariglottis*, grows in this same bog and shows similar variation in numbers of flowering stems from year to year. Unlike *Arethusa*, which produces tiny, grasslike leaves, *P. blephariglottis* produces a conspicuous leaf even when not flowering, and can thus be more easily monitored. Not only do plants of this species growing in openings fail to bloom in the same seasons when pitcher-plants and pink lady's-slippers have clearly been frost-damaged, but the numbers of both flowering and nonflowering individuals drop drastically. I believe that a combination of frost damage to developing flowering plants (affecting seed production), and rodent damage to overwintering roots, accounts for the wide variation in population numbers from season to season.

While I have not observed direct evidence of rodent damage to *P. blephariglottis* in this bog, I did observe extensive destruction of roots and overwintering buds of *P. ciliaris* in a large bog in Kalamazoo County, Michigan. While exploring this bog in the late autumn of 1981, I found that a rodent, probably a vole (*Microtus* sp.), had uprooted the fleshy, aromatic roots and had eaten the winter buds of most of the plants which had flowered that season. In this instance, the damage to the population was significant.

Diseases

Our native orchids, like our other native plants, occasionally suffer from insect pests and disease. Some platantheras and particularly *Cypripedium calceolus* var. *pubescens* suffer from spider mite damage both in gardens and in the wild. Late frost damage to developing leaves seems to predispose the affected plants to much leaf deterioration later in the season. Examination often reveals the presence of numerous spider mites on the injured leaves. Boring larvae, similar in behavior to the familiar cornborers, occasionally attack stems of *Cypripedium reginae*. Developing platantheras can be destroyed by tiny weevils which eat out the heart of the stem growth. Such weevils also occasionally mine away the photosynthetic mesophyll from succulent orchid leaves.

Many native and adventive orchids seem subject to fungal attack. Twayblades (*Listera*), *Platanthera*, and *Epipactis* frequently perish to a blackening of the foliage which rapidly destroys the plants, both in gardens and in the wild. This blackening disease appears on orchid leaves with symptoms much like those of *Botrytis* in garden lilies.

In Port Huron State Game Area, St. Clair County, Michigan, I found a dense stand of *Platanthera flava* var. *herbiola*. The colony, numbering over a thousand plants, grew in the overflow from a sluggish, acid-water, shallow stream. This was the largest and densest stand of *P. flava* var. *herbiola* which I have ever seen. One year, after the plants had been flooded while in leaf, they developed a blackening deterioration of the leaves such as

I described above. All plants in the colony were affected. A year or two later, I could find no plants where this colony had grown. Other botanists checking the spot during another season also failed to locate the colony. Apparently the flooding and fungus attack totally destroyed these plants.

Native Orchids and Plant Succession

The causes and effects of changes in disturbed orchid populations are obvious in the examples cited in the previous sections. The reasons for population changes in seemingly undisturbed colonies of orchids are less commonly understood. Some colonies increase while others decrease or disappear. Such changes are partially due to the fact that the development of the vegetation on any given site produces accompanying changes in the existing light, humidity, humus accumulation, acidity, and water-holding capacity of the soil, as well as producing conditions of competition which did not exist there earlier. The changes may be slow or subtle, occurring over a period of many years, or they may be rapid. Regardless of the time period involved, the continuing interaction of the species present gradually alters the environment sufficiently to prevent their seedlings from developing; or the changes may wipe out established adults as well. At the same time, new species particularly suited to the developing conditions may appear.

On a given site, the general development of vegetation continues toward a state which can maintain itself indefinitely. Such a self-renewing stage of vegetation is called a "climax association." The total process of development and change in plant species on a site is called "plant succession."

The majority of our native orchids are plants of transient successional stages, not climax conditions. They are opportunistic and tend to seed in when a fortuitous environment develops (provided, of course, that colonies exist within sufficient proximity for their seeds to reach the area), establish themselves, and for a time become abundant in suitable niches. Most of our species are relatively delicate herbs which cannot endure severe competition for root space and sunlight, even if other environmental conditions are favorable. Consequently, orchids, like most plants on a given site, invade, develop, flourish, and, with changing habitat conditions, decline and eventually disappear while new colonies develop on suitable sites elsewhere. Most orchid populations are in a state of continuous flux.

Careful observation in the field over a period of time will reveal many examples of orchid population dynamics. It is not uncommon in some districts to find a few old clumps of *Cypripedium calceolus* var. *pubescens* or *C. acaule* in heavy timber, but few or no seedlings will be present. In a nearby area, more open and sunny or with mildly disturbed soils and cover, seedlings may be abundant. In eastern Upper Michigan these species frequently grow more commonly in roadside clearings, ditches, and zones occasionally disturbed by snow ploughs than they do a short distance back into deeper, undisturbed timber.

Eastern prairie fringed-orchid, *Platanthera leucophaea*, formerly a locally frequent species on moist prairie ground around Saginaw Bay, is now one of our rarest species. Its recent demise has been primarily due to drainage and cultivation of these rich prairie soils. One Saginaw County station in 1964 supported a large colony of this species on an abandoned field-prairie near the Saginaw River. However, after 1964 the old field underwent the early stages of natural succession without interference from fire or clearing. Dogwood shrubs (*Cornus* spp.), prickly ash (*Zanthoxylum americanum*), cottonwood (*Populus deltoides*), ash (*Fraxinus* spp.), and willow (*Salix* spp.) seedlings appeared, spread, and grew into thickets entangled with grape vines (*Vitis* spp.). By 1976 there were few open grassy spots, and *P. leucophaea* was largely shaded out. A few pathetic, distorted specimens entangled in brush and vines and struggling to reach full sun were all that remained. In 1984 no prairie fringed-orchids could be found among the thickets and developing forest. On a nearby railroad right-of-way, kept open with brush cutting, a few *Platanthera* remained.

Occasionally, unusually large populations of orchids, often of several species, may develop on certain sites in the Great Lakes region. Such populations occur in enclosed woods, among open sand dunes, or in interdunal troughs, beach flats, or interdunal marshes and old beach ridges (in sand over limestone, such areas as occur on the Bruce Peninsula, Ontario, in Door County, Wisconsin, and in Wilderness State Park, Michigan). Springy hillside fens and sphagnum moss mats in developing bogs can also produce spectacular colonies of orchids. None of these habitats is the only one utilized by any of the species. What is unusual about these superior sites is that they all possess an element of slight, limited, but continuous disturbance provided by blowing sand, moss growth, peat or needle duff accumulation, or changing water table levels (see Case, F. W., Jr. in *North American Terrestrial Orchids, Symposium II*, 1983. p. 138). I believe it is this continuous, mild disturbance which allows the development of exceptionally large and vigorous populations of orchids. Conditions on these sites are, by virtue of the mild disturbance, self-renewing successional stages which provide suitable habitat for the transient orchid species for a much longer time than most habitats do.

Only in climax associations do colonies of appropriate orchid species endure. These species, like the climax plants around them, have seedlings adapted to tolerate the conditions which continually develop there and thus they reproduce easily. Such species, however, form a limited part of our native orchid flora. In most situations, existing orchid plants depend upon the dynamics of change—succession, fire, water table changes, flooding, and developing moss or sedge mats in lakes—to create new habitat into which to seed. Normally, these changes proceed gradually, allowing time for orchid colonies to develop in new locations.

Rapid changes wrought by bulldozers, drainage, land development, lakeshore and recreational usage, off-the-road vehicles, some timber and game management practices, even the visitation of known orchid stations by large numbers of photographers and naturalists, have altered the land so severely in recent years that our native orchid populations have been seriously reduced. In some districts there is little remaining or developing natural habitat into which existing orchids may seed, or the suitable habitats are so few and far between that the chances of propagules reaching them are poor. Conversely, many of our orchids demand specific successional situations and respond favorably to suitable conditions. This makes them appropriate candidates for management programs on suitable sanctuaries. Management of many prairie plants including *Cypripedium candidum* and *Platanthera leucophaea* is already a reality on some preserves.

Orchids and Conservation

Much has been written about the rarity of orchids and the need for strong conservation measures to protect them. Almost all our states and two Canadian provinces today provide some legal protection for rare wildflowers or those popularly perceived to be "rare." Most laws single out orchids for special protection.[10]

In addition to specific state and provincial lists, national laws and international agreements protect orchids. The United States Endangered Species Act lists and protects certain plants in two categories—"endangered" and "threatened." Such listings protect the plants on federal lands from disturbance for any reason without permits from the government. Permits for any activity which disturbs endangered species are seldom issued. Present law (1984) lists only *Isotria medeoloides*, the small whorled pogonia, as a federally endangered orchid species. The status of species considered threatened or endangered is constantly re-

[10]Conservation laws are neither consistent from state to state and province to province, nor do they remain static. Concerned readers should consult their own district's current laws for detailed information.

viewed and other species may be proposed for listing at any time. Authorities are currently reviewing *Platanthera leucophaea* for possible change of its status from threatened to endangered. Another United States law, the Lacey Act, regulates taking or trafficking in certain protected animals and plants. Its provisions allow the prosecution of individuals engaged in illegal interstate movement of species protected by federal or state laws. Canadian national law apparently does not regulate or protect native plants. The Province of Ontario has an endangered species act, but it is very limited in its coverage and presently protects only *Cypripedium candidum* and *Isotria medeoloides*.

Both the Canadian and the United States governments have entered into the Convention on International Trade in Endangered Species of Wild Fauna and Flora (CITES) with other participating nations. This agreement specifies the rare and endangered plants protected from international trade. CITES regulations cover all orchids and a species may be exported from or imported into a participating nation only after both the exporting and the importing countries issue appropriate permits.

State and federal laws in the United States provide, I believe, reasonable legal protection of our native terrestrial orchids from commercial collection or disturbance on public lands. However, the destruction of plants on private lands seldom carries legal penalties. Michigan is one of the few states which protects its endangered and threatened plants on private as well as state land. Like federal law relating to development projects, Michigan law requires an environmental impact statement and permits before any land supporting threatened or endangered species within the state may be disturbed.

While state and federal laws protect our orchids from commercial collecting and illegal collecting on public lands, I believe such activities are rare. In the 43 years I have studied and observed our native orchids, I have seen only one highly organized, terribly destructive, illegal, commercial collecting operation. This activity involved the mass collection of lady's-slippers over a large area and undoubtedly has had a serious impact upon local populations. The perpetrators are currently being prosecuted under federal law.

Although commercial collecting and picking continue to receive much publicity as a major source of wildflower destruction, other kinds of destruction have increased dramatically. These other types of destruction, while receiving little publicity, may cause far more damage to our local orchid populations, in spite of the current "popular" concern for environmental issues. Off-the-road vehicles—dirt bikes, motorcycles, three-wheelers, oversized four-wheel-drive pickups, and dune buggies—do incalculable damage to the soils and delicate vegetation of dunes, beaches, swamps, and steep hillsides. Large colonies of orchids and other rarities are crushed beneath their spinning wheels in soft soils.

At a state game area in Tuscola County, Michigan, I have seen motorcycle trails wipe out colonies of putty-root orchids (*Aplectrum*), a species not at all common in our area. In eastern Upper Michigan our limestone districts support many rare or endangered species in unusually fine beach-bogs and interdunal marshes. In these areas vehicular traffic and camping overflow from nearby state campgrounds has churned up and destroyed many rare plant colonies. In one such location, specifically marked to prohibit vehicular traffic and camping, campers cut down state highway posts to gain access.

Destruction of wetlands continues to threaten many of the rarer species of native plants. Agricultural pressure to drain land coupled with a popular perception that swamplands are "undesirable" poses a threat to these rare wetland species (unless the particular wetland also favors waterfowl hunting). Mosquito control programs which involve draining lands, however desirable for human comfort, can threaten local swamps. Peat mining removes prime open bog orchid habitat and destroys the delicate plants present. Lakeshore "improvement" by cottagers, planting lawns on beaches, building breakwater walls, filling low, swampy shoreline areas to improve bathing beaches, using herbicides and lawn fertilizers—each of these activities can destroy native orchids or their cover. In the more populated regions of the western Great Lakes, few lakes remain in a truly natural state. One must wonder at how much orchid habitat has disappeared.

Management practices for wild game species, either carried out privately or through conservation agencies, can become a double-edged sword. Over a long period of time, wildlife floodings, lumbering to provide food or cover, forestry management projects, or stream improvement ventures can cause favorable orchid habitats to develop as the disturbed areas go through plant succession. However, the immediate effect of some of these projects is the destruction of existing orchid populations by creating such rapid changes that the orchids cannot adjust or recover.

Cedar cover in a large swamp near Atlanta, Michigan was cut, apparently by local sportsmen's clubs, to provide deer feed over a hard winter. The cut area contained colonies of ram's-head lady's-slipper, calypso, and the now endangered small round-leafed orchis. Only a few ram's-head lady's-slippers persist today. The other rarer, less adaptable species disappeared immediately when the forest was opened up and have not reappeared even though more than 20 years have passed. Management practices for larger game animals in the same region include clearing the borders of cedar-balsam fir swamps to provide grazing glades planted to rye and other grains. At least two such clearing projects, to my knowledge, destroyed large numbers of showy lady's-slippers (*Cypripedium reginae*).

These actions were not deliberately undertaken to destroy orchid cover in order to further a game management plan. Ideal orchid cover is often particularly well suited to other conservation or outdoor activities. Those concerned with these land development projects simply did not know that protected plants existed on those lands. But these examples do point out an increasingly frequent conservation problem—how can all potential users of our lands be informed about the plants growing there? How can we protect our rare species from accidental destruction by well-intentioned activities? Many colonies of extremely rare and endangered plants and animals undoubtedly still exist unreported on our wild lands, yet we know almost nothing of what grows on most lands slated for development, whether public or private. We need to make a major effort to identify the locations of such species and to protect them from disturbance.

Another source of damage or destruction to rare orchids comes, surprisingly, from conservationists, educators, and photographers—the very individuals who often profess the greatest concern for them. When groups, classes, or photographers repeatedly make pathways on bog mats, beaches, or dune slopes, the disturbance of the surface can create conditions which allow coarse weeds, sedges, or cattails (*Bidens* spp., *Carex* spp., or *Typha* spp.) to invade. These invaders then compete with the native orchids, often to the orchids' detriment. Orchid lovers usually manage to avoid blooming plants, but frequently trample unnoticed seedlings, causing serious damage to certain species.[11]

The deterioration of certain highly publicized (and protected) orchid habitats at Wilderness State Park, Michigan can be directly traced to the invasion of these areas annually by orchid lovers and photographers. In May 1981, my wife and I observed more than a dozen photographers who spread plastic sheets on the ground and lay on them to photograph *Calypso*. When they had finished, there were large patches of bruised and damaged vegetation. Nonflowering *Calypso* and other orchids were probably hurt because they went unnoticed.

Distressingly, I have seen photographers pluck off the discolored, newly pollinated *Calypso* flowers in order to obtain more

---

[11]In rare instances, however, mild or intermittent disturbance may stimulate clump formation in some species, actually increasing their abundance while causing damage to other species present (see comments under *Platanthera blephariglottis*).

pleasing photographs! Although calypso is a perennial and in theory could live indefinitely, most plants survive only long enough to bloom one or two seasons. Many plants of this species have a short life because they grow rooted on logs or in rotting spruce-cedar duff which quickly becomes so decomposed as to be unsuited to the plant's growth needs. *Calypso* colonies, therefore, must depend on regular seed set to maintain themselves. Picking the newly pollinated flowers can be particularly damaging to the colony's future.

With such a varied onslaught upon our native orchids and other wild species, is there any hope of saving rare or vanishing wildlife? Obviously, *attempts are being made* through laws protecting endangered and threatened species. However, such laws apply only where specific prohibited activities (collecting, picking, international trade) exist. In my experience, such collecting activies constitute a small portion of the total problem. Much of the damage to native plant populations comes from gradual habitat deterioration and destruction brought about by human population pressures, demands for recreational space, and utilization of natural resources.

The past 20 years have brought increased awareness of conservation problems and increased activity by conservation organizations, both public and private. Much land has been acquired and much more needs to be acquired as wildlife habitat. When picking or collecting destroy some of the plants in an area, seeds or seedlings present may continue to develop or new propagules may reach the area. However, when the habitat itself is destroyed all the plants it supports perish as well and new seedlings of those species cannot develop in that location. In order to preserve any rare species of plant or animal, natural areas of sufficient size to maintain breeding populations must be set aside. If the vegetation on such a tract is a climax association, this measure is sufficient since this association is essentially self-maintaining and will continue to produce the conditions necessary to preserve the species present. If a particular stage of vegetation will not normally persist due to plant succession, the habitat can be managed by controlled burning, cutting, water level control, or other tested methods for maintaining the desired vegetational stage. If the required environment is maintained through such management practices, the orchids and other wildlife suited to that habitat may remain there indefinitely.

We need more documented research dealing with management methods for the maintenance and increase of orchid populations. It is still not possible to consistently grow terrestrial orchids from seed or to maintain them in propagating beds for eventual reintroduction into the wild. These skills must be developed.

More benefits might accrue to native flora and fauna if conservation groups and sportsmen's organizations coordinated their efforts. Too often, each group goes its own way. Yet, conditions which improve cedar cover for wintering deer (and thus improve deer hunting) also provide good growing conditions for cypripediums and other cold bog orchids. Trout stream improvement, particularly the protection of headwater sources, can also preserve or develop good orchid habitat. Coordination of effort between organizations with such mutual interests would add political strength to the conservation movement. It could also prevent the inadvertent destruction of plant populations which may occur when one group is unaware of another's activities.

The recent development of outdoor education and nature centers has tremendously enhanced public knowledge and appreciation of the out-of-doors. But, a much more concerted effort is needed to educate our youth about the values of wildlife and wild lands. If our young people have an interest in and love of natural areas for their intrinsic qualities, they will work to protect them.

We must also order our own priorities! We hear much today about "multiple use" of public lands. While "multiple use" can be a wise utilization of such lands, it can also, in some instances, destroy a fragile, beautiful, or irreplaceable resource. Sadly, we still know very little about the interdependence of some species or the qualities or properties they possess which may benefit man in the future. It would, indeed, be a tragedy for them to become extinct. It is essential for us to recognize the fact that some natural areas and wild species are of priceless value in themselves and must not disappear from the earth.

On a short term basis, much can be done to increase conservation awareness and develop conservation policies and programs protecting native plants and animals. Unfortunately, I am not optimistic about the survival of preserves, natural areas, parks, and dedicated public lands under continued pressure from energy crises, food and water shortages, and other manifestations of human population growth.

ORIGINS AND DISTRIBUTION PATTERNS OF GREAT LAKES ORCHIDS

LIKE OTHER plant species, the orchids are subject to changes in geological conditions and climate. A major cause of change in the earth's features is the interplay of the forces of natural erosion which level mountains and carry them off as sediments to the seas and other forces which continually create new features on the earth's surface. The changing land surfaces in turn bring about changes in airflow patterns and ocean currents. Thus, with the changing land, changes develop in climate as well. Forests give way to grasslands, swamp to desert; periods of glaciation wax and wane.

Against the backdrop of geological time, the life span of an individual plant or animal seems insignificant. Yet a species may live through many geological events. Since each species becomes dependent upon a rather limited set of habitat conditions, geological change has a profound effect upon the distribution of many plant species. While some still inhabit the area where they originated, many do not. A species becomes extinct when its necessary habitat is altered too much, unless other events create suitable and accessible habitats to which it can migrate. However, even when conditions change drastically, a few relict colonies may persist in specially favored locations in the place of origin. Such relict colonies give valuable clues to the past distribution of a species. Often it may have moved long distances across the face of the earth to reach its present location.

Most present distribution patterns result directly from the events of geological history, though an occasional plant colony reaches a particular site through the aid of such random agents as man, birds, or railroad trains. Plant geographers are able to understand the distributional relationships and history of certain plant species and of whole regions by careful examination of the clues furnished by the geological history of a region and by the occurrence of relict colonies, present population centers, fossil records, habitat requirements, and distribution patterns of closely related forms.

At present the Great Lakes region is especially favorable to orchids because of its geographic position, its lake-influenced climate, its soil types, and its glacial history. Fifty-eight orchid species grow natively in the region, besides a number of distinct varieties within the species, several adventive species, and a number of hybrids. This region surpasses all others in temperate North America, except Florida, in the number of its orchid species. Yet not one of these species is indigenous to the region. With the possible exception of a very few species in the unglaciated driftless area of Wisconsin, all our orchids have migrated from other regions since Pleistocene glaciation ended about 10,000 years ago.

Regions Which Have Contributed to Our Orchid Flora

Our orchid flora is, therefore, not a discrete unit, but a blend of elements of various other floras which have arrived here because of geological or chance events. The southern half of the Great Lakes region lies generally within the mixed deciduous forest zone—the great belt of hardwood trees that dominates the east, south, and central United States east of the prairies. A great many plants have become adapted to the conditions of shade, humus, and moisture within this zone and follow this forest wherever it develops. Though local, such orchids as *Galearis spectabilis*, *Aplectrum hyemale*, *Corallorhiza odontorhiza*, *Goodyera pubescens*, *Liparis lilifolia*, and *Triphora trianthophora* occur almost throughout this forest zone.

At the northern edge of the deciduous forest in our region, winter hardiness may be a factor in the extremely local distribution of some species. Another hypothesis suggests that this region is still so recently free of glacial ice that many species have not yet been able to fully colonize the available deciduous forest.

To the north of the Great Lakes lies a vast subarctic forest of white spruce (*Picea glauca*), paper birch (*Betula papyrifera*), aspen (*Populus tremuloides*), and a few other trees. It extends from the Atlantic to the Pacific, and virtually the same type of forest extends across Asia and northern Europe. Orchids adapted to the conditions in this forest and climate, such as *Calypso bulbosa*, *Listera cordata*, *Goodyera repens*, and *Corallorhiza trifida*, may occur throughout; or they may be limited to certain regions within this boreal forest zone because their former continuous distribution was disrupted by the enforced southward movement of the forest during the Ice Age.

Where this forest extends south into our region, its typical orchids are present. Such orchids dominate Lake Superior areas. The cooling influence of the northern Great Lakes has produced along their shores stretches of beach bog and evergreen forest which climatically and ecologically resemble the subarctic forest. Orchids typical of the subarctic forest, as well as those of cool Appalachian uplands, appear together here, often in very large numbers. Inland from the lakes the subarctic orchids occur in cold bogs and evergreen forests where glaciation has created favorable conditions for their growth.

A number of our orchid species have affinities with the Appalachian uplands, where they have developed, or at least survived, for centuries. The postglacial climate of New England and the Great Lakes region, similar to that at higher elevations in the mountains, is agreeable to some species, of which *Platanthera psycodes* and *P. grandiflora* are typical.

Certain coastal plain bog or marsh species, if winter hardy, spread wherever suitable acid-sterile cover exists and they can gain a foothold. The many bogs and lake shores created by glaciation provide a huge and readily available area of habitat for them. Such species are *Arethusa bulbosa, Pogonia ophioglossoides, Platanthera ciliaris, P. clavellata,* and *Calopogon tuberosus.* Some of these species, which have close relatives in Japan and China, may have represented remnants of a once worldwide flora before spreading into our region in postglacial times. It is more likely, however, that they represent parallel descendants of common ancestors which have developed since continental drift or other geological events separated portions of the ancestral population.

Platanthera blephariglottis, widespread northward in the East and reaching across south-central Ontario into Michigan, has colonized only the Lower Peninsula. While local but widespread near the tip of the Lower Peninsula and extending southward especially in western Lower Michigan, it is absent from extreme southern Berrien County, all of southeastern Lower Michigan south of Tuscola County, and is very rare in east-central Lower Michigan. It has never been reported from the Upper Peninsula, nor from Wisconsin or Minnesota, although suitable sphagnum bog cover is abundant.[1]

Some of our orchids appear to be remnants of a flora which

---

[1]Sheviak (1974) accepts a report by Higley and Raddin (1891) of the occurrence of two plants of *P. blephariglottis* in Cook County, Illinois. In the absence of other reports or herbarium specimens and in the light of the possibility of confusion with *P. leucophaea,* I prefer not to accept the occurrence of *P. blephariglottis* within the Illinois range of this book until substantiating specimens appear.

formerly spread across North America at this latitude, for such orchids as *Goodyera oblongifolia*, *Piperia unalascensis*, and *Corallorhiza striata* grow today in the Great Lakes region and in the western mountains but not in the regions in between. A number of plants follow this pattern, and some plant geographers suggest that glaciation disrupted a former transcontinental range. Other phytogeographers suggest that certain plants, especially those with minute, easily transported seeds, have simply arrived fortuitously in regions of suitable soils and climate and become established since glacial times. The species mentioned occur in the West most abundantly in coniferous duff over basic, especially limestone-derived, soils. It is in exactly such conditions that these species grow where they occur in the western Great Lakes region.

Within our orchid flora are species of considerable tolerance which occur widely in the region. Other species, needing special soils, unusual plant cover, or combinations of these, and certain temperature conditions, account for the very localized species. Thus our Great Lakes orchid flora is a mosaic of species from a variety of nearby geographic areas.

Descriptions of Frequent Orchid Habitats of the Western Great Lakes Region and Their Typical Species

Biologists and ecologists have devised many different systems to classify the native plant habitats and associations of our region. These classifications are based upon plant associations, soil types, and soil drainage patterns. Complicating this situation is the fact that latitude and longitude alter the species makeup of plant habitats, both wet and dry. We tend to consider the habitats with which we are familiar to be the "typical" form and to judge others against our own experience. Most of us feel we have a good idea of what a marl-fen or a black spruce-tamarack bog is like. But, westward in our area, plants of calcareous open wetlands mingle with the vegetation found in low moist prairies. Northward, bogland species merge into boreal coniferous forest assemblages not confined to wetlands. Even within our region, according to Pringle (1980), "intergradations and intermediate communities . . . are frequently encountered, and basic environments may be subdivided into groups of subordinate units." Consequently, authorities might differ on the assignment of a specific site to a particular category.

All of our habitats have variations in their herbaceous flora influenced by varied conditions within the environment. In the case of the drier, upland habitats, the habitat designations traditionally have included the names of the dominant trees or plants, so that their nature is more or less evident or self-explanatory. What is meant by an "old-field community" or a "beech-maple forest" is fairly understandable to almost any outdoorsman.

Wetland terminology, unfortunately, presents complications. Drainage (or lack of it), soil pH, accumulations of peat (with or without additional minerals), and the amount of calcareous material in the soil all affect the nature of the habitat and the plant species that can grow there. Botanists and ecologists have long attempted to classify wetlands, and there is now considerable published material on this subject which pertains to our region.

In this book I have generally followed the broad classifications set forth in J. S. Pringle's *An Introduction to Wetland Classification in the Great Lakes Region* (1980). Pringle groups our wetlands into marsh, swamp, bog, and fen, and presents a brief discussion of the conditions and the plants found in each. Those who require detailed information on the subject may consult Pringle directly or one of the references cited below.[2] I also include very brief definitions of Pringle's four categories in the glossary.

A word of caution: one should be wary of assigning a species of plant exclusively to any single habitat. A number of our orchids and other native plants tolerate either wet or dry, or acidic or calcareous situations and can occur in bog, fen, or upland. Even in calcareous fens acidic microhabitats occur in which a calciphobe bog species may grow.

It has been my experience that many of our orchids grow in a wider variety of habitats than some authors admit. Furthermore, certain species behave differently in choice of habitat in different districts (perhaps indicating the existence of different physiological races).

In the tables that follow, I have attempted to list a series of

[2]Jeglum, J. K., A. N. Boissonneau, & V. F Haavisto. 1974. Toward a Wetland Classification for Ontario. Canadian Forestry Service Information Rept. 0-X-215. 54 pp.

Reddoch, Joyce M. 1983. Southern Ontario Fens. The Plant Press 1: 76–78.

Schwintzer, C. R. 1981. Vegetation and Nutrient Status of Northern Michigan Bogs and Conifer Swamps with a Comparison of Fens. Canad. Jr. Bot. 59: 842–853.

Schwintzer, C. R. 1982. Chemical and Physical Characteristics of Shallow Ground Waters in Northern Michigan Bogs, Swamps, and Fens. Amer. Jr. Bot. 69: 1231–1239.

Stuckey, R. L., & G. L. Denny. 1981. "Prairie Fens and Bog Fens In Ohio: Floristic Similarities, Differences, and Geographical Affinities." In *Geobotany II*, ed. R. C. Romans. Plenum, New York. 271 pp.

native plant communities or assemblages in a manner which will be recognizable and useful to the inexperienced searcher in his quest for native orchids. While generally adhering to Pringle's terminology in treating habitat, I have attempted in this section merely to list assemblages of native plants which I have found to be dependable in characterizing habitats where one can reasonably be expected to encounter the species listed.

TABLE 1

Descriptions of Some Frequent Orchid Habitats of the Western Great Lakes Region and Typical Species

HABITAT 1

Tamarack-black spruce bogs on mineral-poor, strongly acid brown peats; areas where sphagnum mosses abound. Such areas often have large stands of Michigan holly (*Ilex verticillata*), poison sumac (*Rhus vernix*), or high-bush blueberry (*Vaccinium corymbosum*) southward, and leatherleaf (*Chamaedaphne calyculata*), bog or sheep laurels (*Kalmia polifolia*, *K. angustifolia*), and Labrador tea (*Ledum groenlandicum*) northward. Sphagnum moss is the predominant surface covering, but cranberries (*Vaccinium macrocarpon* or *V. oxycoccus*), sedges, and grasses, and such conspicuous herbs as the northern pitcher-plant (*Sarracenia purpurea*) grow in the moss. Such habitats occur or did occur locally throughout the southern and central parts of the Great Lakes region often on borders of small ponds or lakes. These habitats are widespread in some northern districts. Plate 1A.

Typical Species

Arethusa bulbosa
Calopogon tuberosus
Cypripedium acaule
Isotria verticillata
  (very local, southern
  districts)
Liparis loeselii
  (occasional, mostly on logs,
  tufts in open water)
Listera australis
  (in our area acidic districts
  of Ontario east of Georgian
  Bay)

Listera cordata
  (wooded bogs, or about
  bases of spruces in
  openings)
Malaxis unifolia
Platanthera blephariglottis
  (Lower Michigan, southern
  Ontario, and eastward)
P. ciliaris
  (south half of our area)
P. clavellata
P. lacera
P. leucophaea
  (very rare, may also grow
  in fens and prairies)
Pogonia ophioglossoides

HABITAT 2

Northern, open fens or treed fens with white cedar (*Thuja occidentalis*), tamarack (*Larix laricina*), balsam-fir (*Abies balsamea*), and occasional black spruce (*Picea mariana*). Shrub growth includes Labrador tea (*Ledum*

TABLE 1 (Continued)

groenlandicum), sweet gale (*Myrica gale*), shrubby cinquefoil (*Potentilla fruticosa*) with occasional typical bog shrubs growing in acidic micro-habitats such as on logs or isolated sphagnum hummocks. Sedges and grasses abound in openings and sunny glades. Areas of open wet marl may occur. Peat is more decomposed than in Habitat 1, is blacker, scarcely acid to alkaline, and richer in minerals. Soils are usually cold. Such habitats occur frequently in many of our northern districts and may merge with northern coniferous swamp (Habitat 3).

Typical Species

Amerorchis rotundifolia
(local, very rare except in
far northern districts)
Arethusa bulbosa
Calopogon tuberosus
(*Arethusa* and *Calopogon*
most likely to occur in
acidic microhabitats)
Corallorhiza trifida
Cypripedium acaule
(on logs, hummocks of
acidic substrate only)
C. arietinum
C. calceolus var. parviflorum
C. calceolus var. pubescens

C. candidum
(southern districts mostly
except in far west of our
area)
C. reginae
Liparis loeselii
Platanthera dilatata
P. hyperborea
P. leucophaea
(in Ontario; occurs in more
acidic situations in lake
bogs in Michigan, but may
occur in fenlike habitats
along certain Great Lakes
shores)
Pogonia ophioglossoides
Spiranthes romanzoffiana

HABITAT 3

Heavily wooded, cool, damp, mossy, white cedar, balsam-fir, tamarack, black spruce swamps, often on the headwaters of trout streams, or where springs erupt at or near the bases of glacial moraines. Here sphagnum moss is present primarily as a superficial surface layer and grows along with many other moss species. Dark isles of cedar and fir may create so much shade that few herbs can survive under them. Glades and sunnier areas frequently carpeted with sphagnum and with thickets of Labrador tea. Wettest depressions frequently carpeted with three-leaved false Solomon's-seal (*Smilacina trifolia*). Plate 1B.

Typical Species

Amerorchis rotundifolia
Arethusa bulbosa
(as an occasional plant in
clearings)

G. repens var. ophioides
G. tesselata
Liparis loeselii
Listera convallarioides

TABLE 1 (Continued)

Calypso bulbosa
(always very local)
Corallorhiza maculata vars.
C. striata
C. trifida
Cypripedium acaule
C. arietinum
C. calceolus var. parviflorum
C. calceolus var. pubescens
C. reginae
Goodyera oblongifolia
(occasional, prefers drier
woods in districts it
inhabits)
G. pubescens
(occasional, this is not its
prime habitat)

L. cordata
Malaxis monophylla var.
brachypoda
M. paludosa
(local, Minnesota, Lake
Superior and northward
only)
M. unifolia
Platanthera clavellata
P. dilatata
(occasional, in clearings)
P. hyperborea
P. obtusata
P. orbiculata vars.

HABITAT 4

Damp to dry evergreen woods, mostly of white cedar, balsam-fir, spruce; mainly in the immediate vicinity of the shores of Lakes Michigan, Superior, or Huron, either as interdunal forest or just above the open beaches. Similar in many respects to the damp to dry spruce forests of the boreal forests north of our area. Ground cover of mosses, twinflower (Linnaea borealis), Canada bunchberry (Cornus canadensis), Iris lacustris, and large-leaf aster (Aster macrophyllus). Plate 4A.

Typical Species

Calypso bulbosa
(local, northern)
Corallorhiza maculata vars.
C. striata
C. trifida
Coeloglossum viride var.
virescens
Cypripedium arietinum
C. calceolus vars.
Goodyera spp.

Listera auriculata
(Upper Peninsula and Lake
Superior islands and shores
locally northward along
rivers in similar habitats)
L. convallarioides
Malaxis unifolia
Platanthera hookeri
P. hyperborea
P. obtusata
P. orbiculata vars.
P. psycodes
(local, usually open glades
or on streambanks)

TABLE 1 (Continued)

HABITAT 5

Damp to wet, rather open, aspen-alder thickets along streams, or in brushy meadows in drained, beaver-dammed ponds, or flood plain terraces of smaller creeks and streams.

Typical Species

Corallorhiza maculata vars.
C. striata
  (northward only, usually in
  limestone districts)
C. trifida
Cypripedium calceolus var.
  parviflorum
  (more local than var.
  pubescens)
C. calceolus var. *pubescens*

Platanthera flava var. *herbiola*
  (mainly in southern half of
  region in acidic areas
  subject to periodic flooding)
P. hyperborea
P. psycodes
Spiranthes cernua

HABITAT 6

Marl fens, sandy, swampy lake shores, and floating sedge mats in otherwise more acid lake bogs.

Typical Species

Arethusa bulbosa
  (on logs or more acid
  hummocks)
Calopogon tuberosus
  (mostly on acid hummocks)
Cypripedium calceolus var.
  parviflorum
C. calceolus var. *pubescens*
C. candidum
  (southern half of region)

C. reginae
Liparis loeselii
Platanthera dilatata
P. hyperborea
P. leucophaea
  (very rare and local)
P. psycodes
Pogonia ophioglossoides
Spiranthes cernua
S. lucida
  (always local, Ontario, Lake
  Erie areas; very local in
  central Michigan)

HABITAT 7

Open, wet meadows, damp prairies, fens, marl-fens occurring primarily in the central and southern portions of the region. Common trees, if any, tamarack (*Larix laricina*); shrub cover mostly shrubby cinquefoil (*Potentilla fruticosa*) with occasional clumps of poison sumac (*Rhus vernix*). Sedges, grasses numerous. These fens may occur at the bases of moraines, in basins, or on springy lower slopes of hills and moraines.

TABLE 1 (Continued)

Especially well developed in areas of southeastern and southwestern Lower Michigan. Plate 2A.

Typical Species

Calopogon tuberosus
(local)
Cypripedium calceolus var.
parviflorum
C. candidum
(now generally rare, but
occasionally locally
abundant)
C. ×andrewsii
C. ×favillianum
(both hybrids occur
occasionally with both
parents)

Platanthera leucophaea
(rare or local, fen habitats
seem preferred in Ontario,
not so frequent as damp
sand-prairie or sphagnum
bog mats westward)
Spiranthes magnicamporum
(commonest in eastern edge
of range on Great Lakes
shoreline prairies or sand
ridges, more generally
distributed westward)

HABITAT 8

Dry, jack-pine and red pine forests or barrens on deep, dry sands. Ground covers of smaller blueberries (*Vaccinium* spp.), trailing arbutus (*Epigaea repens*), various ground pines (*Lycopodium* spp.), bearberry (*Arctostaphylos uva-ursi*), and bird-foot violet (*Viola pedata*). Plate 2B.

Typical Species

Cypripedium acaule
C. arietinum
Goodyera tesselata
(local, deeper woods)

Malaxis unifolia
Spiranthes lacera var. lacera
(locally very abundant)

HABITAT 9

Damp to dry meadows, long fallow fields, ditches and roadsides, especially where relatively bare patches of moist soil, moss patches, or earlier mild disturbance has created areas free from grass and sedge competition.

Typical Species in Calcareous Districts

Cypripedium arietinum
(local, mostly northern
districts)
C. calceolus vars.

Platanthera hyperborea
P. leucophaea
(very rare in limestone
districts, but does occur)

TABLE 1 (Continued)

Liparis loeselii

Spiranthes lucida
(rare or local, stations
seldom permanent but can
form large stands)
S. romanzoffiana

Typical Species in Acidic or Sterile, Damp, Sandy Soils

Cypripedium calceolus var.
  pubescens
Liparis lilifolia
(very occasional, in brushy
thickets)
L. loeselii
Platanthera lacera
P. leucophaea
(very rare now, but
occasional large populations
develop)

P. peramoena
(meadows, old fields,
mostly south of our area)
Spiranthes casei
(frequent northward and
eastward)
S. cernua
S. lacera vars.
S. tuberosa
(known in our area from
central and southwestern
Lower Michigan)

HABITAT 10

Mixed deciduous forests of oaks, tulip, sugar maple, hickories, black cherry, American beech, or rich beech-sugar maple stands. This is the forest of the well-known spring wildflowers: hepatica, dogtooth violets, wild leeks, Dutchman's breeches, squirrel corn, and trilliums. Plate 3A.

Typical Species

Aplectrum hyemale
Coeloglossum viride var.
  virescens (very local)
Corallorhiza maculata vars.
C. odontorhiza
C. striata
Cypripedium calceolus var.
  pubescens
Galearis spectabilis
(occasional south, largely
absent northward)

Goodyera pubescens
(occasionally other
  Goodyera species
northward)
Liparis lilifolia
(southern districts only)
Platanthera hookeri
(local)
P. orbiculata and its var.
  macrophylla
Triphora trianthophora
(exceedingly local in our
area, mainly in south of
region)

HABITAT 11

Low, moist to wet, mature red maple (*Acer rubrum*), oak (*Quercus bicolor, Q. velutina*, and other species), paper birch (*Betula papyrifera*),

TABLE 1 (Continued)

and quaking aspen (*Populus tremuloides*) woodlands with a layer of strongly acid humus or duff over a sandy or peaty substrate. Ground cover herbs include: wintergreen (*Gaultheria procumbens*), Canada lily-of-the-valley (*Maianthemum canadense*), New York fern (*Dryopteris novaboracensis*), and bracken fern (*Pteridium aquilinum*).

Such woodlands develop (at least in Lower Michigan) around the outer fringes of sphagnum bog basins and in the vicinity of Saginaw Bay where a series of postglacial former beach ridges lie more or less concentrically ringing the present bay. These ridges, occurring in a number of counties, alternate with low-lying flatwoods, especially on the side away from the present bay. The poorly drained flatwoods and the lower, moister slopes of the old beach ridge commonly develop the flora described here. Similarly, the Indiana and Michigan shores of Lake Michigan's interdunal lowlands, when wooded, produce nearly identical conditions. No single location can be expected to produce all of the species listed. Plate 3B.

Typical Species

Corallorhiza maculata vars.
C. odontorhiza
Cypripedium acaule
C. calceolus var. pubescens
Isotria medeoloides
(extremely rare, but this appears to be the habitat in Michigan and Ontario)
I. verticillata

Liparis lilifolia
L. loeselii
Malaxis unifolia
Platanthera ciliaris
(northern Indiana, south-western Lower Michigan, secondary habitat)
P. clavellata
P. flava var. herbiola
(prime habitat for this species in Michigan)
P. lacera
P. psycodes
Spiranthes ochroleuca
Tipularia discolor
(in Michigan, at least)

HABITAT 12

Low, wet beach-flats, interdunal fens and low dune or shoreline ridges, not so much a single habitat as a melding of several local habitats into a native plant assemblage which gives the impression of being a single, continuous unit. Open, sparsely vegetated, shoreline beach-flats alternate with conifer-covered, low, sandy ridges (actually ancient postglacial shorelines) and sedgy-shrubby interridge sloughs. At times of high water levels, portions of the troughs contain shallow ponds, at least in the

43

TABLE 1 (Continued)

spring (see also comments in section on orchid population changes, page 19).

The soil chemistry on flats and in sloughs is neutral or alkaline (in part because these areas are best developed in limestone districts with much limestone at or near the surface), the vegetation fenlike. On the low dunes and ridges, drier conditions, quartz sands, and abundant conifer needle duff create a surface soil which is acid to subacid and supports appropriately adapted plants.

Minor differences in soil moisture, presence or absence of limestone at the surface, and deep water-sorted sands on the ridges permit vastly different pH conditions in close proximity. Many of the plants growing here, orchid and nonorchid, seem indifferent to the amount of water present provided their pH, humus, and competition requirements are met. Consequently, the same species may be found growing on both the wet beach-flat fens, and on a nearby sandy ridge growing under what appears to be quite different conditions. Close examination, however, usually reveals that both sites meet the essential needs of the particular species.

Vegetation on the wet, sandy-mucky flats may be absent as the result of frequent flooding, or may consist of fen mosses, scattered sedges (*Carex* spp.), algal residue, scattered clumps of pitcher-plant (*Sarracenia purpurea*), colonies of butterwort (*Pinguicula vulgaris*), long-leaved sundew (*Drosera linearis*), bird's-eye primrose (*Primula mistassinica*), shrubby cinquefoil (*Potentilla fruticosa*), and little else. In the more sheltered interridge sloughs sedges grow more densely, and thicker mats of fen and sphagnum moss species develop. A common shrub of sheltered slough borders is sweet gale (*Myrica gale*).

On sandier, drier yet suitably damp, more acidic sites, especially in glades and under coniferous cover grow dense thickets of Labrador tea (*Ledum groenlandicum*), spreading juniper (*Juniperus communis*), bog buckthorn (*Rhamnus alnifolia*), and wild sarsaparilla (*Aralia nudicaulis*). In open, drier, sunny sites, bearberry (*Arctostaphylos uva-ursi*), spreading juniper, and trailing juniper (*Juniperus horizontalis*) occur. Occasionally, one encounters Kalm's St. John's-wort (*Hypericum kalmianum*) on low, open, sandy sites. Coniferous cover consists of white cedar (*Thuja occidentalis*), balsam-fir (*Abies balsamaea*), red pine (*Pinus resinosa*), and black or white spruces (*Picea mariana* or *P. glauca*).

This beach-flat-fen-and-ridge habitat occurs occasionally throughout the western Great Lakes region, but has become particularly well developed in portions of Ontario's Bruce Peninsula, Manitoulin and Drummond islands, northern Lower Michigan and eastern Upper Michigan, and on Wisconsin's Door Peninsula. Plate 4B.

TABLE 1 (Continued)

Typical Species

Typical species of wet, sandy beaches, margins of troughs, and inter-dunal fens, rooted in mosses or sand and muck, and growing in open sunshine.

Arethusa bulbosa
Calopogon tuberosus
Cypripedium calceolus var. *pubescens*
C. reginae
Liparis loeselii
Platanthera dilatata
P. hyperborea
P. psycodes
Pogonia ophioglossoides
Spiranthes cernua
S. lucida (very local, usually in calcareous districts)
S. romanzoffiana

Typical species of drier, more acidic, usually wooded old beach ridges or low dunes; if in wetter situations here, growing usually in superficial layers of sphagnum moss overlying more alkaline soils. These species grow most often in shade or filtered sunlight.

Calypso bulbosa
Coeloglossum viride var. *virescens*
Corallorhiza maculata complex
C. striata
C. trifida
Cypripedium arietinum
C. calceolus var. *parviflorum*
Goodyera oblongifolia
G. repens var. *ophioides*
G. tesselata
Listera convallarioides
L. cordata
Malaxis monophylla var. *brachypoda*
M. unifolia
Platanthera clavellata
P. hookeri
P. hyperborea
P. obtusata
P. orbiculata
Spiranthes lacera var. *lacera*

Some of the species in the preceding tables may grow in the listed habitat in certain districts, but not in others.

GROWING OUR NATIVE ORCHIDS

TERRESTRIAL ORCHIDS, particularly those of North America, are notoriously difficult to cultivate. In addition to the difficulty of their cultivation, many species are rare. Because of this, some people, especially conservationists, feel that any attempt to grow our native species is doomed and hence a bad conservation practice. I cannot agree entirely with this viewpoint. A number of native orchid species respond well to cultivation when given proper environmental conditions. However, unless the gardener is willing to study the ecological needs of the plants in detail and give them the necessary care, he ought not attempt to grow them.

Why Grow Native Orchids?

I believe that scientists, trained horticulturists, and skilled gardeners should learn successful methods for the cultivation of our native orchids for the following reasons:

1. Certain aspects of orchid biology cannot be determined from herbarium material, but require long periods of observation not convenient or even possible with wild colonies. Statements concerning the behavior of certain wild orchid species, without data or verification, appear in print and may be repeated from author to author. Some of these reports, such as the report that plants of *Isotria* may revert to underground, saprophytic growth for years and then reappear and resume normal growth (see comments under the genus *Isotria*, page 148), simply are not borne out by my experience in growing them. Through cultivation of *Isotria*, however, I have learned some facts which might account for this persistent report.[1]

---

[1] Nonblooming stems of *Isotria verticillata* appear up to two weeks after flowering stems. If, in a given colony, no plants possess the strength to bloom that season, the plants will not appear above ground until well after their expected blooming date. A search for the plants at the typical flowering date may fail to locate any plants, whereas two weeks later the sterile plants will be fully in evidence.

Another fact gleaned from experience in cultivating our orchids is that their growth buds have an innate dormancy factor. Before an orchid can initiate new growth, the bud concerned must have been exposed to a period of suitably cold

2. Specifically endangered populations of orchids can be "rescued," grown and propagated for rehabilitation, restocking, and restoration on wild habitat or sanctuaries, if we have the knowledge to grow them.[2]

3. Gardeners and persons with highly specialized interest in certain plant groups, captivated by the great charm or beauty of their favorite plants, desire to grow them. But many gardeners hesitate to attempt the rare and difficult orchids, perhaps fearing the criticism of some conservationists if they do. Other gardeners and plant specialists, driven by their fascination to possess the plants, view their interests as a right to grow the plants which is equal to the interests and rights of those seeking total protection for them. The "to grow or not to grow" conflict between gardeners and conservationists seems to me to result from the high failure rate of orchids in the garden and our present inability to grow them from seed which necessitates collecting garden stock from the wild.[3] We grow most other wild plant groups successfully and, for aesthetic, scientific, and educational reasons, orchids ought to be grown too. Obviously, we lack some fundamental knowledge of the orchids' critical growth factors. If one function of science is to develop new knowledge, then we ought to explore the mysteries of orchid growth requirements so that we can grow orchids as easily as we can grow other plants. Interested parties could then grow propagated stock in gardens without the need to collect plants from the wild.

4. Progress on plant tissue culture and clonal multiplication from meristematic tissue, however, has reached the point where mass propagation of many of our orchid species is now possible or is,

---

temperatures. Once the cold period has broken its dormancy the bud will grow when proper temperatures for growth return. If the young growth is broken, trampled, or grazed off, the plant will not normally send up additional growths or leaves until it again passes through a period of cold to break the dormancy of the remaining buds on the rhizome. Failure of a plant to appear, I believe, results from such bud damage not to a natural reversion to a *saprophytic, underground state.*

[2]It is sometimes suggested that severely endangered plant species could be saved by placing them permanently in the care of botanical gardens. I do not believe that one can "preserve" a species through garden cultivation. Given plants may be maintained in the garden for a time, but if a species is to ultimately survive it must maintain natural populations on natural wild habitat.

[3]The past 25 years have shed little light on the problems of terrestrial orchid seed biology. The techniques to grow our native terrestrial orchids under experimental conditions *in vitro* or in nature have produced, at best, unpredictable results. Many workers have succeeded in obtaining swollen embryos or small protocorms, but few have succeeded in obtaining mature, established, flowering plants.

at most, a few years in the future. Mass cloning of our rarer species will drastically alter the conservation problems concerning them. The reasons for objecting to cultivation of native orchids will no longer be valid. Readily available propagated stock for garden use will reduce the pressure to collect from natural populations and provide abundant material for use in restoration attempts in the wild. To meet the challenges of these rapidly developing new techniques, a sound body of horticultural knowledge concerning our native orchid species is needed. Such knowledge can only be developed by growing these orchids.

Ecological Considerations

In order to grow native orchids successfully, it is necessary to understand and meet the requirements of their biology, particularly their symbiotic way of life and their soil needs. While some orchid ecology is discussed below, the potential orchid grower should also review the more detailed comments in the ecology section of this book. Much additional pertinent information on this subject can be obtained from the publication, *Proceedings from Symposium II and Lectures—North American Terrestrial Orchids* (Michigan Orchid Society, 1983).

Our native orchids maintain complex relationships with soil chemistry and mycorrhizal fungi, but it is not necessary to duplicate these wild conditions exactly in the garden. If the gardener does not intend to attempt to grow orchids from seed, he need only provide certain broad conditions to succeed. In my opinion, the most critical factors for the survival of orchids in the garden are: 1) suitable soil including proper nutrient levels, mineral content, pH range, and texture for drainage; 2) suitable soil temperature, both summer and winter; 3) proper moisture ranges; 4) freedom from competition and encroachment.

Methods of Cultivation

One can grow orchids by two basic methods; naturalize them in suitable habitats, or grow them in special artificially constructed garden beds.

Naturalization

Few people have a variety of orchid habitats available to them. Those so fortunate should determine carefully the native species suitable to the habitats and, assuming that the plants can be obtained legally and in keeping with good conservation practice, plant the stock in the proper sites. As an alternative, scatter fresh seed in suitable places. Plants moved from one site to another very similar site should survive and eventually reproduce. For information on natural orchid habitats in the western Great Lakes region, see the tables and descriptions on pages 37–45. If the gardener carefully matches his habitat with the proper species, he need not be concerned with the critical factors listed above since the environment will provide them.

Gardening With Prepared Soils

If a natural area is not available, the gardener must prepare beds of suitable soils. In these artificial beds, the essential conditions for the particular plants concerned need to be provided. Fortunately, the showier native orchids can be accommodated in the garden in one or two types of beds, in spite of the diversity of habitats in which they occur in the wild.

Bog Gardens

Authors of wildflower culture books and plant catalogs speak glowingly of bog gardens. For the commoner plants of lakeshore, stream, and bog—pickerel weed (*Pontederia*), arrowhead (*Sagittaria*), cardinal flower (*Lobelia cardinalis*), and cattails (*Typha* spp.)—such a garden works well. These plants tolerate a wide range of environmental conditions. However, to create the special conditions necessary for orchids presents a real challenge.

Wet peat, when confined under water-logged conditions as in a container basin, can stagnate, sour, smell foul, and harbor undesirable soil fungi and decay-causing bacteria. These organisms can quickly destroy rhizomes, dormant buds, or even the bases of the flowering stems. If the bog is kept too dry in an attempt to avoid these problems, there can be excessive penetration of oxygen into the soil resulting in accelerated decay of the organic peat or muck. Within a year or so, the soil will have changed to such an extent that the orchids will perish due to incorrect environmental conditions.

Yet, successful bog gardens can be constructed, especially for orchids and companion plants that prefer to grow in beds of live sphagnum moss in full sun. In a bog garden, peat soils and moss beds must be separated from the regular soils for at least two important reasons: 1) to keep the soil properly moist and acid; 2) to prevent earthworms from tunneling into the peat and removing it.

A child's plastic wading pool is an ideal container for a bog garden. Select one of the desired size, poke a few drain holes in it about half-way up the sides (not in the bottom). This placement of the drainage holes will allow the undrained lower portion of the pool to act as a reservoir for some moisture, and will also prevent the entire container filling with standing water. There are two alternatives for obtaining soil to fill the container. If bogs occur locally, blocks of peat and live sphagnum moss can be cut from them and fit into the wading pool. The live sphagnum moss will include native heath plants and natural orchid companions. Plant the desired orchids in the bog garden and provide suitable water to keep the moss wet and growing.[4] This is the most satisfactory bog gardening method.

If peat bogs do not occur in the region, the bog garden container must be filled with a concocted soil. I use a mixture of washed silica sand (available from builder's supply houses as sandblasting sand) and Canadian peat with great success.[5] At the bottom of the wading pool or other container use almost pure sand. Build in more peat as you approach the upper levels. Near the surface use a proportion of 60 percent peat to 40 percent sand. Topdress with almost pure silica sand or a mulch of coarse pine needles to discourage the growth of damp-off fungus on the surface. Pine needles provide both nutrients and soil acidity as they decompose. Either mulch helps to discourage weed seedlings. Thoroughly soak the peat-soil and allow it to cure for several weeks before introducing any of the more delicate bog plants or orchids. During the curing period fungi frequently invade the peat and this could cause the death of any introduced plants. These fungi generally run their course and disappear after a week or two.

Placement of the bog garden or any other prepared flower bed must take into consideration the type of orchids you wish to grow— shaded conditions are necessary for northern forest species, full sun for the southern fringed-orchids, pogonias, or other open bog species. At best, some skill and experience must be developed before a really satisfactory bog garden can be maintained over a long period of time. Fortunately, most of the showier and more horticulturally desirable bog species will grow in other types of beds with more certain success and under conditions much easier to maintain than the bog garden.

Sand-Peat Beds

Orchid species which grow naturally in peaty meadows, in bogs, on beaches or dunes, on granitic outcroppings, or in sterile sandy fields grow well in a carefully prepared sand-peat bed. The bed can be a separate entity, or it can be incorporated as a pocket between rocks in a rock garden or other flower bed. As with the

---

[4]Sphagnum moss resents chlorinated water and will not thrive with it—use rain or distilled water.

[5]Do not use masoner's sand since it may contain limestone grains or other unsuitable materials. Use an inert, silica sand.

bog garden, make some provision to prevent earthworms from introducing unsuitable soil from below or removing the peat for food. If the garden site is well drained, 10–12 inches of native soil can be removed and the resulting excavation lined with a sheet of heavy plastic liberally punctured for drainage. This hole is then filled with the prepared sand-peat mixture.

On poorly drained sites or on clay soils (clays are rarely chemically suited to orchids), or to grow acid soil species on limestone soils, I recommend a raised soil bed. Such a bed will allow rainwater to drain down and away rather than allowing it to evaporate and bring up and concentrate minerals from unsuitable soils below. Do not use cement to line excavations for beds or bogs— its high alkalinity can alter soil pH and adversely affect orchid plants for years. Similarly, do not use metal containers. Metal ions seem to poison orchids and many other bog plants. Railroad ties or garden timbers provide ideal cribbing for raised beds. However, be wary of the new, pressure-treated, decay-resistant garden timbers. The chemical preservatives in the wood are known to adversely affect orchid growth in closed greenhouses and they may have a similar effect on plants in the garden.

Use the same soil for sand-peat beds as for bog gardens—a mixture of 60 percent silica sand to 40 percent Canadian peat. Avoid the product sold as "Michigan peat." It is a sedge peat more highly decomposed and less acid than Canadian peat. "Michigan peat" breaks down and becomes unsuitable quickly. Mulch the bed with coarse pine needles such as those of red pine (*Pinus resinosa*) or Scots pine (*P. sylvestris*) to discourage weeds and to provide an insulating cover to keep the soils cool in summer and less deeply frozen in winter. Special benefits may accrue from the use of Scots pine needles as mulch. In a number of New England and Michigan Scots pine plantations unusually large populations of native orchids have developed (*fide* Case and Case; Champlin 1976). It may be that Scots pine or its needle litter harbors unusually favorable conditions for orchid mycorrhizae.

The raised peat-sand bed is suitable for nearly all orchids of strongly acid soils, both wet and dry. It is not suitable for the orchids of black, mucky swamps, streambank mucks, or moist peat layers over strongly limey soils. To grow these orchids in artificial soils is not easy since there is no convenient way to construct these black mucks so as to attain the proper amount of organic content at the right stage of decay. Native muck can be taken from a streambank or old cedar swamp and placed in a cribbing similar to the raised peat bed. However, problems may arise. In a garden bed, such soils may oxidize too quickly and change chemically. Also, if bog muck dries out too much it can be extremely difficult to wet again. A mulch of pine needles or wood chips will prevent excessive drying and help control weeds, but it may alter the soil significantly as it decays. Regular mulching of the bed with freshly collected bog muck will maintain suitable conditions for long periods, but it is hard work. Plants of marl fens or peaty horizons atop limestone may be grown fairly easily in a bed much like the sand-peat bed, using the same soil but with an equal volume of crushed limestone chips added.

For any of the prepared beds, water can be provided during extremely dry periods, but regular watering will not usually be necessary once the bed is established and mulched. Generally, orchids under cultivation require more light and less water than they receive in the wild.

Greenhouse Culture

Our native orchids are not suitable for greenhouse culture with tropical species because they require a cold rest period to break bud dormancy. They can be grown in a cold or alpine house where a cold rest can be provided. Some of our showiest native orchids including the tongue-fringed *Platanthera* species, *Calopogon* species, *Pogonia ophioglossoides*, and *Isotria verticillata* grow with great vigor in plastic containers filled with living sphagnum moss. Water them with distilled water (water from a refrigeration-type dehumidifier will do). In winter, allow plants in containers to drop to a temperature of about 30° F. Do not allow them to freeze hard since plants in containers will die of the cold where the same species underground, in its native bog soil, would be insulated from temperature extremes and survive. My experience with North American cypripediums has been that many species grow well in slightly acid to neutral loams or even garden soils, if not fertilized, but that few species persist in pot culture.

Do not use any commercial or inorganic mineral fertilizers on any native orchids or bog plants. These usually prove fatal, perhaps by overstimulating the orchid's mycorrhizal fungus or by releasing toxic metal ions (Sheviak 1983). Sadovsky (1968) suggests fertilizing terrestrial orchids with a weak solution made by soaking dead oak leaves in water until the water becomes deep tea-brown. I would use restraint with any fertilizer!

Orchid Pests

Orchid leaves, stems, and especially roots contain sweet and fragrant substances (reputed to be vanillin). Slugs, snails, and deer love to eat them. In greenhouses and garden beds, snails and slugs must be kept to a minimum. Metaldehyde drenches sold under various trade names provide the usual method of control for greenhouse orchids. I do not know their effect on sensitive terrestrial orchids. Use caution! Poisonous pellets used as slug bait contain dangerous chemicals and must be kept away from pets and children.

Thin-leaved orchids suffer heavily from red spider infestations both in cultivation and occasionally in the wild. Hot, dry weather favors both red spiders and other plant mites. Fortunately, sprays such as Kelthane or Malathion control them. Small leaf chafer beetles or weevils sometimes eat the heart out of developing flower stems on cultivated platantheras. They do their damage surprisingly early in the season and their predations often kill the plants. Dust with Rotenone or a general insecticide at intervals starting soon after foliage appears.

Aphid infestations severely damage orchid growth and flower buds, particularly under greenhouse conditions. Watch for them constantly. Any of the commercial insect sprays except the oil-based dormant sprays control aphids without much harm to the plants.

Our native orchids are quite susceptible to fungus rots and leaf spot diseases under cultivation. If blackening of foliage appears or a series of small black streaks develop, fast action is required. Remove the blackened tissue by cutting well back into healthy, green tissue with a sterile razor blade. Then treat the cut surfaces with a fungicide such as Captan or Phaltan. Since many fungus diseases seem to follow an infestation of spider mites or the nearly invisible plant mites, preventative sprayings with Kelthane followed by a fungicide treatment before symptoms appear work well. Suitable fungicides include Captan, Phaltan, Benlate, or Ferbam.

Garden rodents, especially voles and chipmunks, destroy many plants. They dig up tubers, snip off stems, trample plants, and wreak general havoc. Starlings, robins, and sparrows, especially in cities, peck at shoots and leaves and uproot plants (and labels). Coverings of screening material will eliminate bird damage. Traps will control rodents. Avoid metallic screening since it may poison the plants.

Obtaining Plants for Cultivation

Obtaining orchid plants for culture is a sensitive issue. There is great concern over the effects of collecting in the wild on native orchid populations. Many states and provinces protect some or all species of orchids. In some political jurisdictions, plants may be collected from private lands with the written permission of the owner, while in others, protection covers both public and private lands. It is essential for the prospective orchid collector to be knowledgeable concerning local plant protection laws and regulations. Special permission may occasionally be obtained to collect from lands slated for lumbering or development. A few wildflower nurseries sell propagated plants.

One should obtain plants legally and ethically or forego growing them. Assuming that a legal source for obtaining plants from the wild exists, all collection should be carried out with restraint. Clump forming orchids such as lady's-slippers divide as easily as garden iris. It it not necessary to take the entire clump. A clean, sharp knife will sever a portion of rhizome with a bud or two. Part of the clump can then be left in the wild to propagate the plant. The small division, if it prospers in the garden, will soon form a good clump. *Pogonia* produces root bud offsets which, if happily situated, quickly form large patches. A few runners with leaves can be removed to the garden without any permanent damage to the wild colony. *Calopogon* produces offset tubers which may be removed without stripping the whole clump. Platantheras also occasionally produce offsets. Trampled or injured plants tend to form clumps or extra offsets the year following the injury. A small offset of such a clump can be removed while still leaving the plant in the wild to reproduce. Collecting need not be a destructive process.

Within a few years meristematic propagation of outstanding native orchid clones will undoubtedly provide a rich supply of material for gardens without endangering our wild native orchid populations.

Species Especially Amenable to Cultivation in Properly Prepared Soils

> *Cypripedium calceolus* var. *pubescens*
> *Cypripedium calceolus* var. *parviflorum*
> *Cypripedium candidum**
> *Cypripedium reginae**
> *Cypripedium acaule* (difficult to establish, but permanent if happy)
> *Calopogon tuberosus*
> *Pogonia ophioglossoides*
> *Aplectrum hyemale*
> *Goodyera pubescens*
> *Liparis loeselii*
> *Liparis lilifolia*
> *Platanthera psycodes* (difficult)

*Listed as endangered, threatened, or of special concern in some political jurisdictions.

Platanthera blephariglottis
*Platanthera ciliaris**
*Platanthera grandiflora**
Platanthera peramoena
Epipactis helleborine (often weedy)
Spiranthes cernua
Spiranthes ochroleuca
*Spiranthes casei**
Spiranthes lacera var. *lacera*

Other species may, perhaps, grow well in cultivation, but most lack horticultural merit.

*Listed as endangered, threatened, or of special concern in some political jurisdictions.

KEY TO THE GENERA OF ORCHIDS OF THE WESTERN GREAT LAKES REGION

A DEVICE CALLED a KEY offers the simplest method for accurately identifying a plant. Many people shy away from botanical keys fearing they are too difficult to master, but some practice will prove their value and facilitate their use.

The first step in using a key is to acquire the vocabulary necessary to understand the comparisons and differentiations made between the various genera and species. For this purpose a Glossary is provided. The line drawings showing critical differences between similar species and the photographs emphasizing the appearance of each species in its habitat should be freely consulted as aids in identification.

After the genus of the plant has been identified in the Key to Genera, the key to the genus there indicated should be consulted in identifying the species. If no key is given, read the description of the genus and species.

Use of the Key to Genera

To use the Key to Genera of Orchids of the Western Great Lakes Region, examine a typical specimen of the plant to be identified, carefully noting its general features. The important features in identification are variations in structure or size of the sepals, petals, lip, column, rostellum, pollinia, or spur. Figure 2 shows these parts of the orchid flower as they appear in the different lines of development in our native orchids.

Turning to the Key to Genera, start by reading statement A. Then compare both that statement and the plant with statement AA farther along the key. Always check unfamiliar terms in the Glossary before proceeding. From these two statements select the one that corresponds the more closely with the plant in hand. Then proceed to statements B and BB under your choice and compare them. If, for instance, the first of the pair is correct for your plant, proceed to the next letter of the alphabet below it. If the second of the pair should be correct, proceed to the next couplet beyond it. Once a selection has been made, go to the next couplet beyond your selection and repeat the process.

After a number of choices, you will reach a point where you cannot proceed further. At the right of this terminal statement will appear the name of the genus of orchids and a page number. Turn to this page and follow the same procedure with the key to the species of that particular genus. When you have arrived at a tentative identification, read the description concerned and compare your plant with the photograph of this species. Be sure to make a reasonable allowance for individual variation. If the plant agrees with the description, your identification is probably correct. If it does not agree, you have made some error of choice or interpretation. Consult the Key to Genera again and follow it through, checking carefully. No key is infallible, but if used carefully a key is the most rapid and accurate method of identifying plants.

KEY TO THE GENERA OF ORCHIDS OF THE WESTERN GREAT LAKES REGION

A. Lip, or at least the basal one-half of the lip of flower pouched, saclike, or slipper-shaped. (Do not confuse a spur and a saclike lip.)

  B. Lip distinctly a slipperlike pouch, flowers 1–3.

    C. Pouch of lip blunt at distal end, orifice inrolled.

CYPRIPEDIUM
page 70

    CC. Pouch of lip prolonged into two horns distally, orifice with an outward-rolled flat white apron.

CALYPSO
page 212

  BB. Lip saccate, or floor of lip cupped, but not a distinct slipper; flowers 3–many in a somewhat spicate raceme.

    C. Leaves essentially basal, small, usually under 8 cm long, heavy textured, variously veined or tesselated with white markings. Flowers small, 1 cm or less long, white or greenish on outside of segments, lip saccate but ending in a pointed beak.

GOODYERA
page 191

CC. Stem leafy, leaves thin textured, strongly ribbed, largest leaves 4–18 cm long. Flowers relatively large, lowermost, at least, more than 1–1.5 cm long, green, marked with rose or purple. Basal half of lip saccate-cupped, distal half broadly triangular, with a fleshy callus near its base.

EPIPACTIS
page 143

AA. Lip of flower variously lobed, fringed, ridged, or flattened, but not slipperlike or saccate.

B. Base of lip prolonged backward into a hollow spur.

C. Leaves absent at flowering time, or withering, black-streaked or otherwise deteriorating (fugacious).

D. Flowering scape leafless. Flowers slightly asymmetrical. Spur 2–4 times longer than the lip. Leaf solitary, cordate, strongly ribbed, produced in autumn, withering in spring, not present at flowering time. Scape produced from a whitish corm or series of corms.

TIPULARIA
page 210

DD. Scape with 2–4 basal leaves, which deteriorate, wither, or are dried at flowering time. Flowers symmetrical, spur about equaling the lip. Scape from a cluster of fleshy roots and *a pair of ovoid tubers*.

Piperia unalascensis
page 125

CC. Leaves present at flowering time and in good condition.

  D. Flowering plant with one leaf, essentially basal (rarely with an abnormal, enlarged leaflike bract on scape).

    E. Flowers small, green, lip linear to triangular-lanceolate, 1–2 mm wide at base, acute-tipped.

PLATANTHERA (in part)
(*Platanthera obtusata*)
page 93

    EE. Flowers larger, white to pink-mauve, lip 3-lobed, conspicuously spotted or barred with purple, midlobe large, cuneate to obcordate, dilated and notched, 4–6 mm wide at apex.

Amerorchis rotundifolia
page 85

  DD. Flowering plants with two or more leaves.

    E. Sticky disk of pollinia enclosed in a pouch, sepals and petals mauve, lavender, or pink, lip relatively large, 10–20 mm long, 8–12 mm wide, not fringed or dentate on margins.

    F. Leaves two, basal, uniformly dark green, suborbicular to elliptic, 10 cm or more long and wide. Lip ovate to subquadrate, entire, white, rarely pinkish. Sepals and petals free from each other, but forming a hood over the column. Plant widespread in the south of our region.

Galearis spectabilis
page 88

FF. Leaves several, cauline, gradually reduced to bracts above, green with dark purplish madder spots, up to 20 cm long and about 2.5–3 cm wide. Lip 3-lobed, cordate, mauve with darker purple markings. Adventive species known in our region only from the vicinity of Timmins, Ontario.

Dactylorhiza maculata
page 90

EE. Sticky disk of pollinia free, exposed. Sepals and petals variously colored; lip various, green, white, orange, or lavender; if lavender, mauve, or purple, lip fringed or erose-dentate on margins and with three wedge-shaped divisions.

F. Opening to spur of lip clearly visible; spur relatively elongate, cylindrical, tapered-acuminate, saccate, or clavellate.

PLATANTHERA (in part)
page 93

FF. Opening to spur minute, obscured by lip tissue; spur short, scrotiform.

Coeloglossum viride var. *virescens*
page 127

BB. Lip without a distinct hollow spur at its base (in *Corallorhiza*, lip base and lateral sepals may together form a chinlike mentum).

C. Leaves fugacious (drying and falling away at flowering), or if in good condition reduced to cauline sheaths on the flowering scape. Roots fleshy-fasciculate, or absent and replaced by subterranean coralloid stems.

D. Leaves fugacious. Flowers rather densely spiraled, white or cream (floor of lip or back of lip may be variously yellow or greenish); back of dorsal sepal pubescent; roots fleshy, fasciculate.

SPIRANTHES (in part)
page 163

DD. Leaves reduced to slightly inflated, tubular, essentially nonphotosynthetic sheaths on flowering stem. Scape laxly several- to many-flowered; flowers greenish, brown, or reddish purple; backs of sepals glabrous. True roots absent, underground stems coralloid.

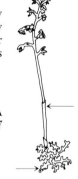

CORALLORHIZA
page 217

CC. Plants with at least one green leaf present or fading at flowering time (if leaf not yet developed or emerging from cauline sheath, flower solitary and showy). Roots fibrous to fleshy, often associated with a corm or tuber.

D. Leaves arranged in a whorl at top of a fleshy-succulent, hollow stem.

ISOTRIA
page 149

DD. Leaves not in a whorl at top of stem.

E. Flowers 1–6 or rarely 10, relatively large and showy, 1 cm or more long, lavender or white. If more than one flower, only 2–4 open at a time, flowers opening in succession.

61

F. Lip uppermost, hinged, bearded with yellow hairs. Flowers 1–10 opening in succession, with only 1–4 open at one time. Medium to dark mauve-lavender, rarely white.

CALOPOGON
page 160

FF. Lip lowermost, not hinged.

G. Flowers typically 3, or several, only one open at a time. Leaves several, small, fleshy, nearly bractlike, borne alternately on stem. Rhizomes stoloniferous, ends of stolons with enlarged tubers.

TRIPHORA
page 145

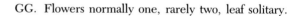

GG. Flowers normally one, rarely two, leaf solitary.

H. Leaf one, rarely two, linear, grasslike, rising from a basal corm, ensheathing the scape. Sepals and petals erect; petals forming a hood over column, sepals reflexed. Floral bract obscure.

ARETHUSA
page 157

HH. Leaf oval, rising from near middle of stem, somewhat fleshy, veins obscure. Roots fleshy-fibrous, widely spreading. Floral bract leaflike, prominent.

POGONIA
page 155

EE. Flowers 6–many, typically with many open at the same time; flowers relatively small, usually less than 1 cm long, or if 1 cm or more, individually dull in color and inconspicuous. Colors mostly green, whitish, or purplish brown.

F. Sepals and petals subordinated in size to lip, which is the largest and most conspicuous part of the flower.

G. Leaves 2.

H. Leaves rising from middle of stem, subopposite. Roots fibrous.

LISTERA
page 130

HH. Leaves basal, similar in size, rising from a subsurface corm.

LIPARIS
page 206

GG. Leaf 1 (appearing to rise from middle of stem [in life], but arising nearer base and ensheathing stem).

MALAXIS (in part)
page 200

FF. Sepals, petals, and lip similar in size and texture; lip not the only conspicuous part of flower.

G. Leaves several.

    H. Leaves narrowly linear to ovate; if ovate, broadly petioled. Flowers white to cream, in a rather dense, often several-ranked, spiral, spicate raceme. Floral bracts conspicuous, mostly 8–10 mm or more long. Roots fleshy-fasciculate.

SPIRANTHES (in part)
page 163

    HH. Leaves ovate to elliptic, not petiolate, rising from above, below, and ensheathing a tiny corm; leaves bearing a few, minute, yellowish bulbils at apex. Floral bracts obscure, appressed, 2–3 mm long. Spike elongate.

MALAXIS (in part)
page 200

GG. Leaf solitary, flowers greenish or brownish madder; floral bracts inconspicuous.

    H. Leaf appearing to rise from middle of flowering scape. Flowers small, 2–4 mm long.

MALAXIS (in part)
page 200

    HH. Leaf arising separately from flowering scape, oval, purple or greenish below, white-veined and wrinkled, weakly erect or lying flat on ground, withering or yellowing at flowering time. Flowers 1 cm or more long.

APLECTRUM
page 215

EXPLANATION OF THE DISTRIBUTION MAPS

T HE SCOPE of this book prohibited the preparation of complete and exhaustive distribution maps. It was necessary to limit the study to show significant distributional trends without making the task impossible. On the following maps distribution is shown by county; i.e., for each species the map shows one mark on each county for which a herbarium specimen was seen. Only one mark per county appears regardless of the number of times the species may have been collected in that county. The only exception to this rule occurs with specimens collected on one of the larger islands in the Great Lakes. In these cases both the island and the county holding political jurisdiction over the island are marked. In the rare instance where a species is known from one of the larger islands but not recorded from the mainland of the county, only the island is marked.

The region covered by the maps includes all of Michigan and Wisconsin and the bordering counties or districts of Minnesota, Illinois, Indiana, Ohio, and western Ontario, Canada. The region covered by the maps is essentially the drainage system of the western Great Lakes region to which has been added a few counties in southeastern Minnesota, much of Wisconsin, and the counties of northern Illinois.

The statements concerning the general North American distribution of Great Lakes orchids given in the species accounts are based upon Correll's *Native Orchids of North America* and Luer's *The Native Orchids of the United States and Canada Excluding Florida*. The orchid collections of the following institutions were examined in the preparation of the distribution maps accompanying each species account:

Cranbrook Institute of Science, Bloomfield Hills, Michigan (BLH)
Indiana University, Bloomington, Indiana (IND)
Lakehead University, Thunder Bay, Ontario, Canada (LKHD)
Biosystematics Research Institute, Agriculture Canada, Ottawa, Canada (DAO)
Michigan State University, East Lansing, Michigan (MSC)

65

Milwaukee Public Museum, Milwaukee, Wisconsin (MIL)
Ohio State University, Columbus, Ohio (OS)
University of Illinois, Urbana, Illinois (ILL)
University of Michigan, Ann Arbor, Michigan (MICH)
University of Minnesota, St. Paul, Minnesota (MIN)
University of Toronto, Toronto, Ontario, Canada (TRT)
University of Western Ontario, London, Ontario, Canada (UWO)
University of Wisconsin, Madison, Wisconsin (WIS)
Oberlin College, Oberlin, Ohio (OC) (provided certain critical specimens)

For the second edition of this book, I again examined all orchid specimens in the listed herbaria except one or two smaller collections where few or no new orchid specimens had been deposited. All specimens were carefully checked for correct identity, and all those containing traceable locality data were recorded. The amount of field work in the Great Lakes region has increased considerably since the 1964 publication of the first edition. Consequently, the number of orchid specimens examined for this new edition was great and the time and effort required to identify, record, and utilize the data would have been prohibitive without the help I received from my wife, Roberta Case, in organizing and recording the data. Much of the work of constructing the county distribution maps is hers and I am most grateful to her for it.

I am also greatly indebted to the institutions cited above, their herbarium directors, curators, staff members, and graduate students for all the courtesies, help, and encouragement so generously extended in the preparation of this second edition. I especially wish to thank those who gave their personal time on evenings or weekends so that these time consuming examinations could be completed within reasonable limits.

It is inevitable that many botanists, both amateur and professional, will know of orchid stations not indicated on these maps. There are many reasons for this: 1) many orchid hunters zealously guard their prized records; 2) many significant voucher specimens have been deposited in herbaria not consulted in this study, 3) certain specimens may have been on loan or under repair at the time I examined the herbarium; 4) a specimen may have been deposited in the herbarium after I completed my work there.

Mapping drawn from herbarium specimens can never be completely up-to-date, since new discoveries regularly come to light. The distribution maps included in this book can really do only one thing — show distributional trends for each species. Other

publications, utilizing county maps for specified districts, may yield
additional information particularly if their authors consulted herbaria other than those I utilized.

Anyone who has a new or unusual record is urged to prepare
adequate specimens and to deposit them in recognized herbaria.
Many scientists will recognize distributional data only if it is backed
by a herbarium voucher specimen properly deposited. Only such
specimens can be utilized by students in future research studies.
Good voucher specimens in herbaria provide a valuable source
of botanical information both now and for generations to come.

The most satisfactory specimens consist of a complete plant including root, stem, leaves, and flowers. The specimen can be
dried inside a folded sheet of newspaper placed between sheets
of blotting paper. The entire packet should be placed under
pressure while drying. Most botanists use a device called a plant

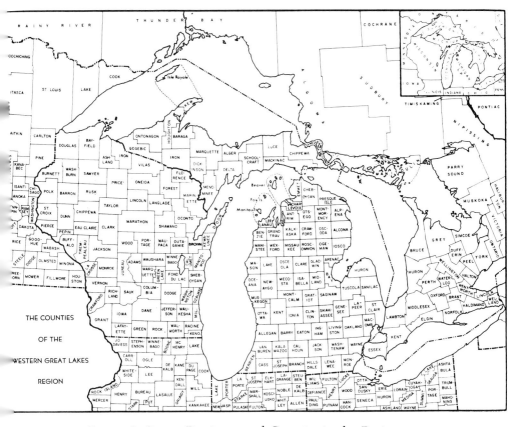

FIGURE 3. States, Provinces, and Counties in the Region

press for this purpose. This device is illustrated in many botany books. When collecting plants to be recorded, select a specimen as nearly typical and perfect as possible. Either a metal collecting can (the vasculum) or a plastic bag prevents wilting and provides a satisfactory means of carrying the plant.

Plant specimens have little scientific value unless they carry the essential data. The most important facts to record are: accurate locality information, including state, county, township or town (if possible with the quarter section in which the plant was found); the collector's name; the date; and the details of the habitat. Estimates of population size or special circumstances may also be of great value to future botanists examining the collection. Though desirable, correct identification of the species is not initially essential, since it can be supplied by botanists at a later date.

No scientific record is sufficiently important to justify the destruction of a station for a rare species. One or a very few specimens from a single locality will suffice. There is no need for botany students to collect vouchers year after year from the same, known stations. Common sense should always guide the collector.

DESCRIPTION OF GENERA AND SPECIES

CYPRIPEDIUM L. (THE LADY'S-SLIPPERS)

The tribe (subfamily) Cypripedieae, to which the lady's-slippers belong, differs from most other orchid tribes in having two fertile anthers instead of one. The sterile third anther forms a special organ, the staminode, which is homologous to the single fertile anther in the rest of the orchid family. Another important difference occurs in the pollen structure. Unlike species with waxy pollen clusters, or pollinia, the cypripediums have loose and granular pollen. Because of these fundamental differences in morphology, some botanists suggest that the Cypripedieae should be considered a separate family.

The lady's-slippers encompass four botanical genera— *Paphiopedilum*, *Phragmipedium*, *Selenipedium*, and *Cypripedium*—which differ in ways too technical to discuss here. The first three genera are mainly tropical, while *Cypripedium* is mainly from temperate regions of the Northern Hemisphere. The name *Cypripedium* derives from two Greek words, *Kypris* (Venus) and *podion* (slipper, little foot), and, by further derivation, lady's-slipper.

Most cypripediums are glandular-pubescent throughout. This pubescence causes an irritation and reaction similar to a severe case of poison ivy in some persons. The roots of some native lady's-slippers have supplied a drug used as a nerve tonic in the past.

Approximately 50 species of *Cypripedium* grow across the world in the Northern Hemisphere; 11 species and several varieties grow in North America. Six species grow in parts of the Great Lakes states, but one of these, Franklin's lady's-slipper (*Cypripedium passerinum* Richards), is known in our region only from a single, very fragile station on Lake Superior, although it is frequent in northern Ontario around Hudson Bay. It is nearly transcontinental in the far North.

Key to *Cypripedium*

A. Pouch opening by a longitudinal fissure; purple, pink, or rarely white. Leaves basal, 2.

C. acaule
page 71

AA. Pouch opening circular; pouch yellow or white, variously streaked with madder, purple, or pink. Stem leafy, leaves normally 3 or more.

B. Pouch color white to madder, variously pink-streaked or with purple spots.

C. Pouch prolonged below into a conical projection. Slipper madder-purple or white, heavily netted with deep madder-purple veinings; upper part of pouch with many long, somewhat matted white hairs. Lateral sepals separate, not fused together.

C. arietinum
page 73

CC. Pouch orbicular or slipper-shaped, not with a conical projection from floor. Lateral sepals fused for most or all their length.

D. Petals acuminate, greenish, streaked with brown or madder, *spirally twisted*

C. candidum
page 79

DD. Petals obtuse to acute, *flat, not spirally twisted*.

E. Pouch not prominently ribbed, essentially white to greenish white, minutely purple spotted within, 12–20 mm long, 9–14 mm wide. Dorsal sepal green, held close over lip orifice, plants usually less than 3 dm tall.

C. passerinum
page 81

EE. Pouch prominently ribbed, white, streaked or blotched with rose or purple (except albinos), 2–4.5 cm long, 1.5–3.5 cm wide. Dorsal sepal white, petaloid, more or less erect; plants usually over 3 dm tall.

C. reginae
page 83

BB. Pouch yellow, often brown or purple spotted, especially within or around orifice rim.

C. calceolus var.
page 75

(A polymorphic species with many races. In our region most material falls into one of two varieties, though many hybrid and intermediate forms occur.)

C. Plant small, graceful, delicate in all proportions. Sepals and petals moderately twisted, nearly solid deep mahogany-maroon; pouch small, mostly less than 4 cm long. Orifice rim usually dark spotted. Plant of wet prairie, marl fen, or cedar swamp.

var. *parviflorum*
page 77

CC. Plant large or small, but, if small, lip of flower disproportionately large. Sepals and petals greenish brown, spotted or streaked with madder-purple. Lip typically more than 4 cm long. Sepals long and narrow, weakly to rather strongly spiraled. Plant of various habitats, both swamp and upland, often in dry habitats.

var. *pubescens*
page 76

PINK LADY'S-SLIPPER, STEMLESS LADY'S-SLIPPER, MOCCASIN-FLOWER

Cypripedium acaule Ait.   Plate 5A, B

The pink lady's-slipper, one of the few native orchids occurring in almost every part of the Great Lakes region, is so common that many persons, even those with little interest in wildflowers, are familiar with it. Correll asserts that although many colonies are quite large, seldom do more than a dozen or so seed capsules ripen in any season. He suggests the reason is lack of pollinating agents and too long a period between pollination and fertilization. My field experience indicates that frost often prevents more capsules from ripening. In the Great Lakes region, the species blooms at a time when late but hard frosts sometimes occur. Observation shows that frost will cut down most scapes, even though the leaves seem little affected. Following a frost-free blooming season, hundreds of seed pods ripen in the larger colonies.

Habit. Scape rising from between two large, strongly ribbed basal leaves; leaves and scape glandular-pubescent. Leaves oblong-elliptic, shiny-silvery beneath, green above, 1–2 dm long, occasionally much larger in deeply shaded specimens growing in rich soils, 5–14 cm wide. Flowers normally solitary, subtended

71

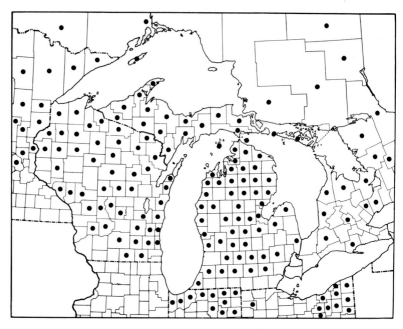

1. *Cypripedium acaule*

by a leaflike bract, bract overarching ovary and blossom. Lip pouch obovoid, pale lavender-pink, crimson, or dark purplish pink, rarely pure white. Lip with branching, darker purple veining. Opening of the lip a longitudinal infolded fissure along top and front surface. Inner lip surface with many hairlike processes and pubescence. Lip 5 cm long, 3.5 cm wide, varying with age and vigor of plant. Sepals and petals yellow-green to purplish brown, frequently darker along veins. Dorsal sepal elliptic-lanceolate, acute, 4–5 cm long, 5–17 mm wide. Lower sepals united, 3–4.5 cm long, 1–2.3 cm wide. Petals lanceolate, widest at base and acuminate at apex, slightly twisted, 4–6 cm long, 1.5 cm wide, variable. Seed capsule erect, strongly ribbed, 3.5 cm long, partially ensheathed by floral bract.

Season. May to late June, depending on latitude and soil temperature of habitat. Plants in cold bogs may bloom many days later than nearby plants on upland. On rocky promontories and exposed rocks of Lake Superior it may be found in bloom as late as early July.

General Distribution. Widespread in northeastern North America, but most abundant in eastern and northeastern parts of range; extends from Newfoundland and Prince Edward Island west to Lake Athabaska, Alberta, southward through Lakes states and

72

in the Cumberland and Appalachian uplands to Georgia and Alabama.[1]

Habitat. Occupies a wide variety of habitats, the apparent requirement being a somewhat sterile, acid soil. Preferred habitats are open or brushy sand ridges, old captured dunes, jack-pine woods, dry to moist aspen-birch groves, and sandy, oak-covered ridges. In such habitats, often associated with bearberry, birdfoot violet, and trailing arbutus. Also grows commonly in intensely acid sphagnum bogs under a cover of black spruce and tamarack, associated with leatherleaf bushes, cranberry, and pitcher-plants, and with other bog orchids. Chooses hummocks and drier areas available in bogs in preference to wetter paths and troughs.

RAM'S-HEAD LADY'S-SLIPPER

Cypripedium arietinum R. Brown   Plate 5C, D

This smallest native *Cypripedium* is one of the most primitive and fascinating. It has long been considered rare, especially in some areas where it occurs; yet, in the heart of its range it is sometimes common. Structurally primitive, its lateral sepals are separate, not fused. Cool soils seem to be essential to this species. All the more southern of Michigan specimens are from cold bogs or cool bluffs in the immediate vicinity of the Great Lakes shores. Only north of central Michigan does it emerge onto the uplands. Even here it is often confined to northern exposures or to troughs on hillsides where cold air channels downward in streamlike fashion.

The blossom is rather short-lived, but it is not, as claimed by some authors, in its prime for a single day. Many plants remain in good flower for a week, provided the weather is cool and the flower is not pollinated. If the bloom is pollinated, a hormone reaction occurs within an hour or two which causes the upper sepal to drop down, sealing the entry to the lip.

Habit. Plant small, inconspicuously glandular-pubescent, 0.7–3 dm tall. Leaves 3–5; where many, lowermost and uppermost often reduced in size; elliptic-lanceolate, noticeably bluish green, *spiraled around stem, not 2-ranked* as in our other cypripediums. Floral bract ovate-lanceolate, acute, 3–5 cm long, 1–1.5 cm wide. Flower solitary or rarely 2; lateral sepals free entirely to base, madder-purple or brownish, green-streaked, 1–2 cm long, 2–5 mm wide, linear. Upper sepal lanceovate, subacuminate, concave. Petals much like sepals in all respects, undulate. Lip saccate, floor pro-

---

[1]Sheviak maps the species from McHenry, Lake, Cook, and Ogle counties in northern Illinois.

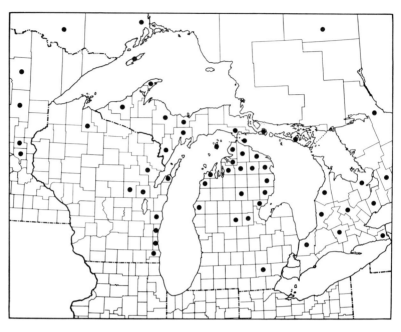

2. *Cypripedium arietinum*

longed downward into a conical pouch. Mouth of sac rather densely long-pubescent. Base color of pouch white, netted and reticulated with madder-purple, crimson, or sometimes with some green. General aspect of lip color white above, madder below. Lip pouch about 1.5–2.5 cm long, 1–2 cm wide; but overall size of plant and all parts vary considerably with type of habitat; those of wet soils usually much larger. Staminode suborbicular and concave. Seed capsule linear-ellipsoid, distinctly less erect when ripe than that of most lady's-slippers.

Season. Late May and June, rarely later around Lake Superior. Blooms a little ahead of other native cypripediums in any area where it occurs. Plants develop rapidly after they appear above ground; flowering plants can appear full blown in spots where, a week before, no cypripediums were in evidence.

General Distribution. Quebec and Manitoba south to Maine, New Hampshire, and Vermont; Connecticut and New York west to Michigan, Wisconsin, and Minnesota. Reports from western China apparently refer to *C. plectrochilon*, an Asiatic species with a similar "ram's-head" pouch.

Habitat. A plant of cool subacid or neutral soils. Two basically different habitats: 1) Cool, dense, balsam-cedar-spruce swamps where mosses, creeping snowberry, Labrador tea, and twinflower abound. Here grows usually as a single flowering stem, rarely in a clump. In such haunts attains its largest size. 2) Nearly pure sand, mulched with pine or cedar needles. If sand is over limestone beach-cobble, so much the better. In such localities, be they north hillsides in jack-pine forest, exposed areas on northern mountainsides, or low, rolling dunes along the Upper Great Lakes shores, this orchid reaches a peak of abundance. Thousands of plants grow along some northern Great Lakes beaches. Needing either shelter from direct sun or cooler soil, the plants grow best around and under low junipers and old, gnarled, deformed cedar, spruce, or balsam. Also grows in this manner, often abundantly, under the last fringe of trees before the open beach.

Yellow Lady's-slipper
Cypripedium calceolus L. var.

One of our better known wildflowers, the yellow lady's-slipper occurs throughout the Lakes states. In one or more of its forms it grows around the world in northern regions. Much geographic variation occurs in this plant, and authorities do not agree on how to treat its forms. The late Dr. Edgar T. Wherry asserted that four distinctive races or varieties grow in the Northeast. I concur, but feel that natural hybridization between races has obscured all but extreme forms.

It seems best to recognize that, owing to hybridization, tremendous variation occurs in the Great Lakes region, where race ranges overlap. Besides a hybrid complex, two rather distinctive varieties can occasionally be found growing in pure populations. These are var. *pubescens*, the large yellow lady's-slipper and var. *parviflorum*, the small yellow lady's-slipper.

The var. *pubescens*, or the hybrid complexes, are more widespread and more cosmopolitan in choice of habitat, and are most likely to be encountered. Again, there may be many small or variable individuals of the large yellow lady's-slipper, but there are no large forms of the small yellow lady's-slipper. In this connection, the amateur botanist should learn to judge plants by population averages, not by an occasional divergent individual. As in human populations, almost all wild plant populations show some variation, whether genetically or environmentally induced. The so-called "species" is only a concept of a type of population as the author of the species interpreted it. No individual of any species, except perhaps the type specimen, exactly fits the published description.

LARGE YELLOW LADY'S-SLIPPER, YELLOW LADY'S-SLIPPER,
WHIPPOORWILL-SHOE

Cypripedium calceolus L. var.   Plate 6A
pubescens (Willd.) Correll

Habit. Plant extremely variable in height; 10–80 cm tall. Leaves
3–5 or 6, elliptic, ovate, or ovate-lanceolate, rather strongly ribbed,
5–20 cm long, 5–10 cm wide. Base of leaf sheathing stem, especially early in the season; leaves pubescent, more or less 2-
ranked. Flowers 1 or 2, subtended by a rather large, leaflike
ovate-acuminate bract of variable size. Peduncle slender, long.
Sepals variable in color, width, and degree of spiral twist, but
usually greenish or yellowish brown, madder-streaked. Upper sepal 3–7.5 cm long, 1–3.5 cm wide, ovate, margins undulate or
slightly spiraled. Lateral sepals united so completely as to appear
as a single, 2-tipped segment; shorter than dorsal sepal and often
obscured by lip. Petals undulate to strongly spiraled, narrow, 4–
9 cm long, often 1 cm or less wide, sometimes linear. Lip an
egg-shaped pouch, though occasionally strongly orbicular and much
inflated; pale to deep clear yellow on outside, streaked and spotted inside, with varying amounts of madder or brownish purple,
1.5–6.5 cm long. Capsule ellipsoid to nearly oval, nearly erect,
frequently broadest above middle.

Season. May to July in its range, depending on type of habitat,
soil temperatures, exposure, and strain of plant.

In growing various strains of this plant for critical study, I discovered that the flowering date in various strains is apparently
genetically fixed. Plants collected in bloom in warm woodlands
early in the season were planted together with plants blooming
late in cold bogs. It was assumed that when grown together under identical conditions they would all bloom at the same time.
The amazing fact is that plants which bloomed early in the wild
continued to do so in the garden, and those that bloomed late
in the wild bloomed late in the garden. This behavior has persisted for years.

General Distribution. Quebec and Newfoundland south to
Georgia and Alabama; through parts of the Gulf states to Texas;
westward in the north through the Lakes states to the Yukon and
British Columbia; south in the western mountains to New Mexico,
Arizona; also Oregon. This distribution may actually represent
the occurrence of more than one race or variety.

Habitat. Tolerant of many habitats—rocky woodland, hillsides,
low areas along small streams, bogs, wooded and open swamps,
lake shores and fens, especially those of the Great Lakes, usually
in subacid to neutral soils. The plant is rare in areas where bot-

76

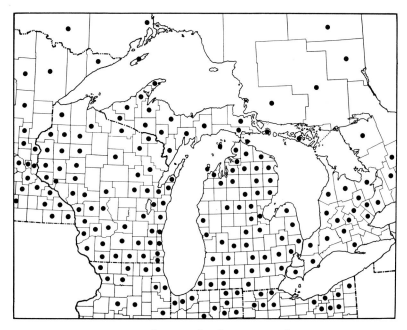

3. *Cypripedium calceolus* var. *pubescens*

tomland alluvium predominates. It seems to thrive in limestone areas where particularly large colonies develop—often in roadside meadows and clearings.

SMALL YELLOW LADY'S-SLIPPER

Cypripedium calceolus L. var.   Plate 6B
parviflorum (Salisb.) Fernald

Correll mentions the recognition of var. *parviflorum* by some botanists, but does not himself recognize it. I consider the variety distinct, in some populations so distinct that it could well be considered a separate species. Unfortunately, diagnostic features other than size become obscured when the plants are preserved.[1]

Habit. Small and dainty, 15–35 cm tall; leaves 3–5, usually 3, distinctly oval, less clasping at bloom time than those of var. *pubescens*; deeply nerved, dark bluish green, 8–15 cm long, strongly 2-ranked. Flowers 1 or 2, floral bract large, sheathing peduncle. Sepals and petals usually solid dark mahogany to madder-purple, polished and glossy. Lateral petals strongly spiral-

[1]Only clearly identifiable herbarium vouchers are mapped for this variety.

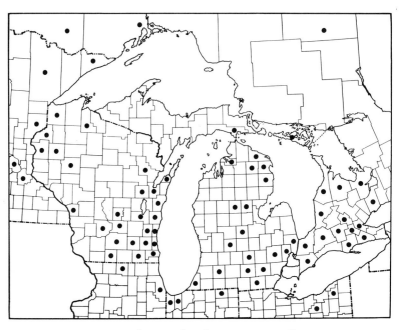

4. *Cypripedium calceolus* var. *parviflorum*

twisted, variable in length, up to 5 cm long, widest at base, tapering to apex. Dorsal sepal up to 5 cm long. Lip soft yellow, 2–3 cm long, distinctly held higher at its apex than at its point of attachment; orifice rim and inside of pouch spotted and streaked with dark purple. Blossom rather strongly fragrant, the odor reminiscent of vanilla.

Season. Late May, June; earlier in open stations, later where it is shaded.

Distribution. Since much of what has been published as the distribution of this variety refers, in my opinion, to a multitude of taxa, only the distribution in the Great Lakes region, based on specimens examined, is given. Here this form has a distinct ecological niche and clear-cut pattern of occurrence. It grows rather abundantly in a narrow band extending from southeastern Lower Michigan across southern Wisconsin and northern Illinois. Many isolated stations are reported both north and south of this band. Many, no doubt, are for this plant, especially in limestone areas. However, many herbarium specimens represent depauperate specimens of the more widespread var. *pubescens.*

Habitat. Old, nonsphagnous tamarack swamps and borders of wet woods, where cowslip and skunk cabbage grow in black, organic muck; or, more frequently, in open, wet meadows, fens or wet prairies where sedge, shrubby cinquefoil, poison sumac, and red osier dogwood abound. Here it grows under shrubbery and in the open among sedges, sometimes by the hundreds. It tends to form large clumps. North of the band defined (under Distribution) it occurs only rarely, and then mostly in cold, marly cedar swamps.

SMALL WHITE LADY'S-SLIPPER

Cypripedium candidum Muhl. ex Willd.   Plate 2A, 7A, B

The small white lady's-slipper is the most sun-loving of all our lady's-slippers. Few plants grow in shade, and those that do are obviously old plants crowded out by shrub growth. One of the loveliest of wildflowers, large colonies still occur locally in the heart of its range. Unfortunately, the mucky meadows it frequents are all too often drained for celery or onion farms. Its choice of habitat and its occurrence only in the more settled portions of the Lakes states has doomed many colonies. The plant is listed as rare, threatened, or endangered over much of its native area today.

Habit. Rather small and dainty, 10–40 cm tall, usually about 20 cm. Leaves 4–5, strongly ribbed, 8–16 cm long, sheathing and erect. Plant developing rapidly at blooming time, flowers often bursting out of the still-furled or stem-sheathing leaves. Flowers 1, rarely 2, floral bract large and sheathing peduncle. Sepals greenish yellow, faintly streaked with crimson-purple. Upper sepal about 2.5 cm long; lower sepals less. Petals colored like sepals, lancelinear, loosely spiraled, about 4 cm long and 8 mm wide. Lip pure waxy white, strongly purple veined within, occasionally with purple spots at pouch orifice, egg-shaped and appearing polished, 2.5–3.3 cm long. Staminode conspicuous, yellow spotted with purple.

Season. Middle to late May and early June; has a rather limited season of bloom, as would be expected for it occurs in fewer and less varied habitats than other native cypripediums.

Distribution. Formerly rare and local and now nearly extinct from New Jersey and New York southward to Pennsylvania, westward through the Lakes states, extreme northern Ohio, and Indiana. Becomes more frequent in southern Michigan, northern Illinois, southern Wisconsin, southern Minnesota, to Nebraska and south locally to Missouri. Now very rare and local in southern Ontario. Long reported from the "barrens" of Kentucky, but without known localities, it was recently located by workers for the Natural Features Inventory, who found a few small colonies in damp depressions in limestone barrens in the north-central region of that state. (M. Medley, pers. comm.)

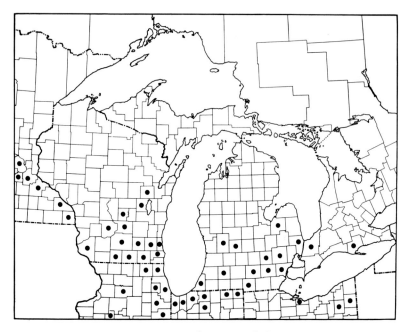

5. *Cypripedium candidum*

Habitat. Marl bogs, fens, and Great Lakes shores in the East, invading the margins of swales, marshes, and wet prairies in the West. Like the small yellow lady's-slipper, which often accompanies it, it is most abundant in wet, open, springy tracts of tamarack, sedge, poison sumac, and red osier dogwood. Unlike it, this orchid stays strictly in full sun or in the meager shade of the shrubby cinquefoil. In Michigan the meadow-parsnip is an almost constant companion of the small white lady's-slipper and is thus a good indicator species. I have found thousands of the white lady's-slipper in a large, springy meadow area, while nearby hundreds more were growing in the cinders of railroad ballast.

Hybrids. It hybridizes with both the large and small yellow lady's-slipper. Both types of hybrid have been named. *Cypripedium ×andrewsii* Fuller (*C. candidum* × *C. calceolus* var. *parviflorum*) (Plate 8A) is a beautiful plant. It has the ivory-white pouch of the white and the dark purple-brown sepals and petals of the yellow parent. It occurs occasionally with its parents in parts of Michigan, Illinois, and Wisconsin. *Cypripedium ×favillianum* Curtis (*C. candidum* × *C. calceolus* var. *pubescens*) (Plate 8B) is intermediate between its parents. The sepals are greenish yellow, streaked with brown, longer and more spiraled than those of the white lady's-slipper; the lip is pale cream, fading to dirty white. The plant often grows taller than the white lady's-slipper, but is rarely as coarse as many of the yellow. *C. ×favillianum* varies much more than *C. ×andrewsii*. One would expect this as *C. calceolus* var. *pubescens* is highly variable. If one does not (as I do) accept that *C. calceolus* var. *pubescens* and *C. calceolus* var. *parviflorum* represent different taxa, then both hybrids must be called *C. ×favillianum*, regardless of their obvious genetic differences.

FRANKLIN'S LADY'S-SLIPPER

Cypripedium passerinum Richards   Plate 8C, D

In the summer of 1964 Dr. James Soper relocated John Macoun's almost century old station for this orchid in the Lake Superior region of Ontario. It remains the only known site for this species in our region. More fascinating than beautiful, this orchid is mainly arctic in distribution.

Habit. Plant of medium size, 1–3.5 dm tall, densely soft-pubescent, with much the aspect of a diminutive *C. reginae*. Leaves 3–5, somewhat clasping at first, obovate to lanceolate, acute, 6–15 cm long, 2–8 cm wide, with rather prominent ribs. Floral bract leaflike, prominent, ovate-lanceolate, 2–8 cm long, 1.5–2.5 cm wide. Flowers normally solitary, borne at summit of a stem frequently elongated above the uppermost leaf. Sepals yellowish green to apple green, pubescent on outer surface. Upper sepal suborbicular, strongly concave, with margins somewhat inrolled, carried closely over the pouch orifice, 1–2 cm long, nearly as wide. Lateral sepals united for most of their length in all specimens I have observed in the field (but, according to Correll, sometimes free nearly to their base), together 1–1.8 cm long, 1–1.5 cm wide. Petals white, close clasping pouch at first, spreading later, 1–2 cm long, about 5 mm wide. Lip obovoid, frequently with a slight chinlike profile below, dull white, pubescent and with dark purplish spots within, 1–2 cm long, 1–1.2 cm wide. Staminode somewhat cordate, grooved dorsally, yellow, brown spotted. Capsule (ovary) rather conspicuously enlarged at flowering compared to that of our other lady's-slippers, becoming much inflated and obovoid, 2–2.5 cm long, 1–1.8 cm wide when mature.[1] Old stems and capsules are more or less persistent.

Season. Late June, July; possibly a little earlier in our region.
General Distribution. Transcontinental in far North. Common

[1]Catling (1983) reports *Cypripedium passerinum* to be self-pollinating (autogamous). Autogamous plants frequently show enlarged ovaries early in the flowering cycle, and more regularly produce seed capsules than do plants which require insect pollination.

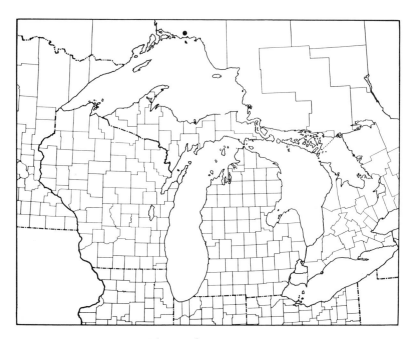

6. *Cypripedium passerinum*

in Alaska and Yukon, locally abundant in Alberta and British Columbia, especially in the Banff and Kootenay National Park areas; northern Manitoba, northern Ontario, Hudson Bay area; Mingan Islands of Quebec, and locally south to area bordering northern Lake Superior.

Habitat. Tolerates a wide variety of habitats in Alaska, Yukon, Alberta, and British Columbia, where I have observed it. Its most frequent habitat is moss-covered, peaty alluvium along arctic rivers or temporary stream beds, usually in openings or lightly shaded thickets in spruce and fir forests. Occasionally grows in open tundra or heathlike situations, on gravelly beaches, and even on borders of sphagnum bogs. Frequent plant companions are Canada buffalo-berry, various shrubby willows, and alpine rhododendron. Its orchid companions include small round-leafed orchis, bluntleaf orchid, early coral-root, and northern twayblade.

Most stations for this cypripedium occur in the far North. It grows near Nome, Alaska (*fide* M. Williams, pers. comm.), and along Hudson Bay shores. On the Mingan Islands, Straits of Belle Isle, it occupies slightly sheltered pockets under stunted spruces along the beach. I have seen it in spruce forest, on river sandbars, on gravelly outwash from glacial flooding, and even in road ballast for the Alaska Highway. In nearly all of its habitats, it pioneers rather early stages of plant succession on new, raw soils, or lightly disturbed, older, mossy areas. Very large colonies commonly occur. In our single known station Franklin's lady's-slipper grows in peaty sand under spruces, firs, and trailing junipers on old lakeshore dunes, surviving precariously apparently as a relict of cooler, postglacial times on an extremely localized and fragile site.

Attempts to cultivate this species south of its natural home have almost uniformly met with failure. Even when plants seem established and flourishing, hot August weather usually causes the leaves to blacken and fall. Next season, the plant fails to appear. This species apparently does not tolerate high soil temperatures. Undoubtedly, this is a major factor in its limited occurrence within our region.

SHOWY LADY'S-SLIPPER, QUEEN'S LADY'S-SLIPPER

Cypripedium reginae Walt.   Plate 9A, B, C

The showy lady's-slipper is the largest and one of the most beautiful of our native orchids, and also one of the best known and most popular of all wildflowers. Of widespread distribution in eastern North America, it is the state flower of Minnesota.

Habit. Plant large, 30–90 cm tall, leafy, with 3–5 strongly ribbed ovate leaves, 10–25 cm long, 6–16 cm wide, strongly hirsute. Flowers 1–2, occasionally 3, each subtended by an erect, leaflike bract, showy. Sepals white or cream-white, petaloid; upper sepal ovate to orbicular, 3–4 cm long, 2.5–3.5 cm wide. Lateral sepals entirely united into one segment similar in texture and size, though narrower, to the dorsal sepal. Petals white to cream, ovate-lanceolate to strap-shaped, 2.5–4 cm long, 1–1.5 cm wide, variable. Lip slipper- or pouch-shaped, spherical, inflated, 2.5–5 cm long, white or more commonly white deeply stained and streaked with rose-purple and marked with distinct vertical white lines along the veins, sometimes with darker madder and green spotting. Staminode prominent, broadly ovate or cordate, white, usually yellow-streaked or yellow-spotted.

Season. In the Great Lakes region flowers from early June to mid-July, depending on locality and type of habitat.

General Distribution. Nova Scotia and western Ontario southward through Illinois, Indiana, and Ohio. From New England southward locally in the mountains to North Carolina and Tennessee, where it is extremely rare. Occasionally disjunct outside this area.

Habitat. Essentially a moisture loving plant, it chooses the wettest open situations available. Found in a variety of wet habitats, but becomes most abundant in openings in balsam-cedar-tamarack

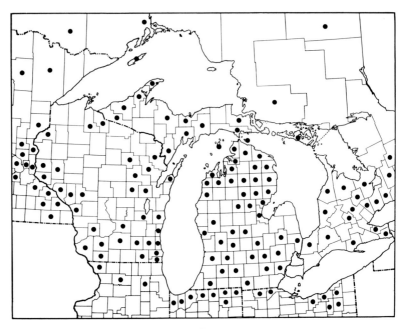

7. *Cypripedium reginae*

swamps, when these are not too acid. Definitely not a plant of
intensely acid, sphagnous, black spruce bogs. When found growing in sphagnum moss, the orchid's roots usually penetrate to a
less acid soil layer. Neutral to slightly alkaline black mucks and
fen marls are favorite soils. In a favorable situation, colonies of
thousands of plants may develop.

Its common companion plants in most swamps are Labrador
tea, marsh fern, bog rosemary, various *Equisetum* species, and
grass-of-Parnassus. A sun lover, it seldom persists long in deep
shade. It is most often seen in bog clearings along old tote-roads
or in tangled "windfalls." Also grows along swampy lake shores
and wet beaches in limestone areas of Lake Huron.

According to the late Professor Warren Waterman, extensive
germination of this orchid's seed takes place only if it is at a
depth of 1–2 inches in a suitable soil. Others have suggested that
this depth provides an ideal oxygen concentration for germination. Waterman concluded that the deer, milling around in their
winter yards, planted the seeds inadvertently. The plant's affinity
for sun or high open shade is also favored by the overbrowsing
of cedar swamps by deer. It is in such old winter deer yards that
the most magnificent colonies of this lovely orchid develop.

Caution. The hairy leaves and stems of the showy lady's-slipper are extremely poisonous to some people producing in them a reaction similar to that caused by poison ivy.

AMERORCHIS Hultén

In recent years it has been the custom of orchid taxonomists, especially those of Europe, to split genera to reflect every small structural difference. American orchid taxonomists, until recently, took a more conservative position. Since about 1970, however, the trend has been to follow the European nomenclature. Consequently, our eastern American "orchis" are now placed in two new genera. *Amerorchis* was proposed as a monotypic genus by Eric Hultén in 1968 to separate *Orchis rotundifolia* Banks ex Pursh from the genus *Orchis*. Among other technical features used to separate this plant from *Orchis* are the single leaf, scapose stem, rhizomatous slender-fleshy roots rather than rounded or lobed fleshy tuberoids, and minor variations in the arrangement and construction of the flower parts. Since there is but one species, the species description will serve for the genus as well.

SMALL ROUND-LEAFED ORCHIS, ONE-LEAF ORCHIS

Amerorchis rotundifolia (Banks) Hultén   Plate 10A, B, C
Orchis rotundifolia Banks ex Pursh (1st ed.)

A small plant, this species has a charm and subdued beauty possessed by few native orchids. It confines itself to cold northern coniferous forests and bogs, moors, and rocky exposed cold headlands. While abundant locally in the Canadian Rocky Mountain areas, and dotting by the thousands woods and bogs in the Yukon and Alaska, it is strictly rare and local in the Great Lakes region. It has become noticeably rarer, even in undisturbed habitat, in recent years. Few, indeed, are the naturalists who have seen it in its native haunts in eastern North America.

Habit. Delicate, but varying considerably in size; somewhat stoloniferous, glabrous throughout, 9–25 cm tall, stem below leaf with 1–2 imbricating sheaths. Leaf basal or nearly so, medium yellow-green, dull, distinctly flat-colored and unpolished; orbicular to ovate-elliptic, rarely as round as specific name implies; 3–10 cm long, width varying from half to equal the length. Scape naked, slender, often slightly curved, raceme loosely 1–several-flowered. Robust plants, with as many as 10–15 or more flowers, each subtended by an inconspicuous lanceolate bract, 6–15 mm long, 3–5 mm wide at base. Flowers showy for their size, on 8–10 mm long pedicellate ovaries. Sepals white to pale mauve-pink, elliptic-subquadrate to ovate-elliptic, obtuse at apex. Dorsal sepal erect, lateral sepals oblique, spreading, longer than dorsal sepal. Petals white to pale pink, smaller and narrower than sepals; petals and dorsal sepal forming a hood over column. Lip 3-lobed, basal lobes relatively small, mid-lobe larger, separated from basal lobes by a broad central portion; middle lobe spatulate to cuneate, notched or truncate at apex, 6–10 mm long, 4–6 mm wide, spurred at base. Lip white, spotted or blotched with deep purple.

In var. f. *lineata* (Mousley) Voss blotching of the lip runs together into two broad longitudinal stripes of purple, or into very irregular, dark, enlarged blotches of color. Floral segments in this variety sometimes show considerable distortion at least in those we examined on the Sibley Peninsula, Ontario, in 1983. This variety, or one extremely similar to it, originally described from the Cypress Hills of Alberta, Canada, has appeared on the Sibley Peninsula near Thunder Bay, Ontario (*Rhodora* 62: 174, June 1960), and correspondents inform me of another small station much farther east in Ontario.

Season. June to late July, throughout its range, varying somewhat in blooming date with degree of exposure within habitat, and with the season, or with individual plants. In one Michigan station there was considerable variation among nearby plants; some have buds just coloring, while others have blossoms nearly faded.

Distribution. Grows from Alaska east to Greenland and south throughout Canada, wherever there are cold evergreen forests and bogs to the latitude of the Canadian-United States border. South of Canada one or two stations are known in Montana and Wyoming. In the eastern United States a few stations are reported from Maine, Vermont, New York, Michigan, and Wisconsin. Becomes more frequent in bog districts of northern Minnesota.

While rare and quite local, small and easily overlooked, it almost certainly occurs more frequently than the record shows. In Michigan, I have found it in three stations, none of which had been recorded previously at state herbaria. Seemingly suitable habitat is frequent in the northern portions of our region.

The behavior of this northern species is most interesting. Individual plants or colonies in known stations tend to "jump around"— that is, some plants disappear while others appear in new areas. In the bog where I first discovered it, all the flowering plants were marked by blazing nearby trees. After a period of 11 years, 25–30 plants still bloomed there, but few were near

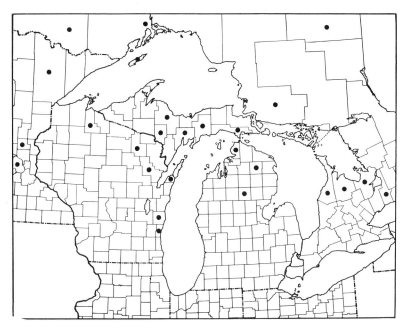

8. *Amerorchis rotundifolia*

any of the original blaze marks. The original plants were not in evidence.

Even more significant is the fact that in recent years (1970's–1984), virtually all known colonies of *Amerorchis* at the southern limit of its range in Michigan, Wisconsin, and New England, have simply disappeared or suffered a tremendous drop in numbers. All stations which I have located in northern Lower Michigan have spontaneously disappeared over the years. One of these, however, dwindled and died out as early as 1954, the others more recently.

Since virtually all of the southernmost colonies are tiny, usually under 25 flowering plants, and since they often occupy only a few square yards of a large suitable habitat, one might speculate that these very southern stations might actually represent a chance arrival of windblown seed from more northern and more suitable climates. These seeds may then develop into a plant or two. If these immigrant plants then manage to become pollinated and to produce seed, as many isolated native orchids do even in the absence of their specially adapted pollinator, a colony would become temporarily established. Given the evidence of short-lived plants, and the known disappearance of most historical colonies in the eastern United States, such a behavior seems to me likely, perhaps also influenced by climatic fluctuations.

Habitat. Throughout its range, habitats have one conspicuously unvarying feature—cold soil. Other factors vary considerably. The plant seems capable of maintaining itself in either sun or shade if the soil is cool and the competition limited; it may occur in both situations at the same location. Soil moisture seems unimportant, for the plant grows in either bog wetness or in dry beds of spruce needles.

At the southern edge of its range, in Michigan and Wisconsin, it inhabits very cold balsam fir-black spruce-white cedar swamps almost exclusively. The swamps in which it occurs usually have underlying layers of marl. Although considerable sphagnum moss is present on the surface, these swamps are not the type where this moss dominates or where the soil is a brown sphagnum peat. Other familiar plants growing with it are Labrador tea, heartleaf twayblade, green adder's-mouth, blunt-leaf orchid, showy lady's-slipper, and perhaps most commonly, the bog false Solomon's-seal. Avoiding competition with larger herbs, it characteristically grows in beds of mosses, or occasionally in cedar or spruce needles, usually in pockets or well-like depressions at the base of trees. North of Lake Superior the species becomes more frequent. In this colder region it occurs in more acid and more open sphagnous situations, in black spruce or spruce-cedar bogs. Even here it tends to grow along streams in mosses other than sphagnum. Still farther north it grows also in dry spruce woods or open tundra.

GALEARIS Rafinesque

Rafinesque proposed the genus *Galearis* for our showy orchis in 1836. Most taxonomists, however, maintained the species in the genus *Orchis* until fairly recently. As understood today, there are two species in the genus, one from North America and one from eastern Asia. The main features which cause botanists to segregate these plants into *Galearis* include the short rhizome without tubers, a pair of basal leaves, the large, leaflike floral bracts, and several highly technical details of column and pollinium structure. In addition, and characteristic of the genus, the sepals and petals all connive (come into contact) to form a hood (galea) over the column. Since there is only one American species, the species description here will serve also for the genus.

SHOWY ORCHIS

Galearis spectabilis (L.) Rafinesque   Plate 11A, B
Orchis spectabilis L. (1st ed.)

The showy orchis, attractive but inconspicuous, cannot be considered as "showy" as the showy lady's-slipper. Because it blooms in deciduous forests at the height of the spring wildflower season, it has become better known than most native orchids. It ranges widely across the eastern deciduous forest, but is much more abundant in some districts than others.

Habit. Plant low, smooth, and succulent throughout, 6–20 cm tall. Roots fleshy-tuberous. Scape stout, naked, 4–5-angled; leaves basal or nearly so, borne above an imbricating sheath or two. Leaves obovate to oblong-ovate, narrowing to an indistinct petiole which sheaths the scape, 6–20 cm long, 3–10 cm wide. Raceme 1–15-flowered, usually 5–8; flowers rather widely spaced but stiff and rigid, stem up to 10 cm long. Floral bracts large, conspicuous, foliar, lanceolate-acuminate, 2.5–6.5 cm long, exceeding the flowers. Flowers 3–10, borne on short and often stubby spikes, large for size of plant, on pedicellate ovaries 1–2 cm long. Sepals and petals free but connivent, forming a hood over column, pink to mauve, fading with age. Sepals ovate-lanceolate, rounded to subacuminate, concave. Petals linear-oblong, obtuse, 1.2–1.5 cm long (Correll), 2.5 mm wide at base. Lip conspicuous, white, entire, ovate-subquadrate, subacuminate at tip, thickened somewhat along median line, and with undulate-crenate margins; lip produced into a spur 1.3–2 cm long. Seed capsules stout, erect.

Season. Mid-May to June, occasionally earlier or later. Generally this orchid is in its prime when the forest leaves have expanded to about three-fourths full size.

General Distribution. Southern Minnesota and Iowa, through south-central Wisconsin and Michigan to New Brunswick and Quebec, south to Georgia and Alabama, west to Arkansas, Missouri, and Kansas. Rather widespread and tolerating many types of woodlands; local.

In Michigan, at least, it is shorter, stubbier, and less colorful than in the Blue Ridge and Cumberland Plateau regions. It can be locally abundant (as it often is in southern Minnesota and Iowa on neutral, rich loess soils), but more commonly it grows as scattered, isolated plants or in small colonies.

Habitat. In the Lakes region reported only from rich deciduous forests and woodlots or their borders (in Minnesota I have seen it persist or actively invade rather grassy old orchards and pastures, but always only if a vigorous colony occurs in an adjacent woodlot). In New England, reported to grow occasionally in

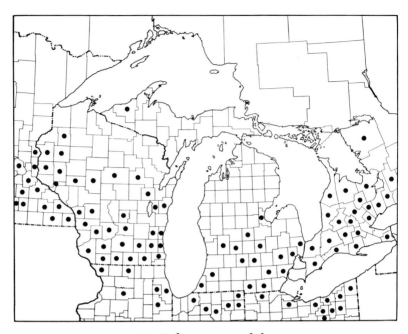

9. *Galearis spectabilis*

hemlock forests. Most frequently it grows in sandy clay or rich loam soils in moist spots not far from temporary spring ponds. In southern Michigan it commonly grows in beech-maple forests under spice-bushes or in beds of leaf mold in open beech groves. Its frequent companion plants are jack-in-the-pulpit, hepatica (especially *Hepatica acutiloba*), white trillium, spring beauty, and spring cress; it frequently chooses more shady, humus-filled hollows than do these companions. Like nearly all our orchids, it shuns competition.

DACTYLORHIZA Necker

Dactylorhiza is an extremely variable group of at least 30 species and many hybrids and intermediate forms found primarily in the Old World. Two species occur in North America, *D. aristata* (Fischer) Soó, in the Aleutians and Alaskan peninsula, and *D. maculata* (L.) Soó, believed to be adventive in our region.

The genus is separated from *Orchis* readily in that its members produce roots with clusters of fingerlike tubers instead of the oval or globular tubers found in *Orchis*. In this genus the leaves frequently but not always show dark brownish purple spotting and the floral raceme is of fairly large, colorful, and showy blooms. The pollinium, instead of being a solid mass of pollen, consists of clusters of pollen grains held together by elastic fibers. Since only one species is known from our region, its description will serve also for the genus.

EUROPEAN SPOTTED ORCHIS

Dactylorhiza maculata (L.) Soó
Orchis purpurella T. & T. A. Stephanson (1st ed.)

This European orchid was first reported in North America by H. Andrews in June 1961 (*Rhodora* 63: 176), as *Orchis purpurella* T. & T. A. Stephanson. A small colony appeared in a marshy spot near a dump at Timmins, Ontario, near the northeastern corner of the region covered by this book. The plant is reported to still persist in very small numbers near Timmins.

Luer (1975) treats the plant as "a member of the *D. maculata* complex close to, if not the same as the common British species, *D. fuchsii*." *D. maculata* and its closely related species constitute one of the most abundant and wide ranging orchid complexes in Europe.

The plant is considered adventive at the Ontario station. Andrews suggested that the orchid was introduced by way of seed contained in packing material or other matter discarded at the dump near which it was discovered.

Habit. (Adapted from Luer, Summerhayes, and other authors.) Plant glabrous, 15–60 cm tall. Leaves, 4–8, dull green with dark purplish brown or madder spotting, lanceolate-elliptic, 2.5–3.5 cm wide, 10–20 cm long, clasping stem and becoming reduced to bracts above. Raceme many-flowered, flowers purple to purplish pink, with darker purple lines and markings, sepals and petals colored more or less alike. Sepals ovate-lanceolate, 9 mm long, 3.5–4 mm wide. Petals lanceolate-falcate (Luer 1975), 7.5–8 mm long, 2.5–3 mm wide. Lip cordate, three-lobed, about 10 mm x 10 mm; lateral lobes rounded, much larger than the short-triangular middle lobe. Spur about 5 mm long.

Season. Late June, July, at our station.

Distribution. All of Europe except arid portions of Spain, Portugal, southern Italy, and far northern Scandinavia, Iceland, east to about the Caspian Sea and the Ural Mountains; vicinity of Timmins, Ontario, Canada, where it is believed to be introduced.

The spotted orchis has persisted for over 20 years at the Ontario site, flourishing in some seasons, declining in others (Luer). How

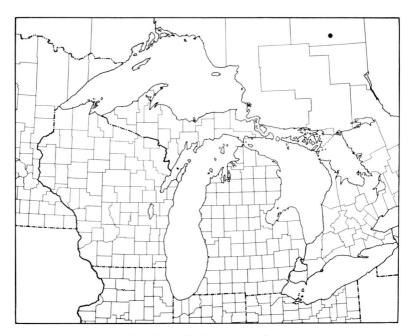

10. *Dactylorhiza maculata*

permanent it will prove to be is uncertain. Two other European species, *Listera ovata* and *Epipactis helleborine* have persisted. They have appeared at several sites, and *E. helleborine* has become a nearly ubiquitous weed in the Northeast. Perhaps *D. maculata* will follow a similar pattern.

PLATANTHERA L. C. M. Richard

Members of this genus formerly were included by Correll (1950) in the genus *Habenaria*. Recent studies and trends toward more detailed splitting of genera now place these plants in the genus *Platanthera*, *Piperia*, or *Coeloglossum*.

Platanthera was founded in 1818 by Louis Claude Marie Richard. According to Luer (1975), the genus today contains about two hundred species. Even with the taxonomic splitting, the genus is rather polymorphic, and sections within it have at times been proposed as genera.

Platantheras are mainly terrestrial, though a few may be semiaquatic. The roots are tapered-fleshy, swollen, or clawlike fascicles. On one of the roots each season is produced a bud that will become next season's plant. Adjacent to the existing plant and during its first year, this bud develops a new set of roots or tubers. At the end of the season the old plant degenerates, leaving the newly formed bud and roots to propagate the plant. Any damage to the main plant or to its food-producing ability during the season results in the reduction of both the size and vigor of the plant produced the following year.

Rein-orchids (platantheras) are erect, glabrous, and leafy-stemmed. In some species most of the leaves are reduced to cauline bracts of various sizes, and in a few species only the lowermost leaves develop; these superficially appear to be basal. Flowers are borne in racemes which, owing to the shortness of the pedicels and ovaries, may be almost spicate. Many have inconspicuous greenish flowers. The petals and sepals are free from each other, but may be connivent and form a hood over the column.

In our species, the lip is lowermost, or nearly so, and variously shaped. The base of the lip extends backward into a hollow spur, which usually contains at its extremity a drop of nectar. The short column bears two anther cells, with granular pollen attached to exposed glands. (This constitutes a main structural difference between the genus *Platanthera* and related *Amerorchis* and *Galearis*, which have the pollen enclosed.)

Except for a few complex species, our platantheras are quite distinct. Hybrids among them do occur. In some cases, these are obvious, but in the *P. dilatata-P. hyperborea* group they are often obscure and very difficult to determine.

Key to *Platanthera*

A. Lip fringed or lacerated on margin.

  B. Lip tongue-shaped or oblong, with a ciliate fringed margin.

    C. Flowers white.

                          Platanthera blephariglottis
                                      page 96

    CC. Flowers orange.

                                Platanthera ciliaris
                                    page 99

  BB. Lip composed of 3 wedge-shaped lobes, lacerate-fringed, erose-dentate, or deeply divided.

    C. Flowers white, cream, or greenish, central lip segment rather deeply fringed.

D. Plant stout, lip full, strongly lacerate-fringed, fringe cut about 1/3–1/2 length of lip segments. Petals wedge-shaped, noticeably eroded or short-fringed across flat apical end. Flowers cream-white.

Platanthera leucophaea
page 114

DD. Plants sparse to stout, lip spare, deeply lacerate-fringed, fringes of lateral lip segments cut nearly to base. Petals linear, barely if at all eroded at apical end; flowers green, yellow-green, or cream.

Platanthera lacera
page 112

CC. Flowers purple or lavender-rose (except in occasional white forms in normal populations).

D. Wedge-lobes of lip erose-denticulate distally, but not distinctly lacerate-fringed, the wedge-shaped lobes often widely spreading.

Platanthera peramoena
page 121

DD. Wedge-lobes of lip distinctly fringed, those of the lateral lobes, at least, cut 1/3 or more of their length.

E. Lip 1.3 cm or less wide, floral raceme often densely flowered, 2.5–3.5 cm in diameter. Pollinaria viscidia held rather closely, about 1–1.5 mm apart. Opening to nectary partially divided by a dorsal projection. Plant widespread throughout our area.

Platanthera psycodes
page 124

EE. Lip 1.3 cm or more wide, raceme often rather laxly few-flowered to many-flowered, raceme 4–5 cm or more in diameter. Pollinaria viscidia 4–5 mm apart, divergent. Opening to nectary undivided or unobstructed. Plant known only from the extreme southeast of our area.

Platanthera grandiflora
page 106

AA. Lip entire, variously strap-shaped, lobed or dilated, or toothed, but not fringed.

B. Major leaf or leaves basal, or appearing basal. Stem leaves, if present, bractlike only.

C. Basal leaf one only (in our region), held somewhat erect or off ground, obovate to oblanceolate. Flower scape rarely over 25 cm tall, often much less, flowers green.

Platanthera obtusata
page 117

CC. Basal leaves 2, more or less orbicular, lying flat on ground. Floral scape usually 30 cm or more tall.

D. Petals divergent-spreading, loosely forming a hood with dorsal sepal. Flowering stem with several small bracts below raceme. Leaves shiny-glossy or slimy in appearance. Sepals and petals greenish white, often with mauve shading.

Platanthera orbiculata
page 119

DD. Petals and upper sepal forming a hood over column (connivent). Flowering stem with not more than one bract, usually none. Flowers greenish yellow to green. (Flower in profile shaped like open ice-tongs.)

Platanthera hookeri
page 108

BB. Major leaves arranged along stem axis (cauline). Upper leaves gradually reduced to bracts.

C. Lip prolonged into a lanceolate-acuminate tip.

D. Lip conspicuously dilated at base. Flowers white, spicy-fragrant.

Platanthera dilatata
page 102

DD. Lip lanceolate to linear, occasionally broadly triangular lanceolate but not conspicuously dilated at base. Flowers green, only faintly if at all fragrant.

Platanthera hyperborea
page 110

(Many populations of *P. dilatata* and *P. hyperborea* intergrade in our region. Plants with all degree of lip dilation can be found, with either green or white flowers, or varying intermediate shades. These intermediate forms are very difficult to place even in fresh material, and impossible in herbarium specimens. See my comments under *P. hyperborea* in text.)

CC. Lip variously 2–3-toothed at apex, never with a simple, acuminate tip, or lip apex blunt and lip bearing a conspicuous tubercle on upper surface near base.

D. Basal half of lip bearing a tooth or small lobelike process on each side, and with a prominent tubercle at middle near base. Cauline leaves gradually reduced to bracts upward.

Platanthera flava var. *herbiola*
page 104

DD. Basal half of lip without a lobe or tooth, or tubercle on its upper surface, 3-toothed at apex. Lowermost cauline leaf large, the others much reduced or bractlike.

Platanthera clavellata
page 101

WHITE FRINGED-ORCHID

Platanthera blephariglottis (Willd.) Lindley   Plate 11C, 12A
Habenaria blephariglottis (Willd.) Hooker (1st ed.)

The white fringed-orchid, one of the loveliest of wildflowers, does not grow in all parts of our region. Although often rare and local, it typically occurs in large numbers in the few suitable localities where it occurs at all.

Habit. Plant 10–100 cm tall, leafy, leaves abruptly reduced to bracts above. Leaves lanceolate to elliptic-lanceolate, acute, rather strongly sheathing stem at base, 5–30 cm long, 1–5 cm wide, silvery green and somewhat keeled below. Raceme usually rather densely flowered, floral bracts short, lanceolate, 1–2 cm long, shorter than the pedicellate ovaries. Flowers brilliant white, dorsal sepal oblong or orbicular, obtuse at apex, concave, 5–10 mm long. Lateral sepal ovate-orbicular, 5–10 mm long. Petals linear-spatulate, truncate, and slightly denticulate at apex, 5–8 mm long, 1–3 mm wide. Lip tongue-shaped, ovate, oblong, solid portion 4–12 mm long, rarely longer, fringed around margin. Fringe segments typically about 6–8 mm long, often quite variable in different locations on same lip. Spur slender, 1.5–5 cm long.

Season. July, early August.

Distribution. Newfoundland and Nova Scotia south along the coastal plain to Florida and Mississippi, west through southern Appalachian Mountains to isolated stations on Cumberland Plateau. In the North, extends across southern and central Ontario into extreme northeast part of Ohio, and also into Lower Michigan. In Lower Michigan seems to be locally frequent in some areas, entirely absent in others. Sheviak (1974) cites an 1891 report of two plants in a Cook County, Illinois, swamp (see my comments in section on distribution patterns, page 33), but without substantiating herbarium specimens. There is a documented record from Macon County, south of our area in Illinois.

Habitat. Through its wide range, occurs mainly in damp, acid sands or in sphagnum bogs. In Michigan and Ontario, the only places where it grows commonly in our region, it is almost exclusively an inhabitant of open black spruce-tamarack bogs, the "cranberry bogs." Here it grows in beds of deep sphagnum, generally where it is rather free from other plant growth, as in lightly shaded areas around clumps of spruce. It may occasionally venture out into dense but sunny tangles of leatherleaf and other heaths. Does not usually grow in the wettest, soggiest mosses, nor in deep shade. Common plant companions are the large cranberry, pitcher-plant, rose pogonia, and grass pink.

The reason this orchid has such a peculiar distribution in our region is unclear. Since it grows much farther north in adjacent Ontario, and in the East northward to Newfoundland, it does not seem that winter hardiness can be a factor. Yet, west of Ontario— except for a few local stations in northeastern Ohio—it occurs certainly only in the Lower Peninsula of Michigan. The plants associated with it are common over a much wider range, and its favored habitat extends far north and west of the areas in which it grows. Indeed, suitable bogs occur in sections of Lower Michigan where the white fringed-orchid does not grow. The plant is frequent in bogs near the Straits of Mackinac in northern Lower Michigan. It is or was abundant in open bogs on the western side of the Lower Peninsula south to Allegan, Van Buren, and Berrien counties, but does not occur in all of the suitable bogs of the extreme southwestern part of Michigan. Similarly, though common locally near the Straits of Mackinac, it has never been reported from Upper Michigan or Wisconsin. It is absent from the bogs of southeastern Lower Michigan south of southern Tuscola County, although *P. ciliaris*, a frequent companion, grows south of there.

In one small bog remnant on the western side of Michigan, the plants grew so abundantly as to cover the ground, and it was impossible to walk without crushing plants with each step. Indeed, it appeared that trampling of the plants by blueberry pickers in

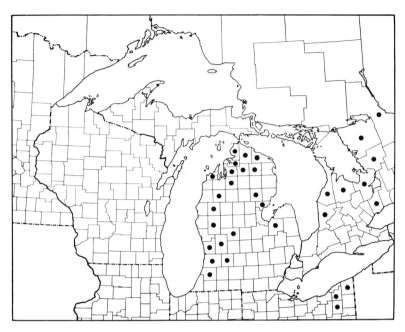

11. *Platanthera blephariglottis*

good berry years was a factor which stimulated clump formation and led to the unusual density of the plants.

Hybrids. In parts of its range, it grows with the yellow fringed-orchid (*P. ciliaris*); there, hybrids (*P.* ×*bicolor* (Raf.) Beckner) are found (Plate 12B). In southwestern Michigan there are at least three such stations, in each of which the hybrid forms actually outnumber the typical parent forms. Here every type of genetic combination for color occurs. Some are buff, some are lemon-yellow, and some even have the orange sepals and petals of the one parent and the white lip of the other. It is interesting to note that the lip color segregates separately from the color of the rest of the flower, as in the tropical *Cattleya* orchids.

In August 1982, in a bog in Otsego County, Michigan, I found a remarkable hybrid of *P. blephariglottis* and *P. clavellata* in a mixed stand of these two species. I named the hybrid *P.* ×*vossii* to honor Edward G. Voss (Plate 13C). To the best of my knowledge no other hybrid with the club-spur orchid has been reported. *P. clavellata* appears to self-pollinate, for all blossoms on a plant typically produce seed pods. Catling also believes it to be self-fertilizing (Catling 1983). Although putatively autogamous, viable pollen seems to be present and insects visiting the flowers could carry away pollinia. Thus, the species could hybridize utilizing the other parent species as the female despite its autogamous nature.

Intermediate in structure, shape carriage of the flower, coloring, fringing on the lip, and lip and spur shape, plants of *P.* ×*vossii* grow nearly as large as the white-fringed parent. Details of the discovery and structure of this unexpected hybrid appear in the article "*Platanthera* ×*vossii,* A New Natural Hybrid Orchid from Northern Lower Michigan," *The Michigan Botanist,* vol. 22, p. 141–144 (Case 1983a).

YELLOW FRINGED-ORCHID

Platanthera ciliaris (L.) Lindley   Plate 12C, D
Habenaria ciliaris (L.) R. Brown (1st ed.)

The yellow fringed-orchid is perhaps the most brilliantly colored of our native orchids. Its rich orange is nothing less than tropical. According to some writers, it is one of the easiest of orchids to cultivate, but this has not been my experience. It is "easy" only when a natural, acid, sandy or peaty soil can be provided, or an artificial bog-soil condition can be maintained in a suitable container. In most garden soils the plants quickly sicken and die.

Habit. Height variable; 20–100 cm tall, rarely taller; stem somewhat stout basally; roots fleshy, rather long, few. Leaves oblong-lanceolate, acuminate, sheathing stem in basal portion, keeled below, 7–30 cm long, to 6 cm wide, varying with available light and degree of exposure. Raceme rather densely flowered. Floral bracts linear-lanceolate, acuminate, shorter than ovaries and pedicels. Flowers rich orange, fading slightly to a yellowish orange in some plants. Dorsal sepals oblong-elliptic, concave, 4–9 mm long, 4–5 mm wide. Lateral sepals ovate to suborbicular, 6–9 mm long, 6 mm wide. Lip (without fringe) 8–12 mm long, 2–4 mm wide; heavily ciliate-fringed, some fringes branched, fringe up to 1 cm long, sometimes less in Great Lakes region. Spur long and slender, 2–3 cm long.

Season. Late July, August

General Distribution. Vermont, Massachusetts, Rhode Island, Ontario, southern Michigan, lake districts of Illinois, Indiana, and Ohio, south into the mountains; south along the coastal plain to Florida and west along Gulf Coast to Texas. Also at several inland localities in South Central states.

Habitat. Within its range occupies a great variety of environments. Does not seem to require any special moisture conditions, but tolerates any acid soil; grows in sun or light shade. In the Great Lakes states, tolerates less habitat variation than elsewhere in its range. Seems to be confined to two basic types of cover: the tamarack-sphagnum bogs of southern Michigan and the

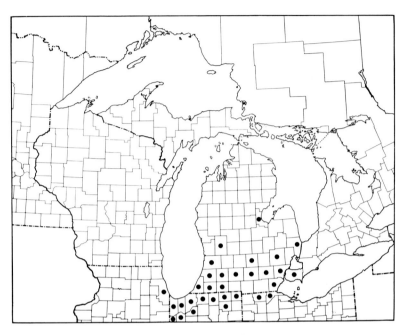

12. *Platanthera ciliaris*

open, damp, sandy meadow or marsh border on acid soils. Very occasionally here, as in the South, grows in relatively dry humus in acid upland woods. May grow in rather deep shade in the Blue Ridge of North Carolina, but nearly all our stations are lightly shaded or open. In Michigan bogs, like the white fringed-orchid, prefers deep beds of sphagnum uncluttered by much other vegetation. Its plant companions in bogs are much the same as those of the white fringed-orchid and the pink lady's-slipper.

Although it is very local, it often forms fairly large colonies where it does occur. A small area of one southwestern Michigan bog has hundreds of plants. The late C. R. Hanes of Schoolcraft once told me of an area in St. Joseph County where this orchid grew so thickly that one could not walk there without trampling the plants. Developing forest shade, however, ultimately destroyed this large colony.

Hybrids. This orchid hybridizes with the white fringed-orchid when the two grow together (*P. ×bicolor*, see comments under *P. blephariglottis*). The hybrids often have great beauty, but they cannot compete with the yellow parent in stateliness or in richness of color. The yellow fringed-orchid is less boreal than the closely related white fringed-orchid, and the two are found growing together only in the southern half of the Great Lakes region.

CLUB-SPUR ORCHID, SMALL GREEN WOOD-ORCHID

Platanthera clavellata (Michx.) Luer   Plate 13A, B
Habenaria clavellata (Michx.) Sprengel (1st ed.)

Like most platantheras of the North, this plant is small, green, and inconspicuous. An interesting and widespread species, it is not too easy to find, but the peculiar "askew look" of the bloom and the frequent dense colonies nevertheless attract attention. To anyone reared in the North, where this species typically grows in bogs, its occurrence in crevices in sandstone cliffs in the Blue Ridge Mountains is always a surprise.

Habit. Plant small, glabrous, 5–40 cm tall. Stem with one well-developed leaf, the others usually reduced and bractlike; main leaf attached just below middle of the stem, though appearing lower if plant is buried in sphagnum. Leaf obovate to oblanceolate, widest above middle, 5–20 cm long, commonly longest in shaded specimens; 1–4 cm wide. Bractlike leaves linear, acute, variable. Raceme few- to many-flowered, floral bracts lanceolate, 3–10 mm long. Flowers greenish to yellowish or whitish. Ovaries 1 cm long, stout. Sepals ovate, rounded, 4–5 mm long, 2 mm wide. Petals ovate, 3–5 mm long, 2 mm wide. Spur longer than ovary and pedicel, club-shaped (giving the name *clavellata*), curved, 10 mm long. Flowers arranged by a turn of the ovary, so that lip is about 45 degrees off the normal lowermost position typical of most orchids.

Season. Late June to August. Floral segments often persist for many weeks in good condition on the developing ovaries.

Distribution. Newfoundland, Nova Scotia, and Quebec to Ontario, west to Minnesota, south through the Great Lakes states and New England, south along the coastal plain and in the mountains to north Florida and Texas. Throughout the Great Lakes region.

Habitat. Widespread and tolerant of many situations; most common in tamarack-spruce bogs, where it grows in sphagnum, in shade or sun. Also grows in loose moss in balsam-cedar-spruce swamps of a less acid nature, but rare and spotty in such places; sometimes in alder thickets or damp woods. Rather common locally on wet sands of lake shores and roadside thickets, especially in Upper Michigan. Most typical bog plants are good indicators: pitcher-plant, wild calla, pink lady's-slipper, leatherleaf. Occasionally pioneers on wet road banks and in borrow pits in Lake Superior areas.

Hybrids. In 1982, in northern Michigan, I found two plants of the hybrid *Platanthera blephariglottis* × *P. clavellata* growing in a mixed stand of both parents (Plate 13C). I named the hybrid

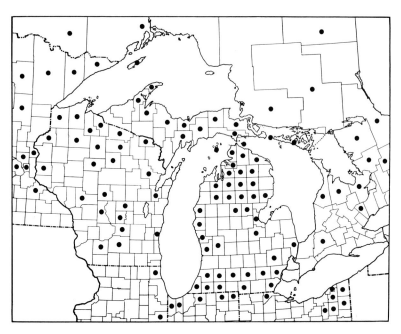

13. *Platanthera clavellata*

P. ×*vossii* (Case 1983a). This hybrid is somewhat unexpected as *P. clavellata* is autogamous (self-fertilizing), its pollen germinating in place (Luer 1975; Catling 1983). In spite of this, apparently, insects can occasionally carry pollen to the *blephariglottis* parent and produce hybrids. To the best of my knowledge no other hybrids involving *P. clavellata* have been reported. (See discussion under *P. blephariglottis*.)

TALL WHITE BOG-ORCHID

Platanthera dilatata (Pursh)   Plate 14A, 15A
    Lindley ex Beck var. *dilatata*
Habenaria dilatata (Pursh) Hooker (1st ed.)

This fascinating plant, with its attractive aroma of cloves and other spices, is as rare in some parts of our region as calypso or the small round-leafed orchis. It reaches maximum size and abundance in the beach bogs of the Upper Great Lakes. There, where conditions often favor the formation of large clumps of up to a dozen stems, the white spires really do suggest the popular name of "bog candles." Though hardly showy, the tall, snowy white spires of this orchid arrayed across a wet, seepy marl flat become a conspicuous part of the bog flora.

Habit. Plant erect, strict, variable in height, glabrous, 10–120 cm tall. Stem variable, slender to stout, leafy; leaves usually rather erect; sheathing, rather linear-lanceolate, rarely obtuse, variable up to 25–30 cm long and 6 cm wide, dark green, gradually reduced to floral bracts upwards. Raceme dense or sparse, up to 40 cm long in robust material, flowers 12–80, sometimes more, each subtended by a bract. Flowers typically white, dorsal sepal ovate, obtuse, with petals forming a hood over column, 3–7 mm long, 3–4 mm wide. Lateral sepals elliptic-lanceolate, blunt or acuminate, 4–9 mm long and 1–2 mm wide. Petals linear, falcate, 4–9 mm long, 2–4 mm wide. Lip in pure material linear, sharply expanded (dilated) at the base so as to be almost lobed; 5–10 mm long, 2–6 mm wide across basal dilation. Lip is pendant during height of anthesis, but after pollination often projects forward or recurves to come in contact with hood formed of petals and sepals. Floral parts may stay crisp and fresh most of season. Spur cylindrical, about equal to lip in length.

Season. June, July, sometimes later; floral parts do not wither immediately after pollination.

General Distribution. Alaska to Greenland, all of arctic America, New England south to Pennsylvania, Michigan, Wisconsin, and Minnesota. In the western mountains south to Colorado, New Mexico, and California.

Not common in our region. Many specimens examined in herbaria and accepted as this species by many authorities are either hybrid material (of this orchid with *P. hyperborea*), or merely *P. hyperborea* itself. Although most authors describe the lip of *P. hyperborea* as linear, not greatly expanded toward its base, the truth is that in many robust specimens the lip is nearly triangular, or definitely widened just above its base. This widening is gradual, not an abrupt dilation as in *P. dilatata*. These wide-lipped forms of *P. hyperborea* are very difficult to distinguish from *P. dilatata* in dried specimens, especially since both of these confusing species usually dry to a dark rich brown, thus obscuring their color differences.

The tall white bog-orchid is less tolerant of habitat variation than the tall green bog-orchid. While the two species do occur together occasionally, *P. hyperborea* grows in many situations where *P. dilatata* would never grow. Where they do grow together, they hybridize. In some populations, moreover, no one could clearly separate the various forms. Nevertheless, that too much herbarium material has been classed as *P. dilatata* is a certainty. Several western forms of *P. dilatata* do occur, but all

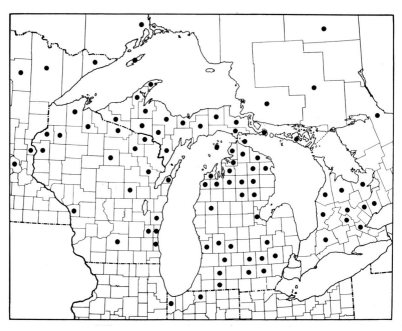

14. *Platanthera dilatata*

eastern material seems to belong to the typical species. (See discussion of hybrids under *P. hyperborea.*)

Habitat. Very wet, open bogs, lake shores, or clearings in bogs. Usually grows in marl or wet sand, never in deep sphagnum beds. When in sphagnum, the moss is a superficial surface layer. Often grows about springy seepages. Common companion plants are: shrubby cinquefoil, bird's-eye primula, pitcher-plant, linear-leaved sundew, and, in some parts of its range, the white lady's-slipper.

TUBERCLED ORCHID

Platanthera flava (L.) Lindley   Plate 13D
   var. *herbiola* (R. Brown) Luer
Habenaria flava (L.) R. Brown ex Sprengel
   var. *herbiola* (R. Brown) Ames and Correll (1st ed.)

Though at first glance this plant appears much like the tall green bog-orchid, close examination reveals distinctive differences of floral structure, especially of the lip. There is also a definite difference in habitat. Of the two varieties of the tubercled orchid, only the more northern var. *herbiola* (R. Brown) Luer occurs in our region.

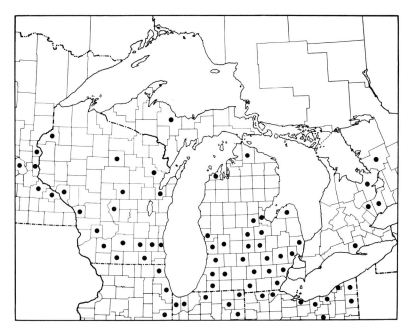

15. *Platanthera flava* var. *herbiola*

Habit. Plant 10–60 cm tall, slender, leafy, lower 2 leaves large, wide, upper ones abruptly narrower and bractlike. Leaves oblong-elliptic to lanceolate, spreading (as contrasted with *P. hyperborea*, where they sheath and ascend the stem); sheathing slightly at base, 6–20 cm long, 1–5 cm wide, peculiarly yellow-green and shiny. Raceme rather lax or compact, flowers 10–40. Lower floral bracts greatly exceed combined pedicel and ovary, upper ones reduced and shorter than flowers. Sepals ovate-oblong or suborbicular, 3 mm or more long and wide. Petals oblong-orbicular, 2–5 mm long, 2–4 mm wide, greenish yellow. Lip ovate to quadrate, with a pair of distinct, lobelike teeth on each side near base, and provided with a distinctive outward projecting tubercle in middle near base; lip 2–6 mm long and wide across widest part. Spur cylindrical, 8–9 mm long, slender.

Season. June. Floral parts persist in fresh condition on developing ovaries over much of the summer.

General Distribution. Nova Scotia, Quebec, through Ontario to Minnesota, southward through Great Lakes states to Appalachian Mountains; grading into southern typical *P. flava*, or remaining discrete but intermingling with the typical variety in the Mississippi drainage from southern Illinois southward.

105

Habitat. Primarily a southern plant in our region, the tuber-cled orchid grows usually in colonies of many plants. It chooses wet, swampy, elm-ash, red maple, and swamp white oak flat-woods, mostly where very shallow puddles and troughs of water stand in the spring and after every rain. Here it characteristically grows in the open floors of these pools and floods, pushing through the matted dead leaves and litter where little else grows, or it may share its home with a tangle of sensitive fern, iris, and even poison ivy. Less commonly, the tubercled orchid grows on lake shores or in open, sandy, moist prairies.

The largest colonies I have seen were along a small, sluggish stream which spilled over at intervals onto a sandy, wooded floodplain where iris, sensitive fern, foamflower, and little else grew. Clumps of 50 to 200 plants were scattered in the stream overflow.

It seems to endure standing water readily. Its manner of form-ing large colonies suggests that offset plants may be formed veg-etatively. In any one colony few plants bloom in a given season.

LARGE PURPLE FRINGED-ORCHID

Platanthera grandiflora (Bigel.) Lindley   Plate 19A, B
Habenaria psycodes var. *grandiflora* (Bigel.) A. Gray (1st ed.)

Many authors, including Correll, regard this orchid as a variety or large race of *P. psycodes*. Others, including myself, find dif-ferences in addition to flower size in petal shape, fringing, lip and petal carriage, and flowering season. Stoutamire (1974), in a thorough study of the races concluded that there were, indeed, two species, *P. psycodes* and *P. grandiflora*, each with distinctive structure, phenology, and distribution.

Large purple fringed-orchid occurs along the Appalachian Mountains and in New England, in meadows, on hillsides, and on mountain balds. Vigorous plants are majestic, with deeply fringed, large flowers in broad, cylindrical racemes. In clearings along the Blue Ridge Parkway, where this orchid grows among clumps of highbush huckleberry, it is richly fragrant about noon-time. Tiger swallowtail butterflies and other long-tongued lepidoptera pollinate it (Stoutamire 1974).

Habit. Plant height variable, erect, glabrous, 3–12 dm tall, often stout, stem with 3–5 leaves, leaves reduced to bracts upward. Leaves elliptic-oblong to lanceolate, keeled below, green to bluish green, 15–25 cm long, 5–7 cm wide. Raceme laxly few- to many-flowered (usually more lax and fewer flowered than *P. psycodes*) 40–60 mm in diameter, up to 25 cm long. Flowers 15–40 per inflorescence (averaging 20, *fide* Stoutamire). Lower floral bracts lanceolate, to 20 mm long, 5–8 mm wide. Flowers rose-purple, purple, or rarely white, showy. Dorsal sepal elliptic, 5–9 mm long, 4–7 mm wide. Petals oblong, less cuneate than in *P. psycodes*, the margins dentate-erose. Lip 3-parted, the divisions cuneate, with the central division widest, 15–25 mm long, 12–18 mm wide, deeply fringed, narrowed at the base into an elongated claw. Column 4 mm by 5 mm, about twice the size of the column of *P. psycodes*. Spur (nectary) directed toward stem, and not recurved toward flower, enlarged in distal portion.

Season. Mid-June through August. There appear to be local races in regard to flowering time, some races blooming early, others late, even in the same district. Generally, authors report that *P. grandiflora* tends to flower earlier in a given district than *P. psycodes*. Stoutamire (*op. cit.*) found considerable overlap on data from herbarium labels. The Ohio specimens from our area were collected between July 27 and August 14.

General Distribution. Ottawa Valley districts of eastern Ontario, Quebec to Newfoundland, all of New England, Pennsylvania and southward along the mountains to North Carolina, westward into extreme northeastern Ohio (Portage and Ashtabula counties). Luer (1975) shows *P. grandiflora* occurring across Michigan and much of Wisconsin. Except for the Ohio material, I have seen no specimens which I consider to be *P. grandiflora* from west of eastern Ontario. In this I concur with the distribution shown by Stoutamire (1974).

Habitat. Northward grows in moist meadows, ditches, open damp woodlands, streambanks, and seaside meadows. Southward, in damp mountain woods, clearings, ditches, and balds. It is locally frequent in ditches of the Blue Ridge Parkway near Craggy Gardens, North Carolina, but road crews usually mow it before it flowers. A favorite habitat in the North Carolina mountains is in relatively dry acid soil of old burns and balds where it grows under or among thickets of highbush blueberry (*Vaccinium corymbosum*). In such situations, it may grow in considerable shade under dense shrubbery. Although large stands sometimes occur, large purple fringed-orchid usually grows in small numbers scattered over a favored habitat.

In Upper Michigan, Wisconsin, and Minnesota, grows a form of purple fringed-orchid which differs (not necessarily in column structure) from the more typical material of *P. psycodes* from the southern Lakes states; it is larger, more robust in all respects, and has denser heads of larger flowers. It also differs from *P. grandiflora* in which the lip segments are deeply fimbriate, often cut nearly halfway to the base. While in this large northwestern form the flowers may be twice as large as those of typical *P. psycodes*, they show no difference in fimbriation. This northern

107

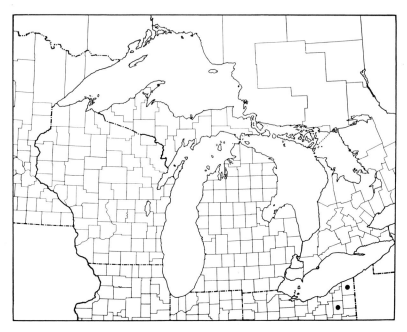

16. *Platanthera grandiflora*

purple fringed-orchid race also tends to grow most often in marshy meadows. This robust form of *P. psycodes* may be responsible for the occasional reports of *P. grandiflora* from northern or western parts of our region.

HOOKER'S ORCHID

Platanthera hookeri (Torr.) Lindl.   Plate 15C, D
Habenaria hookeri Torrey ex Gray (1st ed.)

This orchid and the large round-leaved orchid appear at first to be identical twins. In poorly preserved herbarium material, and probably to the amateur botanist, they do resemble each other enough to make identification difficult. Yet, each has distinct details of structure, habitat, and distribution.

Habit. Plant with scape springing from between 2 basal leaves. Leaves 2, subopposite, orbicular to suborbicular-ovate, outer margins of leaves cupped or slightly ascending at flowering time; later lying flat, distinctly dull, light green, *not shiny*, 6–15 cm long, 5–15 cm wide. Scape bractless or with only one bract near middle. Raceme lax, 6–50-flowered, floral bracts lanceolate, acuminate, and shorter than flowers. Flowers yellowish green, ped-

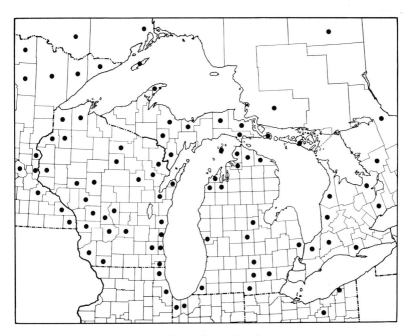

17. *Platanthera hookeri*

icels and flower erect. Dorsal sepal triangular, lanceolate, about 10 mm long, 3–5 mm wide. Lateral sepals reflexed against ovary, lanceolate, acuminate, 9–13 mm long, 3–4 mm wide. Petals linear, 7–9 mm long, 2 mm wide, with dorsal sepal forming a hood over lip. Lip lanceolate to triangular, acuminate, fleshy, *distinctly upcurved, giving the flower, in profile, the appearance of ice tongs*; 9–13 mm long, 3–4 mm wide. Spur widest at base, distinctly tapering evenly downward, 1.5–2 cm long.

Season. June to July. As with some other platantheras, the flower parts do not necessarily wither immediately after pollination, and so the petals and sepals may persist for weeks. Thus the blossom segments are easy to identify over a long season.

General Distribution. Nova Scotia, Quebec, and Ontario, south through New England to Pennsylvania, Ohio, Michigan, west to Minnesota and Iowa. Also the Lake Michigan areas of Indiana and northern Illinois.

Habitat. Almost exclusively a woodland species. Grows mainly in coniferous woods on sandy or humus-rich soils. Sometimes locally abundant. The ideal habitat seems to be the dry, mossy cedar thickets or the balsam and spruce forests of the Upper Great Lakes shorelines. Common on the northern shores of Lakes Huron and Michigan and the south shore of Lake Superior, where it often grows only a few yards above the beach. Here it will be found in the dry conifer rubble with the trailing vines of twin-flower, calypso, ram's-head lady's-slipper, Canada lily-of-the-valley, and the rattlesnake plantains.

Although sometimes found in sand and evergreen needles under spruce, fir, jack-pine, or red pine, it is rather rare in such stations inland from the lakes. Occasionally grows in mixed hardwoods, chiefly in those of beech and maple. These seem to provide the main habitat southward. Only an occasional plant will be found in these hardwoods; the large colonies found on the Upper Great Lakes shores and islands do not develop here.

TALL NORTHERN BOG-ORCHID, TALL LEAFY GREEN BOG-ORCHID

Platanthera hyperborea (L.) Lindl.   Plate 14B, 15B
  var. *hyperborea*
Habenaria hyperborea (L.) R. Brown (1st ed.)

One of the most widespread of American orchids, tolerant of many extremes of habitat, this plant comes as close to being a weed as any of our native orchids do.

Habit. Erect, stout or slender, smooth, very variable; 10–100 cm tall, leafy. Leaves several, cauline, usually linear-elliptic to oblanceolate-lanceolate, obtuse, gradually reduced to bracts, variable, 4–30 cm long, 1–5 cm wide, sheathing and ascending. Raceme densely packed to laxly few-flowered, short or long. Floral bracts lanceolate, acuminate, erect, lower bracts exceeding flowers, upper bracts about equaling them. Flowers green, yellowish in exposed situations. Dorsal sepal suborbicular to ovate, obtuse, concave, 3–7 mm long, 2–4 mm wide, widest near base. Lateral sepals ovate-lanceolate, spreading later, often becoming reflexed, 4–9 mm long, 1.5–4 mm at widest. Petals lanceolate, acute, erect, and with dorsal sepal forming a hood over lip, 3–7 mm long, 1–3 mm wide at base. Lip stiff and fleshy, linear-lanceolate to slightly triangular-lanceolate, *often variable on the same plant*; 3–9 mm long, rarely longer, width variable, usually 1–2 mm wide below middle. Spur somewhat clavellate, cylindrical, 2–8 mm long, about equal to or shorter than lip.

Season. Variable, depending upon nature of habitat; from early June in meadows and on streambanks to August on cold islands and in dark bogs.

General Distribution. Arctic America from Alaska to Greenland, south through our region to Pennsylvania and the southern limits of the Great Lakes; very common northward.

Habitat. A wide variety of wet soils suit this plant. Found here on a streambank, there in a mucky hole among the roots of an-

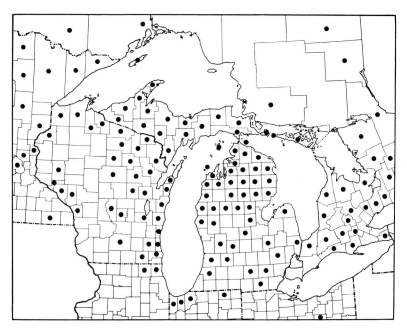

18. *Platanthera hyperborea* var. *hyperborea*

cient bog cedars, it may in yet another spot invade the wet sands
and gravels of Lake Huron beaches. Common among tag alders
in thickets along northern trout streams; often grows in outer
margins of bogs. Frequents black, mucky spots rather than brown
peats or the heart of open cranberry bogs. Perhaps reaches the
peak of vigor and abundance in the wet "beach bogs" of the Bruce
and Sibley peninsulas of Ontario or the Wilderness Park area of
Michigan. Some plants and clumps of plants here are reminiscent
of vigorous young stalks of maize.

In many places in North America, *P. hyperborea* intergrades
with *P. dilatata*. The feature used by most botanists to separate
herbarium material, namely, the degree of dilation of the base
of the lip, is not particularly reliable by itself. Though the plants
often grow together, they have different preferences in our region. *Platanthera dilatata* grows mostly in open, marly clearings
in cedar bogs or in marly meadows and on lake margins; *P.
hyperborea* grows mainly about wooded thickets and swamps or
on streambanks where *P. dilatata* does not grow. Northward on
lakeshore bogs, unfortunately, this habitat separation breaks down;
here the plants intergrade completely, and the flip of a coin
probably becomes as reliable as any structural character for sep-
arating the two species. *P. dilatata* usually has a more delicate,

graceful aspect, and has narrower leaves and a more elongated flower spike. While the flowers of both are fragrant, those of *P. dilatata* are much more so.

Owing to its poor condition or its hybrid nature, a large amount of herbarium material of these two species cannot be distinguished definitely. It seems best to relegate this material to a *P. dilatata-P. hyperborea* complex, but not to *P. dilatata* var. *media*, an entity regarded as a hybrid. This name is not recognized by Correll.

GREEN FRINGED-ORCHID, RAGGED FRINGED-ORCHID

Platanthera lacera (Michx.)   G. Don in Sweet   Plate 16A,B
Habenaria lacera (Michx.) Lodd. (1st ed.)

Though, compared with its fringed relatives in our region, this orchid is inconspicuous and disappointing, it is in reality both delicate and beautiful. More common than the other fringed-orchids, and more cosmopolitan in its choice of habitats, it figures early in the discoveries of the field botanist in the Great Lakes region.

Habit. Variable, slender to stout (bog specimens generally much more robust than those from meadow or ditch); 20–80 cm tall, leafy; leaves, gradually reduced to bracts above, erect and sheathing at first, spreading, barely sheathing later; stem slightly angular, almost winged at angles; raceme usually rather dense, 5–25 cm long. Floral bracts not exceeding combined ovary and flower. Flowers green, greenish white, or yellowish. Dorsal sepal ovate-elliptic, blunt at apex, 5 mm long, 4 mm wide, lateral sepals ovate, obtuse, 4–6 mm long, 3 mm wide, reflexed. Petals linear to spatulate, truncate at apex, erose, 5–7 mm long, 2 mm wide. Lip 3-parted, deeply cut and divided into almost thread-like lacerations; middle lobe less divided, linear-spatulate, 1–1.5 cm long and wide. Spur long, slender, curved, about equaling or slightly exceeding ovary.

Season. Mid-June to August, season varying with type of habitat; average, late June.

Distribution. Newfoundland and Nova Scotia west to Manitoba and Minnesota, south to Georgia, Alabama, Mississippi, Arkansas, Texas, and Missouri.

Habitat. More adaptable than many platantheras; grows in a variety of sterile acid-soil situations. The degree of moisture seems unimportant *as long as the area is not absolutely dry*. Frequent in sphagnum bogs in all parts of our region, the far northwest possibly excepted. Grows in sunny glades and openings in the company of sphagnum, cranberry, leatherleaf, rose pogonia, bog

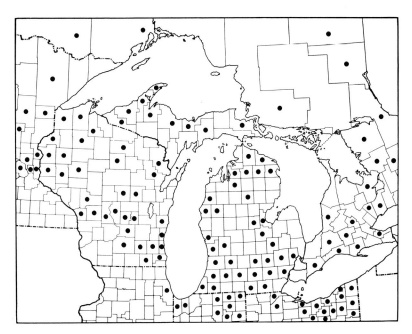

19. *Platanthera lacera*

rosemary, and pitcher-plant. Seldom found in wettest parts of bogs; usually grows on raised hummocks. In areas of sterile, sandy soil, grows in wet meadows and roadside ditches. Any moist field seems suitable. Plant companions here are wild strawberry, goldenrod, Loesel's twayblade, adder's-tongue fern, and horsetails. Although it may be common in such spots, few of the many plants present bloom in any one season.

Hybrids. Hybridizes over parts of its vast range with the purple fringed-orchid to form *P. ×andrewsii* M. White (Plate 16C). Very little herbarium material from the Lakes states represents this hybrid. In central Michigan the blooming seasons barely overlap, and it is doubtful that there is much opportunity for interbreeding. In Upper Michigan, near Lake Superior, and in northwestern Wisconsin, green and purple fringed-orchids flower together in late July. I have seen a few hybrids in northwestern Wisconsin, and large numbers of them in Alger and Schoolcraft counties, Michigan. Many interesting and beautiful backcrosses as well as primary hybrids occur, including those with the flower shape of *P. psycodes* but clear green-colored lips, pale rose-lavender.and green and lavender combinations. Every degree of lip shape and degree of fringe between the two parents appears.

113

In New England, where these species bloom at the same time, reports of hybrids are common.

Eastern Prairie Fringed-Orchid

Platanthera leucophaea (Nutt.) Lindl.   Plate 17A, B, 18A
Habenaria leucophaea (Nutt.) A. Gray (1st ed.)

Few American plants in any family could be lovelier than this orchid. Predominantly a prairie species, it grows also in bog sedge mats and in moist lakeshore situations. Though it has been my experience that many species of platantheras are not long-lived, it is not so with this species. Several of the plants, transplanted from a prospective industrial site to my meadow wild garden, have persisted and bloomed for over 30 years. At dusk the blooms exude a delightful fragrance which can permeate a large area. At this time they are eagerly visited by many small moths, as well as by larger sphinx moths. The plants set seed freely, and heavy seed production does not seem to weaken them to any marked degree.

Habit. Somewhat variable throughout its range, plants nearly always stout, but tall or short, depending upon moisture of season; 20–100 cm tall; stem angled, leafy, 2 lowermost leaves larger than rest, oblong-elliptic to lanceolate, rather acute, sheathing stem below, flaring obliquely away from stem, 8–20 cm long, 2–5 cm wide, widest near base, strongly keeled below, silver-green with darker lines below. Raceme large, showy, very wide for length, loose, 10–40-flowered. Bracts lanceolate-acuminate, 1–4 cm long. Flowers creamy white, on long pedicellate ovaries, 2–2.5 cm long. Sepals and petals connivent, overarching lip and column; dorsal sepal ovate, concave, 8–15 mm long, 5–8 mm wide. Petals cuneate to fan-shaped, more or less truncated at apex and erose-toothed. Lip deeply 3-parted, 1.5–3 cm long, about equally wide, divisions of lip fringed deeply, usually at least halfway to their bases. Spur curved, club-shaped, much longer than pedicel and ovary, 2–5.5 cm long.

Season. June, July; rarely August in cold bogs.

General Distribution. Very rare and local in Nova Scotia, Ontario, Maine, and New York—there mainly in bogs; westward through Michigan, Ohio, Indiana, Illinois, Missouri, and west to Kansas, Nebraska, the Dakotas, and Minnesota, there formerly frequent on wet native prairie; occurring also in a few stations as far south as Arkansas and Louisiana.

Habitat. Sedge mats in open bogs, especially on margins of bog lakes; often growing (in Michigan) on tufts of sedge and grass and on logs out in lake water; or in company with cranberry, rose pogonia, pitcher-plant, and grass pink. Does not usually grow in very acid, sphagnous situations where the white fringed-orchid (*P. blephariglottis*) abounds, although it may occur at the same station. It grows more commonly, also, on rich moist black sandy soils of open prairie. Large colonies sometimes develop in company with blazing star (*Liatris* spp.), blue-eyed grass, various rushes and bulrushes.

Though formerly common in parts of its prairie range, its choice of fertile, moist soil is its undoing. Much of its suitable prairie habitat, being fine truck-garden land, rapidly perishes to the plow.

Prairie fringed-orchid is able to colonize low, moist, recently disturbed fallow land rather rapidly. In a suitable soil plants can flower in about five years from seed. I have even found a few plants colonizing dredgings along drainage ditches amid fields of cabbages and potatoes, but in general, the large scale destruction of the low wet-sand prairies either for agriculture, industrial development, or cottage-recreational purposes has rendered this beautiful orchid nearly extinct over much of its former range. Conservationists, as of this writing, soon hope to have the species listed federally as endangered.

Some comments concerning the endurance and survival problems of the prairie fringed-orchid appear in the section "Conditions Which Affect Native Orchid Populations." These discuss the problems of the plant on its typical sand-muck prairie habitat. We have had occasion, also, to observe this beautiful plant in two inland sphagnum bogs in Michigan.

In 1943, in Arenac County, Michigan, I discovered a colony of *P. leucophaea* growing on the bog mat of a small lake near Lake Huron. About 15 flowering plants grew on a sedge mat near open water. I visited the lake several seasons from 1943–1951. During that time little changed in the bog and the population remained essentially stable. I did not visit the bog from 1951 until 1978. In 1978, while studying the rapid and distressing decline of the prairie fringed-orchid in Michigan and in the process of sharing my information on this species with field workers for the Natural Heritage Survey, I decided to revisit the lake and observe the condition of the prairie fringed-orchid there.

By this time, the surrounding upland woodlands had been lumbered, although the bog forest remained intact. Shrubby growth (apparently from natural succession) had filled the former narrow open bog mat and extended to open water. In two different seasons we completely circled the lake and bog mat. Although we searched diligently, we found no *P. leucophaea*. However, *Arethusa*, *Pogonia*, and *Calopogon* still bloomed sparingly along the lake margin. It appears that the disappearance of *P. leucophaea* here was the result of natural changes in a marginal habitat for the species and was not due to any intensive human disturbance.

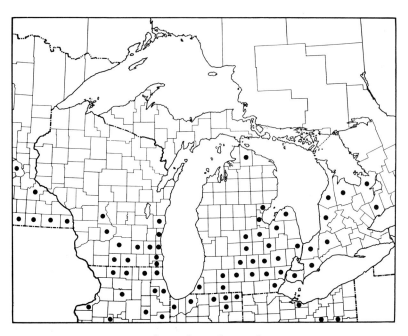

20. *Platanthera leucophaea*

In contrast to this station, is the situation at a bog lake in southern Michigan. I learned of this site from specimens in the University of Michigan Herbarium which had been collected in 1927. (A 1919 collection with only general locality data from the vicinity may represent the same station.) In 1966 a friend of one of my students reported finding this same colony thriving. In the early 1970's my wife and I visited the station and succeeded in locating about 18 blooming stems on an open sphagnum mat. The colony remained in good condition according to my correspondents in 1984. This well documented, small bog station has persisted for at least 55–60 years. In this case, except for willow thickets encroaching upon a small section of the bog, the bog mat has remained open and free of shrub or shade competition. The orchids have flourished in consequence.

After this edition was in press, C. J. Sheviak and M. L. Bowles published a study which separated the western populations of what had been considered *P. leucophaea* into a new species, *Platanthera praeclara* Sheviak and Bowles (see reference below) (Plate 18B).

The authors base their new species on the larger flowers, the fewer-flowered but more compact racemes, the divergent pollinaria, caudicles and viscidia and the differences in column height and size of most flower parts in populations generally west of the Mississippi River. *Platanthera praeclara* (western prairie fringed-orchid) grows in prairie swales and marsh borders west of the Mississippi River from the Canadian border region south to Oklahoma. Its range falls outside the drainage basin of the western Great Lakes region, but it does occur in the counties of southeastern Minnesota which we have included in our maps. According to Sheviak (pers. comm.) and the Sheviak and Bowles article, all Minnesota specimens included on the map as *P. leucophaea* belong to their new species.

Interested readers should refer to the article "The Prairie Fringed Orchids: A Pollinator-Isolated Species Pair, by C. J. Sheviak and M. L. Bowles, *Rhodora*, v. 88, no. 854, pp. 267–290, April 1986. *P. praeclara* may be separated from *P. leucophaea* as follows:

A. Lip 1.7–3.3 cm long, 2.0–4.0 cm wide; *spur 3.5–5.3 cm long*. Column somewhat angular, *pollinia divergent*, the viscidia 6–7.5 mm apart and directed somewhat forward. Raceme short, 8–16-flowered in fully mature plants. Distribution west of the Mississippi River.   *Platanthera praeclara* (not treated further)

AA. Lip 1.4–2.5 cm long, 1.5–2.5 cm wide; *spur 2–3.5 cm long*. Column rounded, *the pollinia closely spaced*, the viscidia essentially parallel, 1.2–3.2 mm apart. Raceme elongate, 12–30-flowered in mature plants. Distribution mostly east of the Mississippi River.
          Platanthera leucophaea (treated above)

BLUNT-LEAF ORCHID

Platanthera obtusata (Banks ex Pursh) Lindley   Plate 16D
Habenaria obtusata (Banks ex Pursh) Richards (1st ed.)

A true northerner, the blunt-leaf orchid does not grow in the southern part of our region. Even in the North it confines itself to cold, dark, evergreen forests and bogs or to shaded headlands and cold, exposed shores.

Habit. Plant small, erect, smooth, 5–20 cm tall, rarely taller. Leaf one (rarely 2), basal, obovate to oblanceolate, rounded to slightly acute at apex, 3–15 cm long, 1–4 cm wide. Scape naked or with 1–2 bracts about midway up stem. Raceme few-flowered, flowers green. Floral bracts lanceolate-acuminate, up to 2 cm long and 5 mm wide, variable. Dorsal sepal ovate, rounded at tip, 3.2–5 mm long, connivent with petals into a hood over column. Lateral sepals reflexed, lanceolate-elliptic, obtuse, 4–5 mm long, 2–3 mm wide. Petals lanceolate, 4–5 mm long, 2 mm wide. Lip fleshy, linear-lanceolate, 6–10 mm long, 2 mm wide, base

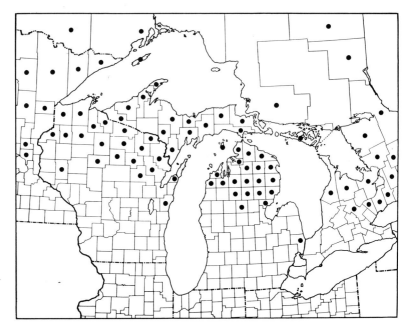

21. *Platanthera obtusata*

auriculate-dilated, bearing a tiny, calluslike excrescence at base. Spur tapered, 4–8 mm long. Capsules rigidly erect, 8 mm long.

Season. June, July. Floral parts often persist as capsules develop.

General Distribution. Arctic forest regions from Alaska to Labrador and Newfoundland, south in the boreal forest and cold bogs of New England, New York, northern Michigan, Wisconsin, and Minnesota; the western mountains south to Colorado and Utah.

Habitat. Cold, wooded bogs and evergreen forests south, becoming more cosmopolitan northward, and occurring sporadically in most situations from open heaths to birch-aspen forest. In our region most often found in white cedar-balsam fir-black spruce swamps. Accompanies twinflower, starflower, bluebead-lily, and creeping snowberry. Sometimes grows in such dark groves that it is the only flowering plant visible in the spruce needle litter.

Cold soil seems to be a requisite for this species. At the south of its range it grows only in cold, shaded bogs. Though many plant species become sporadic in occurrence at the outer limits of their ranges, not so with this orchid. From the moment it appears in the southern fringes of cedar-balsam bog country, it appears abundantly. Of interest in itself, it also serves as an indicator of many rare orchids. Such botanical treasures as calypso, small round-leafed orchis, rattlesnake plantains, and the true twayblades may share the same cover.

LARGE ROUND-LEAVED ORCHID

Platanthera orbiculata (Pursh) Lindl.   Plate 18C,D
Habenaria orbiculata (Pursh) Torrey (1st ed.)

One of the more stately of the so-called green platantheras, this orchid is attractive as well for the otherworldly atmosphere of its deep forest home.

Some authors recognize two varieties of this orchid, others do not. If recognized, the two entities are var. *orbiculata* (the typical variety) and var. *macrophylla* (Goldie) Luer. Most of the authors who recognize the varieties separate them mainly on the basis of the general size of the plant, mentioning especially the very large leaves of the var. *macrophylla*. Correll (1950) did not recognize var. *macrophylla* as anything but extreme-sized individuals of the "typical form." In the first edition I did not recognize var. *macrophylla* because I do not regard size alone as being very important, particularly since unusually large individuals of many orchid species may occur in otherwise typical populations, perhaps due to extraordinary nutrition at that site. Unusually large individuals of *Amerorchis rotundifolia*, *Platanthera obtusata*, *P. hookeri*, *Malaxis unifolia*, *Listera* spp., and *Corallorhiza* spp. occur in all large populations of these species.

Fuller (1933a), however, considers plants from northeastern Wisconsin with spurs 30–40 mm long to be var. *macrophylla*. Fernald (1950) treated the large plant as a distinct species, *Habenaria macrophylla* Goldie. Luer (1975) describes the typical variety as having a spur 20 mm long and the variety *macrophylla* as having a spur 40 mm long. His distribution map for the var. *macrophylla* shows a range from extreme northern Wisconsin and Upper Michigan to New England, Newfoundland, and south in the mountains to North Carolina only. He maps the var. *orbiculata* as having a transcontinental range across Canada and with extensions southward in the Rocky Mountains to Montana and in the Cascade Mountains to northern Oregon. The southward extension of its range in the East is essentially identical to that of the var. *macrophylla*.

Two Canadian researchers, Joyce and Alan Reddoch, are completing a detailed study of this species and its varieties. Their findings, soon to be published, should provide new understanding of the validity of these two varieties, their distribution patterns, and their ecology. Until the Reddochs' work appears, I prefer to treat both varieties as one variable species, while recognizing that the extremely large-leaved, long-spurred plants may represent a distinct taxon.

Habit. Scapose, leaves 2; basal, usually very flat on the ground, subopposite; orbicular in large specimens, frequently oblong-elliptic in small plants, *shining pale bluish green above,* silvery below, 5–25 cm long and broad. Scape rather stiffly erect, 6–60 cm tall, somewhat angled, slender in proportion to width of raceme and size of flowers; provided with several lanceolate bracts. Raceme few–many-flowered, not crowded; floral bracts linear-lanceolate, acute, shorter than flowers. Flowers 5–25 or more, greenish white, sometimes with faint watery mauve shadings. Dorsal sepal suborbicular, erect, 5–10 mm long, 5–8 mm wide. Lateral sepals ovate, obtuse, reflexed, 6–15 mm long, 5– 10 mm wide. Petals ovate to lanceolate, obliquely reflexed, 5–12 mm long, 2–4 mm wide. Lip linear-oblong, obtuse, pendant, somewhat recurved, 10–24 mm long, up to 5 mm wide. Spur cylindrical, thickened toward tip, about equaling pedicel and ovary. Capsules rigidly erect, held parallel with rachis.

Season. Late June to August, depending upon range and habitat. In any area usually blooms later than the similar-appearing Hooker's orchid.

General Distribution. Newfoundland, Labrador, and Quebec, south to Virginia, North Carolina, and Georgia (Correll) in the mountains, westward throughout the Great Lakes states. Also present in Idaho, Washington, Oregon, and Montana; reported from Alaska.

Habitat. A variety of habitats, but nearly always where rather heavily forested. Correll's statement, "usually occurs in dry or moist spots in coniferous hardwood or mixed forests, and rarely in swamps or bogs," illustrates the need for caution in interpretation. While over much of its vast range, and especially in the eastern mountains, it seldom grows in swamps, it should be remembered that few swamps suitable to its growth are found there. In the Lakes states suitable swamp cover is common. Here *P. orbiculata* does sometimes grow in beech-maple or mixed hardwoods and frequently grows in dry evergreen cover along the upper Lakes shores; but it is, nevertheless, mainly a plant of dark-aisled cedar-balsam-spruce wetlands. It seems to show a distinct preference for swamps underlaid with marl strata—definitely not the most acid of cover. It favors dense cedar thickets where there is little else save a few mosses or liverworts.

The largest colonies are found along the upper reaches of the Great Lakes in rather dry, evergreen cover, either along the lakes or behind low sand dunes. In the thick duff of the conifer needles the orchid may actually become common. But, like so many of

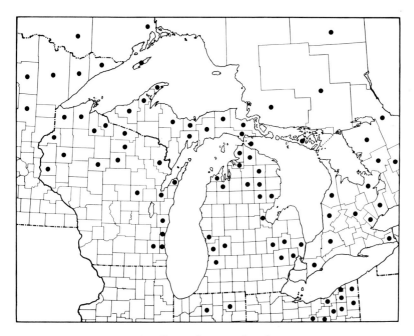

22. *Platanthera orbiculata*

its kin, few of the plants in any one colony will bloom in a given season.

Though structurally quite distinct, the superficial resemblance of this orchid to Hooker's orchid (*P. hookeri*) confuses many people, especially since the two orchids quite frequently share the same cover in drier habitats. Checking the profile of the blossom may help. In *P. hookeri* the sepals are so reflexed and connivent that the lip and the overarching hood give the flower an "ice tongs" appearance. In *P. orbiculata* the floral parts spread, giving a somewhat starlike aspect, with the lip pendent. These aspects are lost in herbarium material. Poorly preserved specimens of the two species can usually be distinguished by the lack of stem bracts in *P. hookeri* and the presence of 2–3 such bracts in *P. orbiculata*.

PURPLE FRINGELESS-ORCHID, PURPLE FRET-LIP

Platanthera peramoena (A. Gray) A. Gray   Plate 19C, D
Habenaria peramoena A. Gray (1st ed.)

At the time of the first edition of this book, I had seen no herbarium specimens of the purple fringeless-orchid from our region, but I did mention its occurrence a very short distance outside our range in central Ohio. One voucher, collected in 1906, is extant from Wayne County, Ohio (OSU), putting this species barely into our area. Whether it still grows within our region is unknown, but it is not unusual for an orchid species to appear, sometimes in great numbers, suddenly, in a district where it had never before been seen. Recently, such a rarity as *Platanthera leucophaea* was reported to have appeared south of its known range in Ohio. *Platanthera peramoena*, too, has had a history of sudden appearances in large numbers. D. M. Spooner and J. S. Shelly discussed the distributional history of this lovely orchid both nationally and in Ohio in a recent issue of *Rhodora* (85: 55–64, 1983).

Purple fringeless-orchid holds its phlox-purple banners high in mid–late July in a broad band across the eastern United States from near the Atlantic coast in New Jersey to Missouri and Arkansas, Mississippi and the Blue Ridge Mountains of North Carolina. Often a tall, stately, and showy plant, it is, nevertheless, infrequently encountered, perhaps because it inhabits rather brushy lowlands, wooded or meadow, in which poison ivy, nettles, and others of its companions make exploration for orchids a chore.

Habit. Plant variable, often stout, 3–10 dm tall, stem leafy, leaves reduced to bracts upward. Leaves 3–5, elliptic-oblong, rarely lanceolate (usually in very well lighted plants only), 7–15 cm long, 2–5 cm wide. Flowers rose- or phlox-purple, very showy. Dorsal sepal oblong-elliptic, 6–8 cm long, 4–8 mm wide, obtuse. Lateral sepals obliquely ovate, obtuse-tipped, weakly reflexed, 7–8 mm long, 4–6 mm wide. Petals oblong-linear to spatulate, the margins erose-crenate, rounded, obtuse, 5–8 mm long, 2–5 mm wide. Lip 3-parted, 1–2 cm long, 1.5–2 cm wide, the lobes remote, cuneate, lateral divisions narrower than the middle lobe, apical margins of the lobes irregular and shallowly erose-toothed, lateral margins of the lobes entire. Spur slender, curved, club-shaped, 2–3 cm long.

Season. Mid-July to early August throughout range, rarely earlier or later. Ohio plants flower strongly in late July.

General Distribution. Eastern Pennsylvania and New Jersey south to Delaware and Maryland, locally southward in the inner coastal plain to South Carolina, largely absent from the piedmont, but locally frequent in mountain valleys from Pennsylvania south to North Carolina, thence westward across Kentucky, Tennessee, extreme northern Alabama, and southward to central Mississippi, eastern Arkansas, and Missouri, southern Illinois, Indiana and Ohio. Spooner and Shelly's (1983) map suggests a strong center of occurrence from southern Ohio westward along

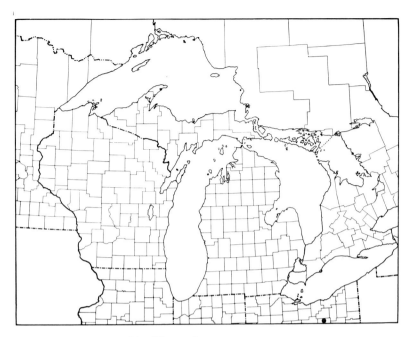

23. *Platanthera peramoena*

the acidic soils north of the Ohio River to Illinois thence southward to Arkansas and western Tennessee, and another strong center of occurrence along the Appalachian Mountain valleys from Pennsylvania to the North Carolina-South Carolina border. The only verified record from our area is in Wayne County, Ohio.

Habitat. Seasonally wet, acid soils, either wooded or open. At its best in wet meadows among phloxes, shrubs, Canada lily (red form), and scattered alders. Also grows on brushy streambanks and in wet flatwoods. I have seen magnificent specimens almost completely obscured by rank jewelweed growths and growing among button-bush (*Cephalanthus*). It also grows in mildly pastured meadows. Spooner and Shelly (*op. cit.*) consider the most vigorous populations to occur on moderately disturbed sites such as "periodically mowed or lightly grazed wet fields or recently logged swampy areas." This also has been my experience with this species.

Correll (1950) described impressively large stands of *P. peramoena* growing near Linville Falls, North Carolina and Caesar's Head, South Carolina. I have botanized extensively in these areas, and made a special effort to locate *P. peramoena* at the Linville Falls site without success. Others have had similar luck. Failure to relocate large stands found by others is a typical experience for orchid hunters. One should realize that wild orchid populations are not static, but rather are dynamic units, thriving briefly in a region of favored ecology (perhaps produced by a minor habitat disturbance). They often fade in a short time because of successional or other change. Although all our orchids are potentially long-lived perennials, few individuals in the wild persist long in the face of the rigors of competition. Rather, existing populations produce the seeds which actively colonize new habitat as it develops, even as the old, formerly vigorous stands decline.

SMALL PURPLE FRINGED-ORCHID, BUTTERFLY ORCHID

Platanthera psycodes (L.) Lindley   Plate 20A, B
Habenaria psycodes (L.) Sprengel (1st ed.)

One of the more cosmopolitan of our native orchids, the purple fringed-orchid possesses considerable beauty. Frequently invading roadside ditches and old pastures, it early becomes a familiar sight to the orchid hunter in those districts where it occurs.

Habit. Plant variable (see discussion of *P. grandiflora*), slender or stout, 1.5–10 dm tall. Stem leafy, leaves gradually reduced to bracts above, elliptic-oblong, obovate, rarely linear-lanceolate, faintly sheathing the stem (less so than in most fringed-orchids), rather dull dark to medium apple-green, 5–20 cm long, 2–7 cm wide. Raceme lax to dense, floral bracts lanceolate, lowermost 4–5 cm long. Flowers lavender, lilac, dark reddish purple, or rarely white; often the lip fades after opening, giving a bicolor appearance to the bloom. Sepals oblong-elliptic to ovate, 5–6 mm long, 3–4 mm wide. Petals (of Michigan material) oblong-cuneate to spatulate, erosely dentate along apical margin, 6–9 mm long, up to 7 mm wide, widest at apex, directed forward over lip. Lip 3-parted, fringed, 8–13 mm long, about the same in width or slightly wider. Spur slender, clubbed, longer than pedicel and ovary.

Season. June, July, August. Quite variable, depending on type of habitat and strain of plant.

General Distribution. Newfoundland, Nova Scotia, and Quebec south to New York, New Jersey, Pennsylvania, and Virginia; in the mountains to North Carolina and Georgia. Westward through Great Lakes region it reaches Minnesota and Iowa.

Habitat. Apparently there are several races of this fine orchid, which seem to have different habitats. The plant grows in low, wet areas in mixed hardwoods, meadows, grassy ditches, and on swampy lake shores, and also in mucky or sandy alluvium along smaller streams and creeks. Although sometimes listed as found

PLATE 1

Explanation of the Color Plates: Genera appear in the same sequence as they appear in the text, and species are arranged alphabetically within the genus, *except* where special groupings aid comparisons of difficult or confusing taxa. Photographs are by the author except where noted.

A. Northern black spruce-tamarack bog.

B. Northern coniferous swamp forest (white cedar, balsam-fir, black spruce).

PLATE 2

A. Mesic prairie and fen with *Cypripedium candidum*.

B. Jack-pine and red pine barrens.

PLATE 3

A. Mixed deciduous forest dominated by American beech and sugar maple.

B. Mature red maple, swamp white oak, red oak and white birch forest on poorly drained, acid soil.

PLATE 4

A. Boreal coniferous forest and dune, Lake Superior, Ontario, Canada.

B. Beach pools, wet sand flats, forested old shoreline ridges and interdunal fens and marshes characteristic of northern Lakes Michigan and Huron.

PLATE 5

A. *Cypripedium acaule*, dark-colored form frequent in the western Great Lakes region.

B. *Cypripedium acaule*, rare white-flowered form.

C. *Cypripedium arietinum*

D. *Cypripedium arietinum*

PLATE 6

A. *Cypripedium calceolus* var. *pubescens*

B. *Cypripedium calceolus* var. *parviflorum*

PLATE 7

A. *Cypripedium candidum*

B. *Cypripedium candidum*

PLATE 8

A. *Cypripedium* ×*andrewsii* (*C. calceolus* var. *parviflorum* × *C. candidum*)

B. *Cypripedium* ×*favillianum* (*C. calceolus* var. *pubescens* × *C. candidum*)

C. *Cypripedium passerinum*

D. *Cypripedium passerinum*

PLATE 9

A. *Cypripedium reginae*, typical coloration.

B. *Cypripedium reginae*, white form.

C. *Cypripedium reginae* in a lakeside fen in Michigan.

PLATE 1(

B. *Amerorchis rotundifolia,* typical coloration in our region.

A. *Amerorchis rotundifolia*

C. *Amerorchis rotundifolia* f. *lineata*

PLATE 11

A. *Galearis spectabilis*, rare white-flowered form.

B. *Galearis spectabilis*, typical coloration.

C. *Platanthera blephariglottis* blooming in a northern black spruce-tamarack bog.

PLATE 12

A. *Platanthera blephariglottis*

B. *Platanthera ×bicolor (P. blephariglottis × P. ciliaris)*

C. *Platanthera ciliaris* in a Michigan bog.

D. *Platanthera ciliaris* flowers with morning dewdrops.

PLATE 13

Platanthera clavellata

B. Platanthera clavellata

Platanthera ×vossii Case (P. clavellata × P. blephariglottis)

D. Platanthera flava var. herbiola

PLATE 14

A. *Platanthera dilatata*

B. *Platanthera hyperborea*

PLATE 15

. *Platanthera dilatata*

B. *Platanthera hyperborea*

Platanthera hookeri

D. *Platanthera hookeri*

PLATE 16

A. *Platanthera lacera*

B. *Platanthera lacera*

C. *Platanthera* ×*andrewsii* (*P. lacera* × *P. psycodes*)

D. *Platanthera obtusata*

PLATE 17

A. *Platanthera leucophaea*

B. *Platanthera leucophaea*

PLATE 18

A. *Platanthera leucophaea;* note spreading petals and parallel pollinaria (compare with 18B).

B. *Platanthera praeclara;* note hoodlike arrangement of sepals and petals over column and lip and divergent pollinaria.

C. *Platanthera orbiculata*

D. *Platanthera orbiculata*

PLATE 19

A. *Platanthera grandiflora*

B. *Platanthera grandiflora*

C. *Platanthera peramoena*

D. *Platanthera peramoena*

PLATE 20

A. *Platanthera psycodes*

B. *Platanthera psycodes*

PLATE 21

A. *Piperia unalascensis*

B. *Piperia unalascensis*

C. *Coeloglossum viride* var. *virescens*

D. *Coeloglossum viride* var. *virescens*

PLATE 22

A. *Listera auriculata* growing among alder trunks on a sandy streambank.

B. *Listera auriculata*

C. *Listera borealis*

PLATE 23

A. *Listera australis*

B. *Listera cordata*

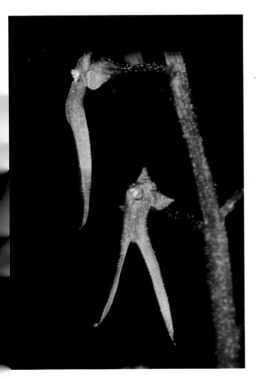

C. *Listera australis*, flower detail with pine pollen.

D. *Listera cordata*, flower detail.
(T. L. Mellichamp)

A. *Listera auriculata*

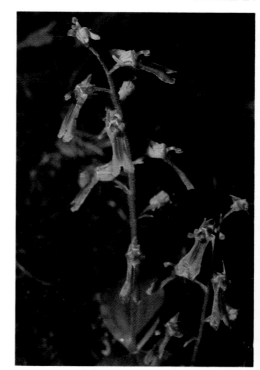

B. *Listera borealis*

C. *Listera convallarioides*

D. *Listera ×veltmanii (L. auriculata × L. convallarioides)*

PLATE 25

A. *Listera convallarioides*

B. *Listera ovata*, photographed in Switzerland.

Epipactis helleborine

D. *Epipactis helleborine*

PLATE 26

A. *Triphora trianthophora*

B. *Triphora trianthophora*

C. *Triphora trianthophora;* these dense clumps result from red squirrels burying numerous tubers in their food caches.

PLATE 27

A. *Isotria medeoloides*
(Erich DeLin)

C. *Isotria verticillata*

B. *Isotria verticillata*

PLATE 28

A. *Pogonia ophioglossoides*

B. *Pogonia ophioglossoides*

PLATE 29

A. *Arethusa bulbosa*

B. *Arethusa bulbosa*

PLATE 30

B. *Calopogon tuberosus*

A. *Calopogon tuberosus*

C. *Calopogon tuberosus*, infrequent white-flowered form.

PLATE 31

Spiranthes casei

B. Spiranthes cernua

Spiranthes lacera var. lacera

D. Spiranthes lucida

PLATE 32

A. *Spiranthes magnicamporum*

B. *Spiranthes ochroleuca*

C. *Spiranthes ovalis* var. *erostellata*

D. *Spiranthes romanzoffiana*

A. *Spiranthes tuberosa*
   (John V. Freudenstein)

B. *Spiranthes lucida*

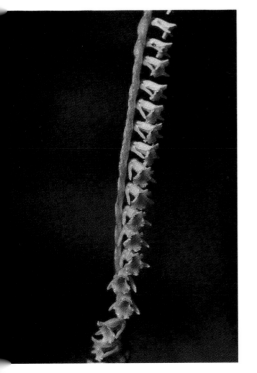

C. *Spiranthes lacera* var. *lacera*

D. *Spiranthes lacera* var. *gracilis*
   (J. Ross Brown)

Comparison of the larger-flowered *Spiranthes* formerly included in *S. cernua* or other species.

A. *Spiranthes casei*

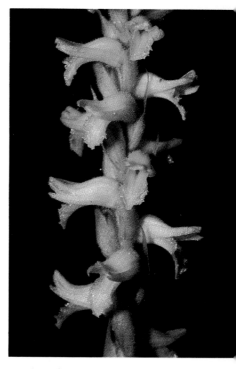

B. *Spiranthes cernua*

C. *Spiranthes magnicamporum*

D. *Spiranthes ochroleuca*

A. *Spiranthes ovalis* var. *erostellata*

B. *Spiranthes tuberosa*

C. *Spiranthes romanzoffiana*

D. *Goodyera* leaf rosettes.
   From top:
   Goodyera repens var. *ophioides*
   Goodyera tesselata
   Goodyera oblongifolia
   Goodyera pubescens

PLATE 36

A. *Goodyera oblongifolia*

B. *Goodyera pubescens*

C. *Goodyera repens* var. *ophioides*

D. *Goodyera tesselata*

PLATE 37

A. *Malaxis monophylla* var. *brachypoda*

B. *Malaxis paludosa*

. *Malaxis unifolia*

D. *Liparis loeselii* growing in tufts of sedges, *Juncus* and mosses in a small Michigan lake.

PLATE 38

A. *Liparis lilifolia*

B. *Liparis lilifolia*

C. *Liparis loeselii*

D. *Liparis loeselii*
   (Erich DeLin)

PLATE 39

A. *Tipulária discolor*, winter leaves.

C. *Tipularia discolor*, note floral asymmetry.

Tipularia discolor, flowering raceme.

PLATE 40

A. *Calypso bulbosa* in northern Lower Michigan (enlarged).

PLATE 41

. *Aplectrum hyemale*, winter leaves.

B. *Aplectrum hyemale*, inflorescence.

Aplectrum hyemale, typical coloration.
(Erich DeLin)

D. *Aplectrum hyemale* f. *pallidum*

A. *Corallorhiza maculata*, early type, raceme.

B. *Corallorhiza maculata*, late type, raceme.

C. *Corallorhiza maculata* var. *flavida*, albino early type. (Erich DeLin)

D. *Corallorhiza maculata*, late type, typic coloration.

PLATE 43

A. *Corallorhiza odontorhiza*, cleistogamous form with less red pigment than is typical.

B. *Corallorhiza odontorhiza*, chasmogamous form with typical coloring.

Corallorhiza striata
(James Wells)

D. *Corallorhiza striata*

PLATE 44

A. *Corallorhiza trifida*

B. *Corallorhiza trifida*
(Erich DeLin)

C. *Corallorhiza wisteriana*

D. *Corallorhiza wisteriana*
(Erich DeLin)

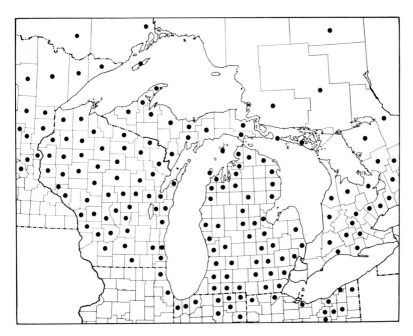

24. *Platanthera psycodes*

in cedar swamps and sphagnum bogs, this information can be misleading. While it may occur in open, wet muckholes on the outer margins of such bogs, it does not grow in the mossy heart of such a swamp, nor is it a part of the cedar swamp community. So far as can be determined from field observations and a study of herbarium annotations, it never grows in sphagnum. A favored situation in the southern Lakes states is a low elm-red maple flatwoods on a sandy soil—just such a location as the tubercled orchid chooses—where there are empty, open aisles with dead and matted leaves covering the soil, and where water stands after every rain and clumps of sensitive fern abound.

In western Upper Michigan, northern Wisconsin, and Minnesota, it grows mainly in wet, soggy meadows or prairies. It becomes very abundant in such situations, lending a purple hue to the "marsh hay."

PIPERIA Rydberg

Founded by Rydberg in 1901, this genus has variously been accepted or rejected by authors since. Luer reinstates it and recognizes three species, all are western and one occurs as well in our region and along the Gulf of St. Lawrence. Plants of this genus produce a few more or less basal leaves which, unlike those of *Platanthera*, wither and fade at or before flowering. In this group, a pair of fleshy ovoid tubers is produced along with some tapered fleshy roots. The lateral sepals, although spreading, are partly fused to the base of the lip.

Since there is but one species within our region, the description of that species will serve for further details of this genus.

ALASKA ORCHID, ALASKA PIPERIA

Piperia unalascensis (Spreng.) Rydberg   Plate 21A, B
Habenaria unalascensis (Spreng.) S. Watson (1st ed.)

A remarkably slender and inconspicuous plant, this orchid grows in a very limited part of our region, its main home being far to the west.

Habit. Very slender to occasionally stout, scapose, 20–80.5 cm tall. Roots short, mostly slender-fleshy, but *including a pair of ovoid to rounded fleshy tubers.* Leaves usually 2, rarely up to 4, basal, oblanceolate to obovate, erect-spreading, obtuse, 7–15 cm long, 1–4 cm wide, pale yellowish green, *withering before or during flowering.* Raceme very narrow, spikelike, cylindrical, or with a tendency for most of the flowers to face in one direction. Floral bracts ovate-lanceolate, acuminate, shorter than flowers. Flowers unusually small, tending to be unequally distributed throughout raceme, greenish white to straw-colored, rancid-sweet. Sepals elliptic-ovate, obtuse, 2–4 mm long, 1 mm wide. Petals fleshy, elliptic-lanceolate, 2–4 mm long, 1 mm wide. Lip fleshier than other floral parts, recurved or thrust forward, triangular, 2–4 mm long, 1–2 mm wide, widest at base. Spur slender, cylindrical, 3–4 mm long.

Season. Late June or early July.

General Distribution. Disjunct in the East and isolated on Anticosti Island, Quebec, the upper Lake Huron-Georgian Bay area, and South Dakota (Black Hills). More generally distributed in western mountains from Mexico to Alaska.

Great Lakes Distribution: Bruce Peninsula, Ontario, adjacent islands, Manitoulin Island, Drummond Island, and extreme eastern Upper Michigan, apparently only on dolomite limestone formations.

Habitat. Mostly open, brushy, rock pavement country, gravelly slopes, and open cedar-balsam woods, usually where burnt over or disturbed. The first record from Michigan's mainland was from the border of a cedar swamp. Plant companions are buffalo-berry, twinflower, Canada lily-of-the-valley, Canada bunchberry, and

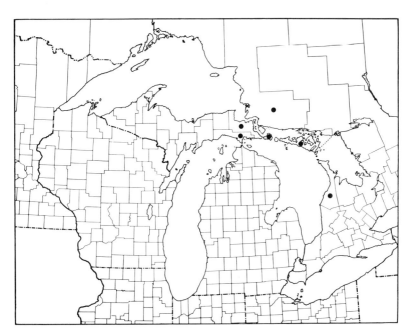

25. *Piperia unalascensis*

round-leaved dogwood. Usually grows in small colonies.

For all its differences, this orchid reminds one of a spike of the tall green bog-orchid stripped of its leaves and pulled out into a slender stem. Yet when expanding its spike it possesses a gracefulness seldom seen in *P. hyperborea*.

Long known from the region of the Bruce Peninsula, rather recently its presence on Drummond Island was ascertained. Not until the 1940s was *P. unalascensis* collected on the mainland of Michigan's Upper Peninsula; the earliest collection I have seen was made by Dr. Rogers McVaugh of the University of Michigan. Apparently it is undergoing population explosion in favored areas of the Georgian Bay region. Old records showed it to be very rare, but now it is apparently locally common. Its choice habitat—dryish rock-rubbled brushlands and open, thin forest—seems to have been bountifully produced by the clearing, lumbering, or burning of the land.

COELOGLOSSUM Hartman

This genus, established in 1820, like some of the others has gone in and out of vogue with taxonomists through the years.

The current trend toward splitting genera in orchid taxonomy has resulted in its being reinstated by European authors and by Luer. There is considerable structural justification for it. The roots of the plant produce a few forked, fleshy, tuberoid roots similar to those of *Dactylorhiza*, a condition not found in our other related species in *Platanthera*. Flower structure is generally much like *Platanthera*, but the viscidium of the pollinarium is covered by a microscopic membrane, not exposed. Openings to the nectary-spur are obscured and minute and some nectar is secreted also on the curved basal lip margins (Luer 1975).

There is but one highly variable species spread across the entire Northern Hemisphere in suitable climates. Several varieties have been proposed with two generally recognized. The var. *bracteata* (Willd.) Gray of most authors (var. *virescens* (Muhlenberg) Luer, of Luer) is the only one found in our area.

LONG-BRACTED GREEN ORCHID, FROG ORCHID

Coeloglossum viride (L.) Hartman   Plate 21C, D
    var. *virescens* (Willd.) Gray
Habenaria viridis (L.) R. Brown var.
    bracteata (Muhl. ex Willd.) A. Gray

A widespread species, this orchid grows from coast to coast in North America and also in parts of Europe and Asia. The greenish flowers, despite their inconspicuous nature, possess an uncommon grace and symmetry. The large, vigorous plants of this species produce offshoots that soon form big clumps.

Habit. Usually fleshy, smooth, and rather tall, occasionally much smaller in exposed positions, 10–60 cm tall (smaller in subarctic regions). Roots distinctive; several simple, fleshy roots and 1 or 2 roots much swollen, palmately divided or bifurcate, and much in contrast to the others. Stem leafy; leaves several, lowermost usually obovate to oblanceolate, upper ones reduced, obtuse or lanceolate. Larger leaves 5–15 cm long, sometimes considerably longer, 2–8 cm wide. Raceme long, dense or lax. Floral bracts linear, acuminate, *lowermost very long, much exceeding flower and pedicel* (2–5 times), conspicuous; upper bracts and flowers often reduced, with bracts barely exceeding the flower. Flowers green to yellow-green, on stout ovaries. Dorsal sepal ovate-orbicular, 3–6 mm long, 3 mm wide. Lateral sepals ovate-oblong, 4–6 mm long, about half as wide. Petals linear, acute, shorter than sepals. Lip oblong, lateral edges roughly parallel, or slightly wider toward apex, rather large in comparison to other floral parts, 5–10 mm long, 3–4 mm wide. Apex of lip with 2 rather conspicuous teeth located at each side, and often with a much smaller tooth between. Spur shorter than lip, saclike.

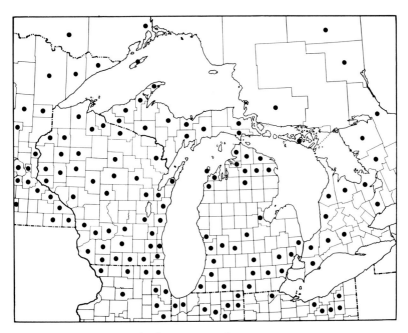

26. *Coeloglossum viride* var. *virescens*

Season. May, at the south of our range, through July or August in Lake Superior areas. Correll gives March as the season in Michigan, but this would surely be only in a most unusual season. In most years almost none of our flora save skunk cabbage and possibly snow trillium or hepatica would be in evidence at this time. The long flowering season of this plant is occasioned by the persistence of the floral parts in good condition on nearly ripened seed capsules.

General Distribution. Newfoundland, Nova Scotia, and Quebec across America to Alaska and the Aleutians; in the East, south to Pennsylvania and Maryland and in the mountains to North Carolina; west through the Lakes states to Minnesota and Iowa. In the western mountains, south locally to Colorado and New Mexico; also in Eurasia.

Habitat. This orchid seems to tolerate most types of acid woodland and arctic heath. In Alaska I have seen it growing on open, turfy hillsides where the only cover was an occasional aspen. In southern Michigan it inhabits low, wet soils, often under spicebush near the margins of temporary ponds. Although rare in the southern part of the Lakes states, it will be seen occasionally. Areas which favor the puttyroot orchid or showy orchis will likewise produce an occasional orchid of this species. Northward it becomes more frequent. Here it often grows in upland beech-maple cover among squirrel-corn, sharp-lobed hepatica, and white trillium; one of its best indicators is the presence of moosewood. Along the upper reaches of Lakes Michigan, Huron, and Superior the orchid becomes really common. Here it grows mostly in lightly wooded yet moist forests of hemlock, fir, spruce, and alder. Particularly abundant near Grand Marais, Michigan, it grows near the lake shore woods which are under the influence of constant blowing sand from nearby dunes. Apparently the continued renewal of rawish soil holds down competition or generally favors orchid seed germination, for in these woods more species of orchids grow in greater abundance than any I have seen in any other plant community of our region.

LISTERA R. Brown

Named for an English naturalist, Martin Lister, these tway-blades are more curious than beautiful. Nearly all the approximately 25 species are small, inconspicuous, and local. In all species a pair of subopposite, subequal, sessile leaves perch midway on a rather short stem. An open raceme of small greenish or madder-stained flowers, appearing superficially to be all lip, completes the picture. The sepals and petals, free, are similar in size and shape; they spread or reflex. The much larger lip is bifid or lobed at the apex. The pollinia are powdery.

All our species, plants of cold, sandy, or humus-rich soils, are absent from the southern parts of the Lakes states, except at higher elevations in eastern Ohio. Five species occur natively in our region and *Listera ovata*, a European species, has appeared recently in two widely separated stations in southern Ontario. Luer (1975) gives a fascinating account of *Listera* pollination.

Key to *Listera*

A. Plants generally robust, 25–60 cm tall, lip abruptly deflexed near its base, cleft about 1/4 of its length into two dilated, blunt lobes.
L. ovata
page 142

AA. Plants less than 25 cm tall, the lip scarcely if at all deflexed at the base, either deeply or shallowly cleft, if deeply cleft, cleft at least half its length, the lobes acute.

B. Lip deeply cleft for half its length into two acuminate tips.

C. Base of lip not auriculate; under magnification is seen to have a pair of conspicuous transverse teeth or horns appearing distinct in texture and color from the surface of lip. Cleft tips of lip tend to be divergent. Flowers reddish, maroon, or green.

L. cordata
page 140

CC. Base of lip slightly auriculate, lacking any basal horns or teeth. Cleft tips of lip not especially divergent.

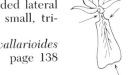

L. australis
page 134

BB. Lip shallowly to scarcely cleft; tips of lip bluntly rounded.

C. Base of lip with a short, slender claw (appearing stalked), cuneate above the claw, bearing two large, rounded lateral lobes with a minute tooth in the sinus, and two small, triangular teeth at base of the lip above the claw.

L. convallarioides
page 138

CC. Base of lip clawless with auricles on either side of the column, sessile, essentially oblong, slightly narrowed at middle, cleft into shallow rounded lobes at apex.

D. Basal lip auricles rounded, curving around (hugging) the column.

L. auriculata
page 131

DD. Basal lip auricles divergent, triangular to somewhat truncate, not rounded nor hugging the column.

L. borealis
page 136

AURICLED TWAYBLADE

Listera auriculata Wiegand   Plate 22A, B, 24A

Confined primarily to the northern parts of our range, this twayblade may be frequent in suitable habitats, especially along the northern shore of Lake Superior. Formerly little known south of the islands of Lake Superior, it has recently been discovered at several stations in Upper Michigan, relocated in northern Wisconsin after not having been reported for about 40 years, and most recently, it has been located in parts of central Ontario south of previously known sites. Botanists also discovered the species in the Adirondack Mountains of New York. Whiting and Catling (1977) examined many herbarium specimens and found that the auricled twayblade had also been collected (although misidentified) farther north toward Hudson Bay than it had previously been known. The species obviously enjoys a wider geographic range than had been realized. Careful searching in its narrow niche may reveal its presence in other districts of our region.

Like Morris and Eames (1929), I at first feared that I would not recognize this species when I found it, but would confuse it with the broad-leaved twayblade. Once seen, however, it cannot be mistaken for that species. The color, unlike its description in the older books, is not always pale green, but often distinctly deep green, yellow-green, or bluish green; the lip, with its column-hugging auricles, is completely unlike that of *L. convallarioides*. Its appearance is very much like that of the northern twayblade (*L. borealis*), and it could more easily be confused with that species.

Habit. Plant height variable, 7–24 cm tall, slender. Leaves distinctly medium–dark green by comparison with related species; oval-elliptic, 2.5–6 cm long, 1.5–4 cm wide. Stem glabrous below leaves, densely glandular-puberulent above. Scape few–many-flowered, bracts, pedicels, and ovaries smooth. Floral bracts oblong-lanceolate, 2–7 mm long, 1–1.5 mm wide. Flowers greenish, fading whitish with age, sepals and petals reflexed away from lip, sepals greenish white, dorsal sepal elliptic-obovate, blunt-tipped, 3–4 mm long, 1.5 mm wide. Lateral sepals oblique, lanceovate, subobtuse 3–4 mm long, 1.5 mm wide. Petals linear, falcate, 3 mm long, less than 1 mm wide. Lip oblong, narrowed just above middle, very faintly ciliate along margins, 6–12 mm long and 3 mm across at narrowest, slightly expanded at apex, and forming 2 blunt lobes. Base of lip prolonged backward into distinct auricles 3 mm long, auricles incurved around column. Center line of lip thickened with a dark emerald green excrescence. Column 2–3 mm long. Capsules about 8 mm long, ripening very early.

Season. Late June to early August, blooming in Upper Michigan from early to middle of July, probably later on islandic stations.

General Distribution. Newfoundland, Quebec, New Brunswick, Ontario, Maine, New Hampshire west to Michigan; in Michigan known from several locations in central Upper Michigan and on

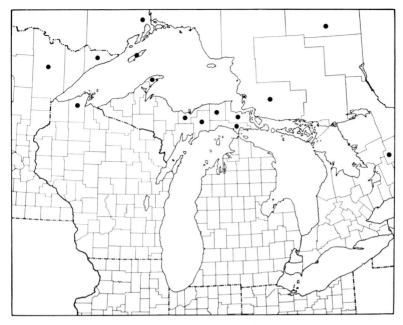

27. *Listera auriculata*

Sugar Island in the St. Mary's River, as well as on Isle Royale. Known from one or two stations along the Lake Superior shore of Wisconsin. Probably much more frequent and overlooked along the larger rivers in the vicinity of Lake Superior.

Habitat. Very distinctive—raw, alluvial sand along rivers. Plants develop at about the high flood water line in sandy wash under alders; often, for members of this genus, in surprisingly open situations. Grows among scattered sedges and grasses; these are often the only plants evident in sandy areas about the base of alders. Along Lake Superior shore, just back of the bare sands and rocky ledges of the shoreline, grows under the row of alders that forms the outer flank of shore vegetation in low areas. Occasionally found on sandy flats along small streams under firs and alders.

Hybrids. In 1962 H. S. Veltman and I discovered a hybrid twayblade at Grand Sable Falls, Alger County, Michigan. The hybrid, subsequently named *L.* ×*veltmanii* Case, is almost exactly intermediate between its putative parents, *L. auriculata* and *L. convallarioides* (Plate 24D). In the course of our searching, we also found the hybrid in Luce County, Michigan. At no time did we find mixed colonies of both parent species although each was present in the same general vicinity as the hybrid. Sometimes the hybrid plants grew with the *L. convallarioides* parent, at other times the identical hybrid grew with *L. auriculata*. As is so often true of hybrid plant stations, the habitat where the hybrid grew was not exactly typical of that of either parent, and it showed evidence of physical disturbance. Catling (see below) found similar circumstances along the Pancake River in Algoma District, Ontario, where he found a number of plants of *L. ×veltmanii* growing in proximity to both parents. *L. ×veltmanii* is described and details of its discovery are reported in *The Michigan Botanist*, v. 3, p. 67–70, May 1964.

In 1976 Paul Catling published (in *Rhodora*) a study of this hybrid in the field and in herbaria. This study demonstrated that although *L. ×veltmanii* is rare it has been collected (often without recognition) at several locations on the north shore of Lake Superior, and in Quebec, Gaspé, New Brunswick, and Newfoundland. He gives details of the hybrid's structure, habitat, and relation to colonies of its putative parents. My herbarium work for this edition has brought to light additional collections from Wisconsin and the north shore of Lake Superior.

Since hybrids vary considerably and since the variability is even greater if backcrossing to either parent has occurred, I give no detailed description of this hybrid here. Interested persons should consult the journal articles cited for descriptions.

SOUTHERN TWAYBLADE

Listera australis Lindl.   Plate 23A, C

This predominantly southern species has been known from the Finger Lakes region of New York, and the Ottawa region of Canada for a very long time. Over the past 50 years, botanists believed it had become extinct in the old Canadian region. In 1973, however, R. E. Whiting, P. Catling, and S. M. McKay discovered plants in an extensive bog not far from the original localities, but east of our region. Inspired by this discovery, A. A. Reznicek, J. R. F. Wiseman, and R. S. W. Bobbette explored a bog near Severn Falls, Simcoe County, Ontario, well within the coverage area of this book. *Listera australis* proved to be present in small numbers. It has since been found in other Muskoka and Algonquin bogs (Whiting and Bobbette 1974). Present evidence suggests that southern twayblade will be discovered in a number of other Canadian stations within our region. A plant known for appearing in widely disjunct localities (Arkansas (*fide* Case), Newfoundland, Quebec) its appearance in Michigan in suitable cover seems a strong possibility.

This early-blooming twayblade, although fairly large, can be very hard to detect when growing, as it does in northern spruce bogs, among leatherleaf (*Chamaedaphne*) stems and tangled bog vegetation. Usually the plant appears as a solitary stem, here or there, across dark, sandy-wet woods floors, or in sphagnous areas among *Osmunda* ferns. In Ontario it grows at the edges of glades in deep mounds of sphagnum. Only rarely does it form loose clumps or clusters as is the manner of the heartleaf twayblade. Deep red and greenish bronze stem and flower colors occur, often in mixed colonies. Although the flowers are tiny, the deep red forms are striking. Deep red or maroon flowered forms predominate in Ontario.

Habit. Plant variable, slender, somewhat stiffly erect, 6–25 cm tall, green to dark purplish red overall, glabrous below, slightly glandular above the leaves. Leaves subopposite, attached at or below midstem, elongate-ovate, obtuse to apiculate, occasionally subcordate, smooth, and except for the midrib, appearing almost veinless, green to dark purplish red, 1–4 cm long, 0.5–2 cm wide, widest near the base. Raceme somewhat elongate, few- to many-flowered, often longer than subfoliar stem. Floral bracts minute, about 1–2 mm long and wide. Flowers few to many (2–25), small, superficially similar to those of *L. cordata*, on filiform pedicels. Dorsal sepal obtuse, ovate-elliptic, about 1 mm long and wide. Lateral sepals obtuse, ovate, 1 mm x 1 mm. Petals oblong, obtuse, about 1 mm long and wide. The much larger lip is sessile, linear, cleft 1/3 to 1/2 its length into two linear-attenuate, acuminate lobes separated by a minute tooth in the sinus (absent in the superficially similar lip of *L. cordata*). Base of lip with small, incurved auricles less than 1 mm long on each side of the column. Disk of lip with a slightly raised, papillose, T-shaped area beneath the column, but lacking the divergent basal horns of *L. cordata*. Column short, 0.5 mm long, thick.

Season. February to July (Correll) across entire range, blooming in the Great Lakes region in early June–early July. Entire plant often withering early in the season.

General Distribution. Coastal regions of Texas, along the Gulf Coast to central Florida, thence northward in coastal plain and outer piedmont to New Jersey, Pennsylvania, and New York into Ontario, Quebec, and Maine. Disjunct stations occur on the Cumberland Plateau in Tennessee and in Arkansas (*fide* Case). In our region known from Simcoe County, Muskoka and Algonquin districts, Ontario.

Habitat. Widely tolerant of a variety of moist, acid habitats in the South, preferring sandy flatwoods with pine humus or leaf litter. Northward, especially in the newly discovered Ontario stations, *L. australis* grows in surprisingly boreal black spruce-tamarack bogs. In such situations, it grows in open beds of

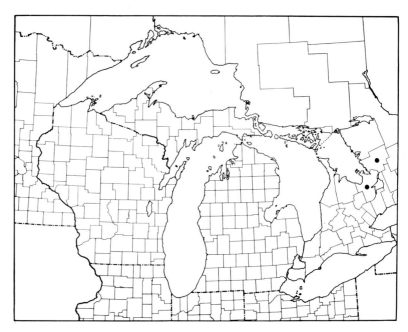

28. *Listera australis*

sphagnum moss, often that which is reddish in color, among leatherleaf stems, Virginia chain-fern (*Woodwardia virginica*), pitcher-plant, and three-leaved false Solomon's-seal (*Smilacina trifolia*). Such situations in this region as are ideal for the white fringed-orchid (*P. blephariglottis*).

NORTHERN TWAYBLADE

Listera borealis Morong   Plate 22C, 24B

In 1965 Roberta Case and I discovered the northern twayblade growing in a deep, mossy, wooded ravine in company with *Cypripedium passerinum*, Franklin's lady's-slipper, on the north shore of Lake Superior. At that time about 40 plants grew in the colony. In 1983 we could not locate any *L. borealis* in our original location, but another colony has been seen by others nearby. Disappearance of the original plants is not, in itself, alarming since all our twayblades appear short-lived; at least blooming plants seem not to reappear at the same spot the next season. Rather, twayblade plants spread by budding of the underground rhizome or by seed. In this respect, they grow like the rattle-snake plantains in which, after flowering and fruiting, the flowering growth degenerates. However, before the death of the flowering growth, buds along the rhizome immediately behind the flowering offshoot form new branches or leaf rosettes.

Although the northern twayblade has a very large range across northern Canada and in the Rocky Mountains, this station remains the only known one for the western Great Lakes region.

Habit. Plant height variable, 4–26 cm tall, relatively slender, somewhat stiff in aspect. Leaves 2, subequal, green to slightly bluish green, elliptic to ovate-elliptic (in eastern material especially), 1.5–6 cm long, 0.5–3 cm wide, midrib prominent. Stem glabrous below, sparsely glandular-puberulent above, faintly four-angled. Raceme rather short, few-flowered, glandular-puberulent. Floral bracts tiny, ovate to oblong, blunt-tipped, 2 mm long. Flowers irregularly wide-spreading, pale green, darker on nerves and disk of lip. Sepals and petals strongly reflexed from lip, green; dorsal sepal elliptic-linear, rounded at apex, 5–6 mm long, 1.5–2 mm wide, one-nerved; lateral sepals elliptic-lanceolate, obtuse, falcate, 4–7 mm long, 1.5–2 mm wide, one-nerved, nerve darker green. Petals linear-oblong, obtuse, 4–6 mm long, 0.5–1.5 mm wide, green, darker along nerve. Lip conspicuous, oblong, slightly dilated at distal end into two shallow rounded lobes, each about 3 mm long and wide and bearing an apiculate tooth in the sinus between them. Lip 6–12 mm long, 4–7 mm wide, widest above the middle, dilated at the base into two divergent almost triangular auricles which project away from the column. Central disk of lip with a somewhat ridged, dark shiny green thickening ending at two raised pads of tissue below the column. Column stout, arcuate-curved, 3–4 mm long. Capsules oval-elliptic when ripe. Old stem and capsules frequently persist for one season.

Season. Late June–August, later northward and on islandic sites. Blooming along Lake Superior about July 1–10.

General Distribution. Newfoundland, Anticosti and Mingan islands, Gulf of St. Lawrence, northern Lake Superior shores, Hudson Bay regions, across the continent to central Alaska and south along the Rocky Mountains to Montana and very locally to Colorado. Widespread and frequent in Alaska, Yukon, and British Columbia.

Habitat. On Lake Superior, northern twayblade grows on deeply wooded, captured sand dunes and sandy flatwoods in the immediate vicinity of the cool lake shore only. Plant companions here are *Calypso bulbosa*, *Goodyera repens* var. *ophioides*, *Listera convallarioides*, mosses, white cedar (*Thuja*), Canada fir (*Abies balsamaea*), and white spruce (*Picea glauca*). Twinflower (*Linnaea borealis*) carpets the ground. Nearby shrubs include buffalo-berry (*Shepherdia canadensis*) and bearberry (*Arctostaphylos uva-ursi*).

Northward *L. borealis* grows in spruce thickets, often where

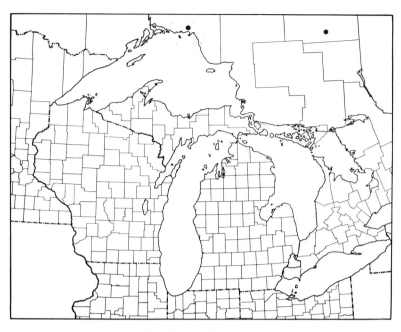

29. *Listera borealis*

very dark and dense, in needle litter and mosses, or in spruce groves and turfy humus-filled pockets along lake shores. This species becomes less selective of habitat in the northern parts of its range.

L. borealis should be sought elsewhere on northern Lake Superior shores and islands. Its suitable habitat is more widespread on Lake Superior than is that of *C. passerinum* and I believe the potential for additional colonies is good. Nonetheless, northern twayblade should be considered very rare and possibly an endangered species within our area.

BROAD-LEAVED TWAYBLADE

Listera convallarioides (Swartz) Nutt.   Plate 24C, 25A

The specific name of this orchid refers to the lily-of-the-valley, but it has very little resemblance to that plant. A wide-ranging species of cold soils, it is sometimes abundant enough to attract attention despite its inconspicuousness. Though not beautiful in the usual sense, it has a graceful habit and a soft translucence which are pleasing.

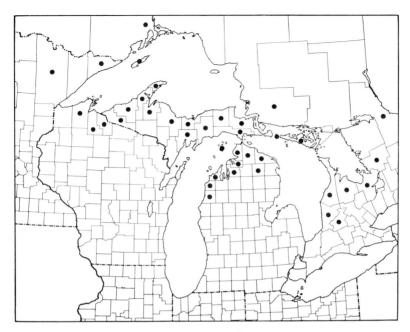

30. *Listera convallarioides*

Habit. Plants somewhat stoloniferous, glabrous below leaves, minutely glandular-pubescent above, 6–37 cm tall. Leaves 2, opposite, borne about a rather stout stem, ovate-elliptic to suborbicular, blunt-tipped, smooth, 2–7 cm long, 2–5 cm wide. Raceme loosely many-flowered, 3–12 cm long. Floral bracts 3–4 mm long, semitransparent. Flowers pale, translucent, green, on slender pedicels, sepals linear-lanceolate, 4–5 mm long, 1 mm wide, reflexed upon ovary. Petals similar in appearance, narrower and paler, also reflexed. Lip large and very conspicuous, clawed, cuneate, rounded and lobed at apex, with a tiny tooth in sinus of lobes; bears a tiny tooth on each side just above claw; 8–14 mm long, 7–8 mm wide at widest point. Column relatively conspicuous, slightly curved, 2–3 mm long.

Season. Late June to August; mostly early July.

General Distribution. Transcontinental, or possibly absent from the center of North America; rather frequent on both eastern and western sides of continent. Frequent from Newfoundland and Ontario south to Vermont, New York, and Michigan, also in the mountains of the Carolinas (Correll). In the West, grows from Alaska and the Aleutians south to Utah and Arizona.

Habitat. At the south of its range, in the northern portions of Michigan's Lower Peninsula, grows mostly at the base of steep hills, along bog borders. Here most frequently met in sandy seepage areas and in mucky, springy areas under white cedar and balsam fir. Common plant companions are dwarf bishop's-cap, horsetails, and jack-in-the-pulpit. Although a few blooming stalks are dotted here and there in such habitats, many nonflowering plants dominate. In the upper Lakes it is more cosmopolitan, occurring not only as it does further south, but also in cedar swamps or in swamp woods of red maple, aspen, and fir. In areas where the forest floor is awash with freshets during heavy rains, the plant forms extensive colonies; here the plants are robust and most of them flower. However, they seem to be subject to some disease or early withering, and many blackened stems are usually found in the large colonies. Especially abundant in moist, interdunal woods near Grand Marais, Michigan.

Hybrids. Crosses with *L. auriculata* to form *L. ×veltmanii.* See discussion under that species, page 133.

HEARTLEAF TWAYBLADE

Listera cordata (L.) R. Br.   Plate 23B, D

One of the widest ranging of all our orchids, the heartleaf twayblade is found in all boreal regions of North America, as well as in Japan, Iceland, Greenland, and Europe. Western forms, more robust than ours, grow in moist spruce forest and dry, turfy woods, as well as in bogs. Our plants are mostly confined to cold bogs and swamps.

Habit. Slender, delicate, and smooth, 6–25 cm tall, roots fibrous-fleshy, rambling, brownish or white. Leaves 2, opposite to subopposite, broadly ovate-cordate, sometimes obscurely deltoid, 1–4 cm long, 0.8–4 cm wide. Raceme rather densely flowered, flowers 8–25 or more. Bracts small, 1–4 mm long, inconspicuous. Sepals ovate-oblong to elliptic, 2–3 mm long, 1 mm wide. Petals narrower, similar. Lip linear-oblong, sharply cleft into 2 acuminate lobes for at least half its length, upper surface of lip bearing 2 divergent curved horns near lip base, the horns of a distinct texture and darker than rest of lip. Column very short and inconspicuous, 0.5 mm long. Seed capsules ripen so quickly that plants are commonly found with the flower parts still fresh, but with the seed already dispersed.

Season. Late May (in more open bogs) to mid-July.

Distribution. Transcontinental in boreal forests and cold bogs, extending southward in both eastern and western mountains, to North Carolina and Oregon respectively.

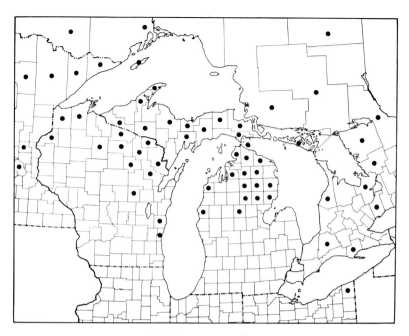

31. *Listera cordata*

Habitat. Cold mossy bogs and woods. In the Lakes region most common in old balsam-cedar-spruce bogs where mosses and twinflower carpet the ground, and where Labrador tea dominates sunny spots. An ideal habitat is found in shady bogs having open floors where bog Solomon's-seal luxuriates, where logs are lined with sundews, and where, in clearings, clumps of ram's-head, showy, or yellow lady's-slippers abound. Here this twayblade grows mostly in rich, pure stands of loose sphagnum. Large colonies often occur, numbering 25–40 plants.

Few native flowering plants can be less conspicuous than this orchid. It is easy to walk through large colonies and miss them completely. In the North, few wooded sphagnum bogs are without this species. The growth of the colonies suggests that, in addition to seedlings, small offset plants are formed. It is possible that this twayblade and the others are monocarpic; that the terminal growth on the rhizome dies after flowering. It may be that the lateral buds on the rhizome continue, thus in time forming the colonies so typical of the species. At any rate, in marked colonies plants do not reappear in the exact same location in the season following the flowering, although many smaller plants may grow nearby. North of Lake Superior, or on Isle Royale, the heartleaf twayblade sometimes grows in rather dry, but thick, moss mats on headlands and in fir-spruce forests.

COMMON TWAYBLADE

Listera ovata (L.) R. Brown   Plate 25B

In 1968 Canadian naturalists first discovered this large European twayblade near Red Bay on the Bruce Peninsula, Ontario (Elliott 1969; Elliott and Cook 1970). In 1982 Anderson and Glotz discovered a small colony of common twayblade in Wellington County, Ontario, about 200 km from the Bruce Peninsula site. These same authors mention another herbarium specimen identified as *L. ovata* from Wellington County which they believe came from a different station than theirs.

How this plant became established in Ontario can only be conjectured; there is no record of its deliberate introduction. But *L. ovata* appears to be successfully colonizing the Bruce Peninsula, where it has appeared in several locations a short distance from the original plants. The plant behaves as a weed in Europe and it may well join *Epipactis helleborine* in spreading rapidly in our region.

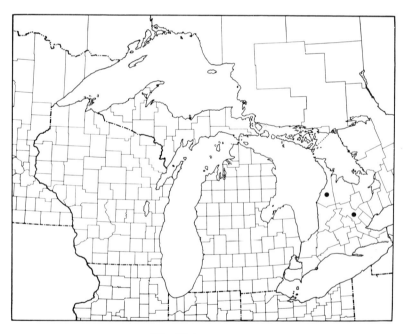

32. *Listera ovata*

Habit. Much larger than our native listeras, relatively stout, especially below the leaves, 20–60 cm tall. Stem glabrous below the yellow-green, ovate-elliptic, acute-tipped leaves, pubescent above. Leaves 2, opposite, attached at about the lower 1/3 of stem, 10–17 cm long, 10–12 cm wide. Raceme many-flowered, usually dense, bearing up to 75–100 flowers. Bracts small and narrow to 3 mm long. Dorsal sepal concave-ovate, 5–6 mm long, 2–3 mm wide. Lateral sepals ovate, oblique, about 4 mm long, 2–3 mm wide. Petals linear, 4 mm long. Lip linear, 8–10 mm long, up to 4 mm wide, slightly dilated toward apex and divided into two bluntly rounded lobes separated by a tooth in the sinus. Lip sharply deflexed at a slight constriction just above the base, disk with a longitudinally thickened ridge. Column short, 1 mm by 2 mm.

Season. In Europe, May through July; in the known Great Lakes stations, flowering in late June and July.

General Distribution. Boreal and temperate Eurasia, from Siberia and the Himalayas to Great Britain, where it is the commonest orchid (Summerhayes 1959). In North America it is adventive on the Bruce Peninsula and in Wellington County, Ontario.

EPIPACTIS Swartz

Only one species of this genus occurs in the eastern United States. It is described in the following account.

HELLEBORINE

Epipactis helleborine (L.) Crantz   Plate 25C, D

The helleborine is an attractive European species which is now established and spreading throughout the northeastern states.

Habit. Variable, 20–120 cm tall, leafy, like a *Cypripedium* in general aspect, puberulent-pubescent above. Leaves more or less clasping, smaller below and above, with largest leaves near middle of stem; leaves orbicular-ovate to elliptic-lanceolate, acuminate, plicate, somewhat erect. Leaves rather rough-puberulent. Raceme usually rather densely many-flowered, up to 30–40 cm long. Floral bracts leaflike, lowermost very conspicuous, longer than flowers. Flowers green, whitish green, or rose-purple streaked. Ovary and pedicel together about 1 cm long. Sepals concave, ovate-lanceolate, prominently nerved, 1–1.5 cm long, 5 mm wide. Petals ovate-elliptic, 1 cm long, 5 mm wide. Lip porrect, constricted near middle, lower half fleshy-thickened, somewhat saccate-concave; apical half ovate-triangular, less fleshy;

overall lip length about 1–1.5 cm, 4–8 mm or more wide, widest just above constriction. Base of apical half of lip with a raised fleshy callus. Capsule obovate-ellipsoidal, 1 cm long. Lowermost capsules of raceme often near full size while uppermost buds are still opening.

Season. June to September; early to mid-August usual in the Great Lakes region.

General Distribution. Not a native species and therefore has an irregular pattern, but appears now at many widely separated places in New England, the Lakes states, Missouri, and even Montana. First collected in the United States near Syracuse, New York, in August 1879. At the time of the publication of the first edition of this book, the plant was common to abundant in New York and eastern Ontario, and had begun to appear within our region. At that time, I mapped five Michigan stations, and one each in Indiana, Illinois, and Wisconsin. In the herbaria consulted for this edition, there are now specimens for 24 Michigan counties, two in Indiana, three in Illinois, and records in Illinois and Wisconsin for most of the counties along the west shore of Lake Michigan.

Habitat. Apparently rather indifferent to kind of habitat, for it has been collected on floodplain banks, clayey soils in hardwoods, wooded sand dunes, and brushy waste places. It occurs mostly under deciduous trees, but near Barrie, Ontario, in 1983, we observed the plant growing in a sphagnum bog!

Few botanists regard it as a native North American species. It is common in Europe, where it is widely used in folk medicine. Botanists theorize that it was brought to America by immigrants before the time of strict plant quarantine laws, or was accidentally introduced as seed in soil with nursery stock. Evidence for this explanation is the fact that helleborine was not detected in our flora until late in the history of plant exploration and that all early records were from the vicinity of large eastern cities. When this species does appear, it quickly spreads, weedlike, across the woodland, often forming colonies of hundreds of plants. Though not showy, it is graceful and attractive.

In 1965, I introduced a single clump of the helleborine into my woodland garden. By 1969 plants began to appear in flower beds, on lawns, and even in a driveway. Now (1985) it is well established in my five acres of woods and garden.

Epipactis helleborine appears able to live saprophytically from germination till flowering. I regularly find large, underground rhizome systems while spading the garden. Each year large flowering stems appear on our mowed lawns, plants which have never previously produced green, photosynthetic leaves above the ground.

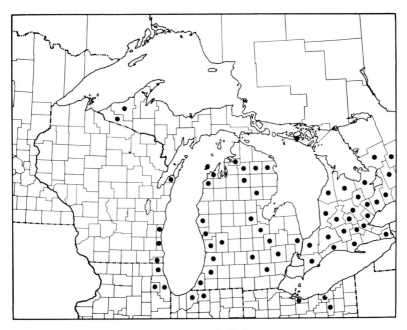

33. *Epipactis helleborine*

A correspondent from Illinois reports the presence of pure white (albino) leaved plants in a colony there. We have seen the same phenomenon at La Malbaie, Quebec. Helleborine seems, at times, to be able to subsist entirely upon nutrients furnished by its symbiotic fungus partner.

TRIPHORA Nutt.

The genus *Triphora* occurs only in the Western Hemisphere. Structurally and physiologically members of this genus appear to be intermediate between independent, free-living green plants and dependent saprophytes. Their habit of developing root systems only in rich leaf mold or rotten wood, never in mineral soil, plus the failure of some plants to produce normal leaves in some seasons, emphasizes their semisaprophytic position.

A small genus of about ten species, *Triphora* is characterized by generally small size and a stoloniferous, tuber-bearing habit. The slender, succulent stems bear flowers in the leaf axils. All floral parts are distinct. The lip is 3-crested. The column remains free of the perianth throughout its length, and bears the erect anther rigidly attached to the top of the column. Two pollen masses, having granular pollen, are present. Only one species is present in North America north of central Florida.

NODDING POGONIA, THREE BIRDS ORCHID

Triphora trianthophora (Swartz) Rydb.   Plate 26A, B, C

One of the rarer orchids of the Lakes states, nodding pogonia offers a great challenge to the orchid hunter. Not only are stations for this orchid rare and confined to the southern parts of our region, but its habit of producing in some seasons only a handful of plants—even though in other seasons it may carpet the woods—makes it difficult to detect in most years.

Triphora does not appear above ground until late July or early August. The plants develop rapidly, almost funguslike, and within a week or two approach blooming size. After this rapid development, the opening of the flower buds can be very slow. Following a week or two of slow enlargement, the lowermost bud of the plant turns pinkish white; it will open the next day. The flower opens fully by noon or shortly thereafter, and by evening it collapses. Thus the bloom is open and available for pollination less than one full day. Curiously, in the colonies I have observed nearly all the blooming plants had one flower each open at the same time. After the collapse of that bloom, the next flower bud slowly enlarges; this enlargement often takes a week. Again, all the plants of a colony will bloom together. This cycle of open blossom, development, open blossom, is repeated during August and early September until all buds have flowered. On certain days no flowers are in evidence; on others nearly all plants are in bloom. The seed pods develop rapidly after pollination, but remain pendent for about three weeks. Then, suddenly, there is a more rapid elongation of the peduncle, the capsule becomes erect, and while the pod is still fleshy and green, longitudinal slits appear in the capsule. In just a day or two all seed is dispersed.

The tendency to produce numbers of stoloniferous offsets, so that plants at one station multiply rapidly in a good growing season and slowly in a poor season, results in a fluctuating population level. This habit, with intermittent production of blooms and the very rapid development of the plant body in late summer, makes *Triphora* seem sporadic in appearance, and probably thwarts the discovery of many plants. Thus, the species may be more frequent locally than the record shows.

Triphora, under favorable conditions, can persist on a site for many years. The late Florence and Clarence Hanes, noted local botanists from Kalamazoo County, Michigan, explored their county and became truly accomplished authorities on its native plants. One of their rare finds, in 1937, was the three birds orchid (*T. trianthophora*) in a low mixed woodland with much American beech (*Fagus grandifolia*) (Hanes and Hanes 1947). Their station was tiny. Only about 15–20 plants grew in a relatively young but undisturbed grove of beeches at the edge of a swale in an otherwise pastured and disturbed low woodland. The Haneses visited the site and observed plants in most years from 1937 to 1945.

In 1960 H. Veltman, B. Horne, Roberta Case and I, guided by instructions from Florence Hanes, visited the Hanes station and found *Triphora* in bloom. About five plants were seen at this time. When I last visited this station in 1965, *Triphora* still grew there. This particular colony, occupying less than a square yard of woodland, is known to have persisted for at least 30 years. Such documentation of longevity for specific plants or colonies of our native orchids is rare. In my experience, few individuals or colonies of meadow or bog orchids survive the rigors of competition in a given spot for a long period of time. This behavior of *Triphora*, however, is consistent with that of most herbs of the mature forest floor—they are not temporary, successional species, but rather enduring members of the forest community.

Habit. Plant 6–30 cm tall, usually under 15 cm, from a whitish tuber. Roots and stem stoloniferous, producing offset plants from tubers produced at ends of stolons. Stem smooth, succulent, greenish purple. Leaves ovate-acute, concave and partially clasping stem, 8–20 mm long, 6–12 mm wide, alternate. Flowers usually 3, rarely 1–6, borne in axils of upper leaves, nodding, typically only one maturing at a time. Upper sepal oblong, lanceolate, more or less acute, 1–1.5 cm long, 5 mm wide. Lateral sepals oblong, lanceolate, falcate, 1.3 cm long, 4 mm wide. Petals elliptic, spatulate, 1.5 cm long, up to 5 mm wide. Floor of lip with 3 interrupted, crested keels. Seed capsules pendent, 1.5 cm long.

Season. Early August, September, rarely late July.

General Distribution. In rich deciduous forests, southern New England and southern Ontario through south-central Michigan and in the Lake Michigan wooded sand dunes north to Leelanau County. Also southern Wisconsin south to central Florida, Texas, Mexico, and Panama. Rare to very rare at northern edge of its range, it becomes frequent in the south-central United States and the Appalachian Mountains.

Habitat. Rich beech-sugar maple woodlands or mixed deciduous forests, where it grows in pockets of deep humus, never in predominantly mineral soil. Occasionally reported from sphagnum bogs or mixed forest borders of bogs where sphagnum moss

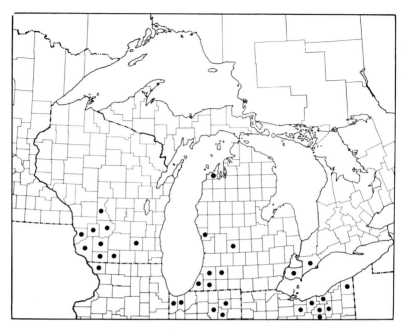

34. *Triphora trianthophora*

occurs as a surface layer over damp leaf mold.

Usually, *Triphora* grows as scattered small groups or single plants. But at one Cass County, Michigan, station we observed several massive, tight clusters of 50–150 stems. Upon digging into the soil, we found the masses to consist of layers of large tubers, often so crowded that the lower ones could not reach the surface. After some consternation concerning this obviously abnormal growth pattern, we concluded that we had found squirrel food caches. *Triphora* tubers, like the roots and tissues of many native orchids, exude a rich fragrance, in part similar to that of vanilla. Squirrels seem to enjoy the delicate flavor.

ISOTRIA Raf.

Plants of this genus have a whorl of leaves perched atop a succulent stem, and differ radically in appearance from other native orchids. The flower, large for the plant, is more bizarre and curious than beautiful. The erratic blooming habits and sporadic appearance of some add to the charm of these orchids.

Closely related to the genus *Pogonia*, and formerly placed in it by some botanists, the genus is characterized by the following features. The plants are relatively large, with long, dark brown-hairy roots and a whorl of five or six leaves at the summit of the stem. One or two flowers may be borne above the leaves. All the perianth parts are distinct. The lip is conspicuously tuberculate-crested, the sepals rather large and equal, giving the group its name (*Isotria* = "equal" and "three"). The column is toothed at the apex, the anther terminal. Seed capsules, if set, become rigidly erect. The plants, especially of *Isotria verticillata*, spread vegetatively as well as by seed and commonly form clumps or colonies. There are two species, both of eastern North America.

Key to *Isotria*

A. Stem purplish, flower pedicel below ovary 2–3 times longer than ovary. Sepals purplish brown, at least 3 times longer than petals, plants stoloniferous, often forming clumps.

Isotria verticillata

page 152

AA. Stem green with a whitish bloom, flower pedicel below ovary shorter than or barely equaling the ovary. Sepals clear green, 1.5 times petal length. Plant solitary, or with only one or two nearby plants.

Isotria medeoloides

page 149

SMALL WHORLED POGONIA

Isotria medeoloides (Pursh) Raf.   Plate 27A

William Schwab first discovered the smaller whorled pogonia in the Great Lakes region in 1968. It was discovered in southwestern Lower Michigan (Case with Schwab 1971). Since that time, it has also been found in southern Illinois and in southwestern Ontario. In August 1985, Roberta Case and I found a single plant in a southern Ohio woodland; to my knowledge this is the first Ohio record.

The small whorled pogonia is the only North American terrestrial orchid listed under United States law as legally "endangered." Certainly it is one of the least discovered native orchids, although it ranges widely over the eastern United States.

A denizen of moderately rich, acid hardwood forests, the orchid has been reported officially from Maine to North Carolina along the piedmont and Appalachian Mountains, with outlying stations in Missouri, Illinois, Michigan, Ohio, and Ontario, the latter four all recent discoveries. I am aware of several colonies, correctly identified, but without substantiating herbarium specimens, in northern Georgia, Pennsylvania, and New Hampshire. It is my opinion that the plant occurs much more widely in suitable soils of the eastern deciduous forest than is currently believed.

While the species is truly rare, it does not form extensive clumps vegetatively, as does *I. verticillata*. Widely scattered single plants are the rule. Since it often grows in the same woods as *I. verticillata*, and the overall aspect of the two is so similar, many nonflowering stems may well go undetected. Out of bloom, the aspect of either species is so like that of Virginia cucumber-root (*Medeola virginiana*), that anyone not specifically seeking the pogonia might not notice it.

Older writers and some recent ones speak of the whorled pogonias as having extended periods of underground dormancy, lasting up to 20 years. I first commented upon this theory under the species *I. verticillata* in the 1964 edition of this book. Nothing I have observed since then has changed my opinion. *I. verticillata* planted on my property in 1968 and carefully marked, continues to appear every year. In fact, a colony of about eight plants has expanded to over twenty-six. Never have the plants failed to appear each season. Plants in a nearby wild colony show a continuous row of old stem stumps at the base of the present season's plant. The late Erich DeLin of Fort Montgomery, New York, kept a New Jersey colony of *I. medeoloides* under observation for many years and found no evidence of prolonged underground dormancy.

The reports of dormancy for years *may* stem from the behavior of the plant. If it behaves as does *I. verticillata* (see that species account), then, in nonblooming years, the vegetative growth will appear at a later date. A naturalist checking on a certain date based upon past blooming would not find any plant in evidence. Of course, any individual plant may meet with an accident or be grazed in any one season. All of our native orchids upon meeting such a fate would not appear again until the next season, as the plant requires a cold, dormancy-breaking rest before it can again initiate buds or growth.

Whether it is as rare as most believe or less so, the small whorled pogonia presents a severe challenge to any orchid hunter.

Indeed, there are few botanists who have succeeded in discovering a new station for this plant as the result of a deliberate search.

Habit. Usually shorter than *I. verticillata*, but variable, 9–25 cm tall, stem faintly stout, glabrous, clear green with no purplish coloring and hollow. Entire plant with a whitish bloom. Leaves 5–6, in a whorl at top of stem, elliptic to elliptic-obovate, usually *widest at the middle* and tapering gradually to an acuminate tip, clear green and covered with whitish bloom, 2–8 cm long and 1–3.5 cm wide, strongly drooping at early anthesis, but becoming more or less at right angles to the stem when fully expanded. Roots fleshy-slender, hairy, less rambling and extensive than in *I. verticillata*, and not giving rise to offset shoots. Flowers 1 or 2, usually 1, from stem apex above the leaves, yellowish green, somewhat gaping. Sepals equal, linear-oblanceolate, concave on inner (toward column) surface, up to 20 mm long, 3–4 mm wide, green. Petals oblanceolate-elliptic, obtusely rounded at the tip, about 17 mm long, 3–4 mm wide, forming a hood over the column. Lip nearly white with a pale green, veined crest, obovate-cuneate, 3-lobed, the side lobes erect and sheathing the column, 1.5 cm long, 5–7 mm wide. Disk of lip with a 2-ridged callus and wartlike excrescences on the nerves. Column round, about 9 mm long. Capsule erect, narrowly cylindrical, about 2–3 cm long, borne on a pedicel of about equal length. In *I. verticillata* the capsule is larger, thicker, and the pedicel is at least twice as long as the capsule (see illustrations in Case with Schwab 1971).

Season. May in the south to early June in the north of its range. The Michigan colony blooms about the first of June.

Distribution. Apparently rare and very local throughout its range. Maine, New Hampshire, New York, Pennsylvania, and New Jersey south to Virginia and North Carolina (northern Georgia, *fide* B. Frye, pers. comm. and photographs). Missouri, southwestern Illinois, Michigan, and southern Ontario, Canada.

Habitat. Unlike the larger whorled pogonia, *I. medeoloides* has not been reported from sphagnum bogs. It grows in a wide variety of rich, acid-soil deciduous forest or mixed hemlock (*Tsuga*) and deciduous woods. In its southern range, it often grows in deep humus under tulip (*Liriodendron*), beech (*Fagus*), maples, sweet-gum, or near hemlock groves. In the Michigan station it grew on a sandy-damp flatwoods floor, formerly an orchard, under large red maples (*Acer rubrum*) and with scattered oaks and black gum (*Nyssa sylvatica*). There was little other ground cover except a few scattered royal ferns (*Osmunda regalis*). Humus at this station was thin and near the surface of the damp, sandy soil only.

The habitat at the Michigan station was typical of the low, sandy,

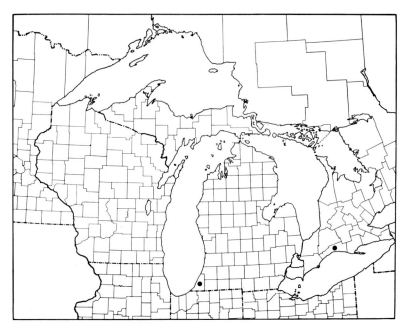

35. *Isotria medeoloides*

acid, second growth forest so very common in southwestern Michigan and on the postglacial shoreline ridges which concentrically ring Saginaw Bay. I could find nothing distinctive about the habitat that could furnish a clue to the presence of *I. medeoloides*. With further exploration I expect additional Michigan colonies of this species will be discovered.

WHORLED POGONIA, WHORL-CREST

Isotria verticillata (Muhl. ex Willd.) Raf.   Plate 27B, C

This fascinating plant, whose large, fantastic flowers suggest some of the tropical *Epidendrum* species, is common in parts of its range, but rare in the Great Lakes region.

Several writers mention the long periods of dormancy of the whorled pogonia and its sister species. Though the related *Isotria medeoloides* may remain inactive for 10–20 years as reported, this has not actually been documented. The reports of these long periods of dormancy for the genus *Isotria* trouble me. I can find no evidence for this in 32 years of observing many colonies and growing *I. verticillata*. All plants in all colonies I have observed have produced plants and additional offshoots each year. If one probes about the base of a plant, the old stem scars and bases are found in an unbroken line going back many years.

I have, however, observed one interesting phenomenon. Blooming shoots, always in the minority in a colony, appear well ahead of the nonflowering shoots (sometimes 10 days ahead of nonflowering stems). The reports of dormancy could arise from a situation in which a botanist, expecting flowering at a given date, visited a colony which, that season, produced no flowers. Since he had arrived too early for the appearance of the non-flowering shoots, he would find no plants. A week or so later the situation would be significantly altered.

Habit. Rather variable, depending on age, vigor of plant, and whether or not it is a main growth or an offshoot. Stems 10–40 cm tall, purplish or reddish maroon, with a faint bloom, smooth, hollow. Leaves 5–6, in a whorl at top of stem, oblong-lanceolate, broadly obovate, widest beyond middle, often narrowed rather sharply into a subacuminate tip. Leaves small and somewhat erect at first, gradually enlarging with season and tending to droop, 3–9 cm long, 2–5 cm wide, expanding during season. Roots brown, very long, rambling, fleshy-fibrous, densely covered with hairs, giving rise at intervals to shoots. Thus the plants form large colonies. Flowers 1–2, at top of stem, borne on pedicels 3–5 cm long, somewhat gaping. Sepals nearly equal, lanceolate-acuminate, thickened, brittle, 4–6 cm long, 3–5 mm or more wide, greenish, heavily stained with purple-brown or madder. Petals yellow-green, elliptic-obovate to elliptic-lanceolate, obtuse, 2.5 cm long, 5 mm wide. Lip whitish green, yellowing with age, oblong-cuneate, 3-lobed near tip, 1.5–2.5 cm long, 1 cm wide, crested along median line with a fleshy-papillose ridge, truncate at tip. Column 1 cm long. Capsule rigidly erect, ellipsoid, 2–3 cm long. Dry fruiting stems often persist till second season.

Season. Late May in drier woods and upland habitats; late May to early June in bogs. Flowers are transient, seldom lasting more than 3–4 days in good condition.

Distribution. Of local occurrence throughout the eastern deciduous forests from the southern part of the Lakes states and New England, south to Florida and Texas, occurring also in Missouri and Arkansas. Frequent in parts of Atlantic coastal plain, the Cumberland Plateau, and in the Blue Ridge uplands, local to rare elsewhere.

Habitat. Occupies two superficially distinct habitats in the Great Lakes region. (1) Moist, acid woods, mostly second growth in nature, dominated by oaks, red maple, aspen, scattered white pine, and sassafras. Such woods occur on rather poor, sandy soils, ancient glacial-lake shores, and back of the present Great Lakes shores. Here *Isotria* grows in thick beds of brown, acid duff in

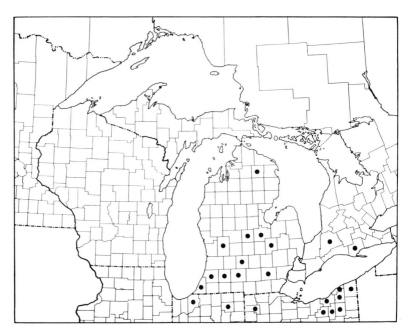

36. *Isotria verticillata*

company with Indian cucumber-root, goldthread, fringed poly-
gala, pink lady's-slipper, and sometimes with Canada dogwood.
Because the plants are usually heavily shaded, few bloom in any
one season. (2) Deep beds of sphagnum moss in rich tamarack
or spruce bogs, where it occupies lightly to heavily shaded positions where leatherleaf bushes are dying out because of shade,
or where little else but moss grows. Also grows below highbush
blueberry and holly in the same types of bogs, in company with
pink lady's-slipper, yellow fringed-orchid, pitcher-plant, sundews, and green fringed-orchid.

Although the sandy red maple woods and the sphagnum bog
appear quite different, the two habitats are distinctly similar in
terms of soil acidity, heavy humus, and relative sterility. Almost
certainly the degree of moisture is unimportant and the basic
needs of the whorled pogonia are met in both habitats.

The whorled pogonia is typically a southern or mild-climate
speoies, and all records but one from the Great Lakes region are
from southern Michigan or the lake areas of Ohio and Indiana.
The one colony considerably north of other reported stations, at
East Twin Lake, Montmorency County, Michigan, is in a distinctly boreal area. Here *Isotria* grew in a red maple, aspen,

white pine grove a few feet from the lake. The existence of this colony, over 130 miles north of other stations in this region, suggests that the species may grow over a wider area of the aspen-maple, second-growth forests of central Michigan than known at present. It may easily be overlooked because of its sparse flowering habits and its resemblance to Indian cucumber-root, with which it often grows.

Although the whorled pogonia can be very local in occurrence, and its behavior and appearance suggest a delicate and difficult plant to grow, it is easy to cultivate given a strongly acid, humus-filled soil. In 1968 I introduced eight plants of *I. verticillata* onto a small, shady knoll of acid humus with *Gaultheria procumbens* (wintergreen) and other acid-soil plants. The plants survived, flourished, and increased. By 1984 the colony had reproduced vegetatively into 26 stems. Between 8 and 11 of the plants bloom annually. It is most interesting that some of the current stems are located from several inches to over two feet from where the original plants were placed, indicating not only that this species relies on strong vegetative reproduction to produce its dense colonies, but also that there is considerable underground movement of the plants over the years.

POGONIA Juss.

Pogonia is a small genus found in both hemispheres. There are about 10 species, most of which grow in sterile, acid soils. One species of rather wide distribution grows in eastern North America. A similar and closely related species is found in Japan and China. Pogonias are terrestrial herbs bearing a solitary, rather fleshy leaf midway on the flowering stem; in nonblooming plants one or two similar leaves are produced directly from the fibrous roots. One to three flowers terminate the stem. The floral parts are about equal in length, distinct, and often showy. The lip is bearded with fleshy, bristlelike structures. This bearded lip gives the genus its name (from the Greek *pogonias*, bearded). The column is free, toothed at the apex, with a terminal anther. The pollinia have simple pollen grains.

ROSE POGONIA, ADDER'S-MOUTH, SNAKE MOUTH

Pogonia ophioglossoides (L.) Jussieu   Plate 28 A, B
Pogonia ophioglossoides (L.) Ker-Gawl. (1st ed.)

Rose pogonia is a showy orchid, frequent in most of our wetter bogs and swamps, and not particularly rare in boggy spots among sand dunes and old beaches of the Upper Great Lakes. It varies considerably in color and size, very likely because of environmental conditions. Flower buds developing in clear, cool weather will often open deeper in color than those developing rapidly in warm weather. Exposure to wind and weather often slightly dwarfs many plants. There is no doubt, however, that genetically distinct strains do occur. Pure white, very deep-colored, and unusually marked or veined forms occur locally and seem to be characteristic of certain areas.

The fragrance of this orchid has been compared to many things. Perhaps the most startling comparison was made by Thoreau, who likened its odor to that of snakes. Many find the odor pleasing and like that of red raspberries. A person familiar with the odor can sometimes detect the presence of the plants before seeing them.

Habit. Plant fleshy-slender, 8–70 cm tall, stem green. Flowering stem with a single, fleshy, ovate-elliptic or ovate-lanceolate leaf, 2–12 cm long, 1–3 cm wide, placed about halfway up. More or less long-petiolate leaves of similar size occur at base and on scattered offshoot plants, these often much more numerous than flowering stems. Floral bract leaflike, rather large, 1–3 cm long. Flowers normally solitary, rarely 2–3, terminal, dark to pale rose-pink, rarely white, fragrant. Sepals and petals oblong-elliptic, 1.5–2.3 cm long, 3–6 mm or more wide, petals broader and more obtuse than sepals. Lip spatulate, narrowing to point of attachment, tip of lip lacerate-tuberculate along margin, heavily fleshy-bearded along main veins. Lip with mottlings of dark madder-purple and yellow, variable. Capsule ellipsoid, prominently ribbed, 2 cm long.

Season. June, July. Since the time of bloom varies greatly for different plants at any given station, individual colonies have a long season.

General Distribution. Newfoundland, Maritime Provinces, Quebec, and Ontario, west to Minnesota, south along the coastal plain to Florida and west to Texas. Local in the interior north to Illinois and Missouri.

Habitat. Sphagnum bogs, sedge mats, marsh borders, shore bogs, and sandy depressions along shoreline dunes in our region, commonly in company with arethusa, calopogon, pitcher-plant, sundews, buckbean, and such shrubs as leatherleaf and bog rosemary. It usually grows in the wettest parts of the bog, often on floating tufts of sedge or on logs at lake margins. If present at all, it is usually abundant. It spreads by means of root shoots and forms dense colonies. Occasionally few or no plants will bloom for several years, and then, suddenly, when conditions are again favorable, the bog will appear to burst forth with blooms.

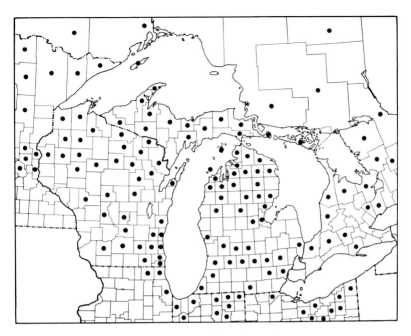

37. *Pogonia ophioglossoides*

Though primarily a bog plant in our region, it grows also in damp, sandy depressions in the pine barrens and coastal plain. The most unusual habitat I have seen for it was in islands of moss on dripping wet cliffs and ledges on Caesar's Head, a granitic outcropping in the Blue Ridge Mountains of North Carolina.

ARETHUSA L.

Arethusa is named for a river nymph of classical Greek mythology—aptly, since the strikingly beautiful flowers grow in the wettest of bog cover. A single large flower, a single leaf appearing after anthesis, an operculate anther on the ventral side of the column, and a pair of mealy pollinia characterize this monotypic genus.

ARETHUSA, DRAGON'S-MOUTH, WILD PINK

Arethusa bulbosa L.   Plate 29A, B

No orchid in our flora is lovelier than arethusa. The peculiarly facelike blooms are aptly named "Dragon's-mouth." Morris and

Eames perhaps most nearly capture the fanciful spirit of this exquisite orchid stating, "we shall never forget the moment when our eyes first fell on its blossom in the lonely depths of a sphagnum bog. The feeling was irresistible that we had surprised some strange sentient creature in its secret bower of moss; that it was alert and listening intently with pricked-up ears."

There are conflicting reports on the abundance of arethusa. Some authors call it rare; others, common. Actually, blooming populations of this orchid can fluctuate considerably at a given station. At one northern Michigan bog observed for over 30 years, the number of blooming plants varied from as low as 12 to over 1,000 in different seasons. During this time water levels remained fairly constant. Populations of later-blooming orchids and most other bog plants showed little fluctuation. However, there were years when late frost, coinciding with the flowering season of arethusa, cut down most of the flowers, thus preventing seed production. When this occurred in successive years, the number of flowering plants declined sharply in succeeding frost-free years. These observations suggest that arethusa may be short-lived, depending upon heavy seed production for population maintenance. It seldom produces offsets or forms loose clumps in the manner of calopogon.

Arethusa, rose pogonia, and calopogon regularly occur together. Rarely indeed in northern Michigan or Wisconsin does one of these species occur without the other two; yet, at times, each does grow where the other two do not.

Arethusa would be a coveted plant for wildflower gardens, or even for the greenhouse, because of its spectacular and distinctive flower. Unfortunately, few can claim lasting success with it, for it seems to resent disturbance. Any attempt to move it during the blooming season usually results in damage from which the plant never recovers.

Habit. Scape variable, 4–40 cm tall, rising from a bulbous corm and a few spreading fleshy, fibrous roots. Scape erect, enclosed in 1–2 scarious, lightly inflated sheaths, from which the single grasslike leaf emerges. The leaf is often not evident at the onset of flowering. The floral bract is minute or absent. Flowers 1, rarely 2, rather large, rose-purple, very showy, with sepals and petals arched over column; lip clawed, oblong, very slightly if at all 3-lobed, recurved, notched to lobate at apex, crenulate-undulate at margin; margin erose, 2–3.5 cm long, 1–2 cm wide, strongly veined. Disks of lip have veins crested with fleshy-hairy projections. Lip color variable, commonly with floor of lip pale yellow with dark madder-purple blotching; plants also occur with a white lip and obscure blotching. Sepals and petals rose-magenta and arched over column. Dorsal sepal linear-oblong, obtuse, 3–5 cm

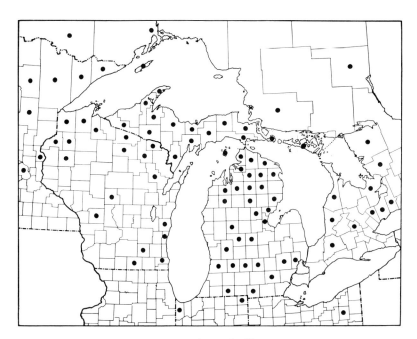

38. *Arethusa bulbosa*

long, 5–10 mm wide. Capsule ovoid, 2–3 cm long, column becoming firm, almost woody in texture, and persisting atop capsule. In large populations plants with white flowers occur occasionally.

Season. From earliest June to mid-July in the Lakes states. Occasionally plants flower in August, usually in areas that have been inundated earlier.

General Distribution. From Minnesota and Ontario eastward to Newfoundland and Nova Scotia and Anticosti Island in the North, south through the Lakes states (reported only twice from Illinois), and following the mountains south to the piedmont plateau of North Carolina. Reported, but without good substantiating evidence, from South Carolina and Louisiana.

Habitat. In the Lakes region grows most commonly in deep, open, sunny sphagnum bogs, especially in black spruce-tamarack bogs surrounding small lakes. Preferred habitat is near open water; indeed, it may occasionally be found growing on logs or in tufts of sedge surrounded by open water. It may also grow in marl fens, where it is usually found in low runnels and wet tracts where peaty materials collect, or on isolated sphagnum hummocks, but rarely in the marl itself. It can also be found in sandy shore bogs of the northern Great Lakes. In sphagnum bogs its frequent companions are pitcher-plant, cranberry, leatherleaf, sundews, rose pogonia, and the fringed-orchids. In marly situations it grows with tall white bog-orchid, linear-leaved sundews, and arctic primrose. On the peaty moors of southwestern Newfoundland, I have seen beds of thousands of plants, enough to impart a rosey hue to the entire land surface. This is truly a thrilling sight! In North Carolina it grows very sparingly on grassy, peaty, upland hillsides under mountain laurel and rhododendron, a type of habitat very different from those it inhabits in the Great Lakes region.

CALOPOGON R. Br.

Correll and Luer recognize four species in this genus. All are native to the southeastern United States and adjacent areas, but only one grass pink ranges north into our region. Members of this genus are all showy and often locally abundant. The grass pink is one of the most conspicuous plants of bog or wet meadow. The generic name *Calopogon*, from the Greek, means "beautiful beard" and refers to the delicate hairs on the lip.

In this genus the flower scapes rise from a globose or ellipsoid corm and bear one or two grasslike, strongly ribbed leaves. The raceme bears one to several flowers. Unlike most orchids, *Calopogon* blooms carry the lip uppermost, and there is no twisting of the ovary to bring the lip into a lowermost, resupinate position. The floral segments, free and spreading, are lavender, crimson, or rarely white; the lip, spreading at the apex, is bearded and has a tiny lobe on each side near the base. The column is free and incurved. The pollen grains are attached to each other by filaments.

Grass Pink, Calopogon

Calopogon tuberosus (L.) B.S.P.　　　　　　　Plate 30A, B, C
Calopogon pulchellus (Salisb.) R. Br. (1st ed.)

This orchid is a rare example of beauty accompanied by abundance. Not only is it very showy, it is also one of the most familiar orchids of the Lakes states. Morris and Eames aver that it is one of the most perfectly beautiful of all wildflowers.

Habit. Plant rising from a corm having slender-fleshy white roots below. Scape wiry, slender, smooth, 10–45 cm high. Leaves 1 or 2, sub-basal, grasslike, linear, ribbed, 5 cm wide. Leaves emerge from 1 or 2 sheathing, scarious, somewhat inflated bracts. Raceme lax, elongate, flowers few, widely spaced and opening one to few at a time over a rather long period; 2–10-flowered.

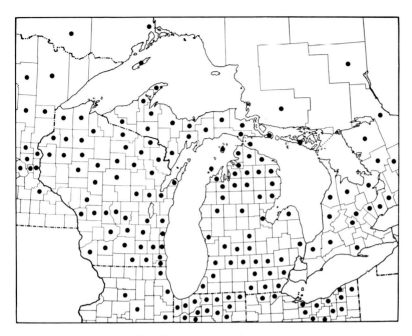

39. *Calopogon tuberosus*

Bracts subtending flowers, ovate-acuminate, 3–9 mm long. Flowers purplish pink or magenta, rarely white. Dorsal sepal narrowly oblong, acute, 2–2.5 cm long, 5–10 mm wide. Lateral sepals ovate to ovate-lanceolate, oblique, abruptly acute, somewhat concave, 1.5–2.5 cm long, 10–13 mm wide. Petals short-clawed, longer and narrower than sepals, pandurate to ovate-lanceolate, 1.3–2.5 cm long, 4–10 mm wide. Lip uppermost, 1–2 cm long, obscurely 3-lobed, lateral lobes ill-defined, middle lobe becoming most prominent portion of lip. Central portion or disk of lip densely bearded with short, knobbed hairs arranged in rows. Column incurved, 1–2 cm long, winged on each side, 6–9 mm across.

Season. June or July, occasionally August.

General Distribution. Newfoundland to Florida and Cuba, west to Texas, and north to Iowa and Minnesota.

Habitat. Tolerates many habitats. In its most common habitat—rich sphagnum or sphagnum-sedge mats in bogs— it grows in company with pitcher-plant, rose pogonia, arethusa, bog rosemary, bog laurel, cranberry, and other typical bog vegetation. Frequent in spruce-tamarack bogs, it grows around the bases of the spruces and on the edges of hummocks. It also grows in beach bogs and similar wet areas along the shores of the Great Lakes, especially along the upper reaches of Lake Huron, on both the Michigan and Canadian shores. It may occur on moist prairie in company with the eastern prairie fringed-orchid. It has been reported to grow on sandy oak ridges and in dry sandy areas, but I have not seen it in such habitats in the Lakes region, nor have I seen notations to that effect on herbarium sheets.

Calopogon multiplies by offset corms as well as by seed, and consequently may build large colonies where conditions are favorable. At one spot in northern Michigan I once found over 1,000 plants growing in a spruce-tamarack bog in less than one square yard of sphagnum moss. Like other orchids producing a corm, each season it builds an entirely new corm for the next season's growth. This new corm is produced through enlargement of the basal section of the flowering scape, just above the old corm. Thus, as the moss grows deeper, the position of the corm is kept relatively constant in relation to the surface of the moss.

Various forms of calopogon have been described from both the northern and southern parts of its range, but the plants in the Lakes region seem fairly uniform and are best considered typical of the species.

SPIRANTHES L. C. M. Rich.

Spiranthes of various species occur throughout the world and in both hemispheres, running the gamut in size from tiny, threadlike, inconspicuously white-flowered plants to rather large, brightly colored ones which some taxonomists separate into other genera. Differences between species, often in very technical and minute features, make the separation of the taxa a difficult task.

Most American species, though not necessarily weedy, tend to be somewhat invasive plants, pioneering the plant succession in fallow fields, damp meadows, on shores, and in roadside ditches. The genus name *Spiranthes* is derived from the Greek words meaning "coiled flowers"—an allusion to the spiraled arrangement of the blossoms, most strikingly evident in such single-ranked forms as the slender ladies'-tresses (*S. lacera*).

Structurally close to the rattlesnake plantains, the ladies'-tresses differ from them in several ways. They lack evergreen leaves and their leaves are never white-tesselated. The flowers, borne on a spicate raceme, are not spurred. In contrast to the rattlesnake plantains, the labellum never has a saccate basal portion. In *Spiranthes*, the base of the lip has rather prominent, more or less incurved calli (inflated tubercles).

162

Our knowledge of the genus *Spiranthes* has changed more since the publication of the first edition of this book than that of any other genus of Great Lakes region orchids. The species formerly called *S. cernua* is now known to be a complex of similar-appearing species, often difficult to identify from preserved material, yet distinct in structure, season of bloom, and habitat. The intensive study and subsequent splitting of this complex orchid group into several species by Catling, Sheviak, Cruise, and others seems to be sound and to represent accurately the situation as it occurs in the western Great Lakes region. All of these new species occur in our area. At least two southern species, previously unknown from our area, have been found here, one of them at several widely separated localities.

Although some authorities disagree concerning the occurrence of certain hybrid *Spiranthes*, I continue to see plants, especially in eastern Upper Michigan, which appear to be hybrids. Certainly, the opportunity for hybridization exists in numerous colonies of mixed species throughout the state. Several hybrids reported from east of our region can be expected to appear here.

Spiranthes are by no means easy to identify. Identification can be best accomplished with fresh plants for study and the use of more than one key by more than one author. The lowermost flowers on an inflorescence yield blooms more typical in size and structure than those opening later and higher on the spike. Occasional aberrant plants of several species simply will not key.

Spiranthes vernalis Engelm. and Gray is not presently known to occur within the region covered by this book. In the earlier edition I included it, primarily on the authority of Correll who annotated a specimen from Cheyboygan County, Michigan (E. G. Voss #509, MICH) as that species, and on the basis of several confusing plants from other collections. It is now known that these specimens represent either *S. ochroleuca* or *S. casei*. Nevertheless, *S. vernalis* has been collected in southern Ohio (specimens in OSU) and its occurrence within the region of this book would be no more surprising than the newly discovered occurrences here of *S. tuberosa* and *S. ovalis*.

Key to *Spiranthes*

The intent of this key is to provide an aid to field identification of fresh plants without the use of a microscope (although a 10× hand lens is very useful). For best results, use the lowermost two or three flowers on a raceme, as these provide the most typical specific features. In most cases, an entire plant with leaves is necessary for accurate determination. Aberrant, growth-curtailed, and deformed specimens rarely key satisfactorily. Take care to select average, typical specimens for study and identification.

Identification of *Spiranthes* is difficult and presents a challenge even to the professional botanist. Those who require a more detailed key utilizing more technical structural features under laboratory conditions, may refer to the key to Michigan *Spiranthes* in Case and Catling (1983). This publication covers all of the species known to occur in the western Great Lakes region. The distribution and biology of Great Lakes *Spiranthes* are imperfectly known and provide a rich area for field study.

A. Lip less than 6 mm long.

    B. Floor of lip with a strip of bright yellow or green color in the central region.

      C. Floor of lip bright chrome-yellow, rarely with added greenish tones. Leaves present at flowering, ascending, broadly oblong-elliptic to lanceolate, shining. Sepals slightly fused at base.

                  S. lucida
                  page 175

     CC. Floor of lip dark green. Leaves forming a basal rosette, withering at or before flowering, ovate to ovate-lanceolate, with a distinct petiole. Sepals free to their base.

                  S. lacera var.

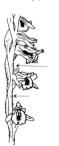

      D. Flower spike one-sided, or with one or two widely spaced twists; lowermost flowers widely spaced in the spike. Lip color extending only a short distance onto the flared, deflexed apex.

                  S. lacera var. *lacera*
                  page 173

DD. Flower spike strongly spiraled, the flowers sometimes appearing in up to four secund ranks, lowermost flowers not separated in the spike. Lip color extending almost to the apex, leaving only a narrow white margin.

S. *lacera* var. *gracilis*
page 174

BB. Floor of lip pure white, or pale creamy yellow throughout, no strongly colored central portion.

C. Flowers 2–4 mm long, pure white. Leaves basal, ovate to ovate-lanceolate, with a definite petiole, withering at or before flowering.

S. *tuberosa*
page 187

CC. Flowers 4–7 mm long, white, creamy white, or faintly yellow-white. Leaves basal and cauline, lacking a definite petiole, oblong-elliptic to lanceolate, gradually reduced to bracts upwards; at least some of the lower leaves persisting through the flowering period.

D. Flowers about 5 mm long, white, several ranked in very short, compact spikes atop a relatively tall scape; lip ovate-rhombic, usually tapered, very rarely dilated, distinctly arcuate-recurved in distal half; tissue of the central region of the lip not conspicuously thickened; backs of floral segments at most only faintly puberulent. Leaves present at flowering, elongate-ascending, slightly narrowed below middle, submembranaceous, oblanceolate, dull bluish green. Flowering late September into mid-October.

S. *ovalis*
page 183

DD. Flowers 6–7 mm long, cream, usually single ranked, spike typically rather elongate. Lip ovate, tissue of the central portion conspicuously thickened, apical region slightly dilated, the margins erose. Backs of flowers covered at least in proximal half with reddish, glandular hairs. Lowermost leaves often deteriorating or withering at flowering, oblanceolate, relatively short (to 7 cm), if in good condition, firm and green. Flowering late August to early September.

S. casei
page 168

AA. Lip 6–11 mm long.

B. Lip pandurate (fiddle-shaped), i.e. sharply constricted near the middle, flaring beyond the constriction; basal callosities minute. Sepals and petals connivent, forming a hood. Inflorescence heavy and thick, not strongly spiraled; flowers in each rank often strongly secund, producing an angular spike.

S. romanzoffiana
page 185

BB. Lip not pandurate, with little or no constriction at the middle; basal callosities relatively prominent. Sepals and petals variously associated, but not forming a distinct hood. Spikes mostly strongly spiraled, the ranks rarely secund.

C. Leaves absent at flowering. Lip somewhat deflexed, giving the flower a gaping aspect; central portion of the underside of lip yellow, thickened and creamy white above; basal callosities short, conical, as wide as high. Lateral sepals free, spreading, with incurved tips, often meeting above the flower. Flowers strongly fragrant.

S. magnicamporum
page 177

CC. Leaves present at flowering. Lip white or uniformly pale cream; basal callosities longer than wide. Lateral sepals appressed.

D. Flowers pale cream, yellowish, or with faint creamy green tones, the under surface of the lip sometimes deeper yellowish cream. Flowers single or multiple ranked.

E. Lip 6–7 mm long. Dorsal sepal and lateral petals directed forward, scarcely or not at all upcurved; lateral sepals directed forward. Lower perianths less than 7.5 mm long. Flowers usually borne in a single, loose rank but more robust, several ranked plants occur. Flowers in a continuous spiral but the spacing is such that a side view gives a false impression of flowers grouped in twos. Lowermost leaves usually shriveling at flowering time, upper leaves somewhat persistent.

S. *casei*
page 168

EE. Lip 7–10 mm long, rarely longer. Dorsal sepal and lateral petals connivent-recurved, giving the flower a strongly two-lipped appearance; lateral sepals usually somewhat ascending. Lowermost perianths usually 8–9 mm long; basal callosities of lip very prominent, strongly incurved. Flowers one–several-ranked, usually several. Lowermost leaves normally present in good condition at flowering.

S. *ochroleuca*
page 180

DD. Flowers white, crystalline, occurring in multiple ranks. Lip white throughout. Dorsal sepal and lateral sepals and petals approximate (close together), slightly recurved, but not two-lipped in aspect. Leaves normally present and in good condition at flowering, ascending, linear-lanceolate.

S. *cernua* var. *cernua*
page 170

Spiranthes casei Catling and Cruise   Plate 31A, 34A

Among the *Spiranthes* taxa which were until recently included within the concept of *S. cernua* and now recognized as distinct species is this moderate-sized, essentially northern population given specific status in 1974 by P. Catling and J. Cruise. The plant has been a source of confusion to northern naturalists for some time. Earlier botanists confused *S. casei* with *S. cernua* var. *ochroleuca*. Later D. S. Correll identified some herbarium material as a form of the southern *S. vernalis*. Luer (1975) used Ames' *S.* ×*intermedia* for this species (Ames, however, considered *S.* ×*intermedia* a hybrid). In the first edition of this book, I assigned these confusing plants to *S. vernalis* or *S. cernua* var. *ochroleuca* while questioning the name. Correll (1950) had identified them as *S. vernalis* from herbarium material at the University of Michigan, but I did not feel that they truly fit the description of that species. Voss (1972) in his *Michigan Flora* retained *S. vernalis* Englm. and Gray for these confusing plants, with reservations, on the basis of the identifications by Correll and my comments regarding their possible origin.

Spiranthes casei occurs primarily on the Canadian Shield rocks and soils of Ontario, but it also occurs across Upper Michigan, in the driftless region of Wisconsin, and in the northern tip of Lower Michigan. Because it grows largely away from population centers, it is not a familiar plant to most botanists, amateur or professional.

Habit. Stem slender to stout, tall, up to 40 cm, pubescent above with capitate hairs. Leaves glabrous, ascending, basal leaves ovate-lanceolate, up to 2 cm wide, 6–7 cm long, lowermost withering at or before anthesis. Cauline sheath-leaves persistent into the flowering season, oblanceolate to linear-lanceolate, 12–20 cm long, 0.5–1 cm wide, becoming reduced to bladeless sheaths above. Flower spike elongate, 6–15 cm long, many-flowered, flowers arranged in a loose single spiral so that, although continuous, a side view of the spike gives the impression of florets in groups of twos or threes with gaps around the stem. Floral bracts ovate to lanceolate, long tapering, acuminate, 8–12 mm long, basally pubescent. Ovary 5 mm long, swollen on upper side at anthesis, pubescent. Flowers cream-colored; dorsal sepal directed forward, barely if at all upturned, 5–7 mm long, lateral sepals 5–7 mm long, 2 mm wide. Petals 5–7 mm long, with three distinct veins, scarcely reflexed or upturned. Lip 6–7 mm long, 4–5 mm wide, ovate, calli short, stout, papillose-pubescent, 0.8–1 mm long. Both surfaces of the lip may be papillose-pubescent. Flower in side

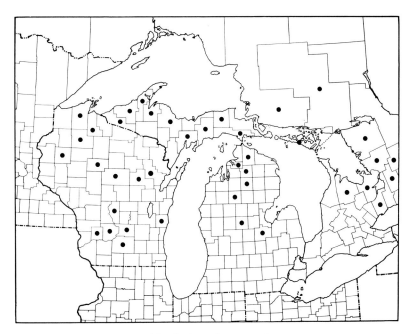

40. *Spiranthes casei*

view with the least two-lipped appearance of any *S. cernua*-like *Spiranthes* owing to the forward-directed dorsal sepal and petals.

Season. Late mid-August to mid-September throughout its range.

General Distribution. Nova Scotia (*S. casei* var. *novaescotiae* Catling), Maritime Provinces, Quebec, and New England, across Ontario, mainly on the Canadian Shield (with its distribution center between Quebec and Georgian Bay), across the Upper Peninsula of Michigan, northern and driftless region of Wisconsin, and locally into Lower Michigan north of Saginaw Bay. *Spiranthes casei* is so recently described as to still be unfamiliar to many botanists. As it becomes better known and collected, our knowledge of its range, particularly northward, may be expanded.

Habitat. Dry to moderately moist, sandy, sterile soils, crevices in igneous rocks, roadsides and pastures. Often growing with aspen (*Populus tremuloides*), paper birch, sumac, bracken fern and sweet fern. Occasional in drier, sandy borrow pits. Like many of its kin, *S. casei* is a colonizer of disturbed sites, developing large colonies briefly then waning rapidly. Although it may appear in ditches with *S. cernua* occasionally, it prefers drier conditions. Catling (pers. comm.) found it colonizing dry sandstone ledges and bluffs in the driftless area of southwestern Wisconsin.

NODDING LADIES'-TRESSES, AUTUMN TRESSES

Spiranthes cernua (L.) L. C. M. Rich.   Plate 31B, 34B

This orchid is by far the most familiar *Spiranthes* in the Great Lakes region. Its dainty, pearly white blooms may be seen not only in wet meadows and marly bogs, but commonly in roadside ditches and even on lawns. Probably no other orchid is so widespread and frequent in our region.

Habit. Quite variable, erect, leaves glabrous, scape densely downy-pubescent above, 10–50 cm tall, mostly 20–30 cm. Leaves mostly basal, linear or lanceolate, and broadest above base, acuminate, 4–25 cm long, 0.5–2 cm wide. Raceme densely flowered, flowers directed slightly downward (nodding). Floral bracts ovate-lanceolate, 8–15 mm long. Dorsal sepal oblong-lanceolate, 6–11 mm long, 1–3 mm wide; lateral sepals lanceolate, acute, free and somewhat spreading, 6–11 mm long, 1–2.5 mm wide. Petals linear, 6–11 mm long, 1–2 mm wide, connivent with dorsal sepal. Lip oblong to ovate, curved downward at apex, very slightly constricted or tapering from middle, margins undulate-crisped, crystalline, 6–11 mm long, 3–6 mm wide. Basal callosities prominent, slightly incurved, pubescent. Seeds polyembryonic (an unusual situation where each has several embryos) at least in some strains.

Season. August, September, and until killing frost, occasionally earlier (primarily late August–early September in our region).

General Distribution. Nova Scotia, Quebec, and Ontario, westward to Minnesota, south through eastern states to Florida and Texas, west to Kansas and the eastern Dakotas (especially South Dakota).

Habitat. Almost any type of open, moist cover on neutral or slightly acid soils. Prefers sandy, acid, wet soils, and distinctly shuns clay. Commonest in damp meadows, pastures, roadside ditches, open marly bogs, recent excavations, and along lake shores. This species has benefited from the construction of our superhighway system. In northern Lower Michigan, highway banks and grassy medians with their regular mowing have become prime habitat and have been heavily colonized in places.

Varieties and Hybrids. In such a widespread plant a great variation in structure and physiology is expected and various races have been recognized. Some of these have recently been segregated into distinct species (*S. casei*, *S. magnicamporum*, *S. ochroleuca*). One variety, var. *odorata* (Nutt.) Correll, had been regarded as a separate species until Correll reduced its status in 1940. Luer (1975) restored it to independent species status stating: "Certain other criteria exist for maintaining *S. odorata* as a

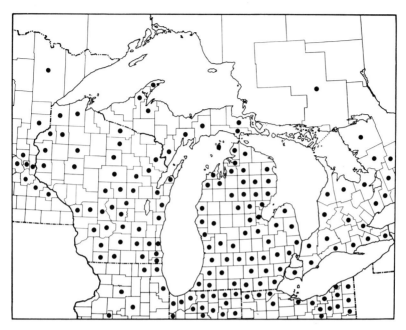

41. *Spiranthes cernua*

species." While he gives several unique features of var. *odorata*, he does not make clear exactly how it differs sufficiently from *S. cernua* to be maintained as a species. Species or variety, the taxon *odorata* has not been collected in the western Great Lakes region. It is primarily a southern taxon.

Several hybrids of *S. cernua* with other taxa have been described and named in the literature. The best known is *S. ×steigeri* Correll. I have seen plants, especially in Upper Michigan, that appear intermediate and grow with both *S. cernua* and *S. romanzoffiana*. Others continue to report such hybrids. Paul Catling recently studied putative hybrids which I collected at Deep Lake, Barry County, Michigan. He does not believe that the specimens which he examined represent hybrids, but rather abnormal plants of *S. romanzoffiana* (Catling, pers. comm.). Since *S. cernua* exhibits characteristics of apomictic or autogamous behavior (i.e. polyembryony and the entire flower spike open at the same time), opportunity for hybridization may be limited. Plants of this species do, however, produce pollen and are visited by insects, so some hybridization may occur.

Spiranthes lacera (Raf.) Raf.
Spiranthes gracilis (Bigel.) Beck (1st ed.)

Although widespread in our flora and one of the most distinctive in appearance of our ladies'-tresses, this orchid is nonetheless inconspicuous and often overlooked. Long known as *S. gracilis*, this species' status was revised by Fernald in 1946. He applied Rafinesque's name, *S. lacera*, to the northern populations, and the epithet *S. gracilis* to southern populations. Correll (1950) rejected this treatment considering the separation invalid. In the first edition of this book I followed Correll. Sheviak (1974), a student of *Spiranthes*, followed many recent authors in combining Fernald's two species. Luer (1975), however, treated *S. lacera* and *S. gracilis* as varieties of one species, *S. lacera*, generally following Fernald's descriptions, but mapping the ranges of the two varieties as widely overlapping in the North.

Paul Catling, another specialist in *Spiranthes*, recognizes Luer's treatment of *S. lacera* (i.e. having two distinct varieties). In our paper, "The Genus Spiranthes in Michigan" (*Michigan Botanist* 22: 79–92, 1983), we mapped both varieties based upon Catling's

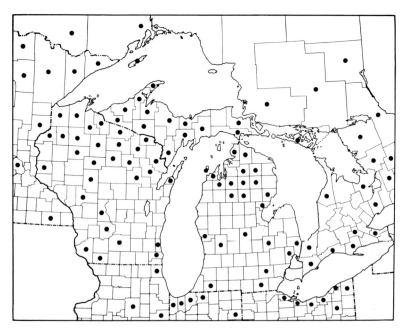

42. *Spiranthes lacera*

thesis studies, with var. *lacera* occurring mostly in northern and western Michigan, and var. *gracilis* occurring mainly in the southeastern quarter of the Lower Peninsula. I have since reexamined many herbarium specimens for the revision of this book, and I have found that the distinctions between the two varieties here are frequently obscured. Specimens from many populations in our northern jack-pine barrens show many overlapping features of the two varieties. A very few specimens from southeastern Michigan do approach the var. *gracilis* in spike characteristics and flowering time, but are not always clear-cut.

Thus, I make no distinction of varieties in mapping this species, but I do include a short description of var. *gracilis* following the more detailed description of *S. lacera* var. *lacera*. All plants of the *S. lacera* type in our region should be carefully checked, not only to elucidate the nature of this species here, but also to detect the presence of very similar species which occur adjacent to our region in the East and South.

Northern Slender Ladies'-tresses

S. lacera (Raf.) Raf. var. *lacera*   Plate 31C, 33C

Habit. Leaves basal, fading at or just before flowering time; broadly ovate to elliptic, in size and shape closely resembling those of the lesser rattlesnake plantain; short-petioled, 1–6 cm long, 1–2 cm wide, unmarked light green, shiny. Scape very slender, gradually to strongly spiraled or occasionally secund. Floral bracts ovate-lanceolate, sheathing pedicellate ovaries. Flowers small, crystalline white, lowermost flowers often widely separated. Sepals and petals about 4–5 mm long. Sepals lanceolate, lateral sepals usually spreading, clearly separate from and flanking the lip. Petals linear, adherent to dorsal sepal. Lip oblong-quadrate, 4–6 mm long, 2–3 mm wide, crystalline, crenulate-erose, the floor of lip having a stripe of rich green but with green coloring not extending to the apex of the lip; apex lacerate. Basal callosities of lip small, erect, not curved.

Season. Mid-July to mid-August. Frequently at full bloom when lowbush blueberries (*Vaccinium* spp.) are ready to harvest.

General Distribution. Nova Scotia, New Brunswick, Quebec, and across Ontario to Manitoba, south through Minnesota, Wisconsin, eastern Iowa, Illinois, and northern Missouri, eastward to Kentucky, northern Virginia, and New Jersey, thence northward through New England. In our districts more common northward; abundant in northern Lower Michigan, the Upper Peninsula, northern Wisconsin, Minnesota and Lake Superior districts of Ontario.

173

Habitat. S. lacera var. *lacera* occurs in dry, acid soils, either wooded or open. Especially common in dry, sandy, jack-pine woodlands, in clearings or in beds of reindeer lichen, or with lowbush blueberry. Also frequent on Great Lakes shores and dunes. I have also seen it growing with small purple fringed-orchid (*P. psycodes*) in quite damp sandy ditches in Upper Michigan.

SOUTHERN SLENDER LADIES'-TRESSES

S. lacera (Raf.) Raf. var. *gracilis* (Bigelow) Luer   Plate 33D

Habit. Plant generally similar to var. *lacera*, but more sparsely pubescent. Leaves fugacious, absent at onset of flowering. Scape usually rather tightly coiled, giving it a somewhàt broader aspect (than var. *lacera*), flowers closely spaced. Spike length (in mm) to flower number ratio less than 2.3 (Case and Catling 1983). Flower parts, except lip, similar to var. *lacera*; lip apex more rounded, crenulate or finely lacerate, the green color on the floor of the lip broader, less clearly defined, and extending almost to the apex.

Season. S. lacera var. *gracilis* flowers later in a given district than var. *lacera*. In our area var. *gracilis* usually flowers from mid-August to mid-September.

General Distribution. In the Great Lakes region, northeastern Illinois and northern Indiana, southern and southeastern Lower Michigan, southern Ontario, and northern Ohio. Generally more southern in occurrence than var. *lacera*, its southern range includes all states east of the prairies and south of our region except peninsular Florida.

Habitat. Rather open old fields, prairies, roadsides, in dry, slightly acid or neutral substrates. Common plant associates in our area include Canada blue-grass (*Poa compressa*), poverty-grass (*Danthonia spicata*), and wild strawberry.

Both varieties of slender ladies'-tresses are plants of old, open fields, clearings in forests, or dry, sandy dunes and roadsides. The var. *lacera* grows in great abundance in some of our jack-pine barrens. In Roscommon and Crawford counties, Michigan, the plant abounds in open jack-pine and scrub oak forests, flowering at the time blueberries ripen. The var. *lacera* grows, as well, in damp ground along beaches, ditch banks, roadsides, and dunes, and even in granite crevices along Lake Superior. It is very abundant in similar habitats in Minnesota.

Hybrids. Ames (1921) reported hybrids between slender ladies'-tresses and nodding ladies'-tresses (*S. lacera* × *S. cernua*) from New England and Texas. Sheviak (1974) reports the hybrid between S. *lacera* and S. *magnicamporum* from DuPage, Hancock, and Kane counties, Illinois. The most recent specimen listed by Sheviak was collected in 1912. Simpson and Catling (1978) report the hybrid of S. *lacera* var. *lacera* and S. *romanzoffiana* from the Parry Sound District, Ontario, with careful documentation of the nature of the hybrid.

Since S. *lacera* and its varieties frequently grow with other *Spiranthes* species in our region, it seems likely that additional hybrids may appear from time to time. In most reported hybrids the characteristics are intermediate between the putative parents, making the parentage fairly obvious.

SHINING LADIES'-TRESSES, WIDE-LEAVED LADIES'-TRESSES

Spiranthes lucida (H. H. Eaton) Ames   Plate 31D, 33B

Earliest blooming of our ladies'-tresses and possessed of considerable charm and beauty, this orchid offers a great challenge to the orchid hunter. It has a very local distribution in the western part of our region, and the plants are generally so diminutive that, even when they are present in some numbers, detection among the grasses and swamp vegetation is difficult. Of our native ladies'-tresses, it is the only species where the leaves remain green and functioning after flowering. However, in the other species a new rosette of leaves forms in the late fall.

Habit. From less than 8 cm to 37 cm tall (Correll), usually about 12–20 cm. Leaves appear basal and clustered, though occasionally some leaves are cauline; glabrous, fleshy, and shiny; broadly oblong-lanceolate, blunt-tipped to acuminate, 3–12 cm long, 0.5–1.5 cm wide. Scape glabrous to slightly pubescent above, spike cylindrical, spiraled, flowers in 1 or 2 ranks. Floral bracts scarious, lanceolate, longer than ovary. Flowers crystalline, white, nodding or drooped, in outline rather tubular-flaring. Sepals linear-oblong, 4–5 mm long, 1–2 mm wide, dorsal sepal with petals more or less forming a hood over column, but not forming a conspicuous hoodlike structure; lateral sepals free, carried forward and more or less parallel with lip. Petals linear, 5–6 mm long, 1–1.5 mm wide. Lip oblong-quadrate, truncate or rounded at apex, folded around column in life, about 5 mm long, 2–2.5 mm wide, with a small callus at base on each side; floor of lip with a bright, rich yellow stripe.

Season. Late May to mid-July; commonly mid–late June.

General Distribution. Irregular, and with disjunct stations, from New Brunswick, Quebec, and the limestone areas of Ontario's Lake Huron region, northeastern Ontario, south through New York to Virginia, west through northern Ohio, south-central

175

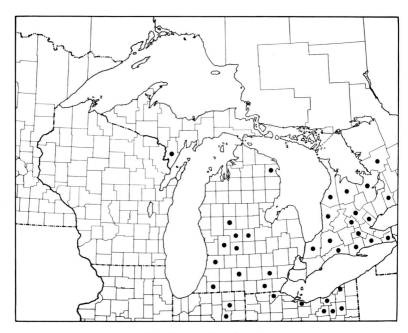

43. *Spiranthes lucida*

Indiana, Kentucky, and Michigan; also Missouri and Kansas.[1] West of Ontario exceedingly rare or local. Frequent along Lake Erie on both the Ohio and Ontario shores, it grows also on the Canadian shore areas of Lake Huron. Throughout its range, reported colonies persist only a few years then wane. In addition, its oft-recorded habitat, rich pastures along streams, holds few plants of great interest to botanists in June and is thus infrequently examined. The combination of these two facts may be responsible for naturalists considering this plant rarer than it actually is.

Habitat. Gravelly sand bars and river banks, lake shores, crevices in limestone rock, wet ledges, wet meadows and swales, especially in calcareous regions, mossy pads in fens, damp lime-

[1] Correll and others report this plant from Wisconsin. I have seen no material referable to this species from that state. The specimen cited by Ames (1924) in *An Enumeration of the Orchids of the United States and Canada,* "Bluffs, Devil's Lake, August 23, 1900, Umbach No. 12,228," is *S. casei* Catling and Cruise. Don Henson, in 1984, found the species along the Menominee River on the Wisconsin/Michigan border in western Upper Michigan, a remarkable range extension (but a characteristic behavior pattern) for this species. Its occurrence at a site this close to Wisconsin indicates it may occur in that state as well.

stone cobble, and damp floors of gravel pits. Where I have seen it in Michigan, it grows in black, sandy-mucky pastures along a medium-sized stream, among wild iris, sweet flag, sedges, and sometimes scattered white cedars. This orchid prefers open, sunny, damp spots where grass has been cropped or where black soil is exposed, i.e. somewhat raw, disturbed spots. One of its most constant plant companions is meadow spikemoss (*Selaginella apoda*) which thrives in similar habitats. Where this tiny fern relative grows, shining ladies'-tresses may also be found. In limestone districts such as the lake district of Alpena County, Michigan, *S. lucida* grows along sandy-cobbly shores. In such habitats, the plants grow in peaty turf right on the rim of vegetation as it stops at the high wave mark.

Occasionally, man inadvertently creates ideal habitat for this orchid. At a lake in Kent County, Michigan, a resident filled the low lake shore with yellow sand to raise it for a better lawn. Within 2–3 years hundreds of *S. lucida* plants appeared. They persisted for a season or two and then gradually disappeared. Similarly, in 1983, I found (with A. A. Reznicek) near Collingwood, Ontario, a sand-filled low lawn on which grew thousands of specimens of *S. lucida*. In nearby natural wet areas, shores, and ditches, only a handful of these plants could be found. More shining ladies'-tresses grew on this one lawn than I ever expected to see.

PRAIRIE LADIES'-TRESSES

Spiranthes magnicamporum Sheviak   Plate 32A, 34C

One of the most interesting new species which has been segregated from the *S. cernua* complex is the prairie or Great Plains ladies'-tresses, *S. magnicamporum*. Described by Charles Sheviak in 1973, it was originally believed to occur mainly from northwestern Indiana westward to the Dakotas and southward to Texas and the Black Belt soils of Alabama. This species is now known to have a fairly widespread occurrence on prairie remnants, fen borders, and interdunal soils in eastern Michigan and southwestern Ontario.

This is a fairly large and handsome plant. In my opinion it is very distinct with an intriguing and strong fragrance of coumarin. Once one is familiar with the subtle but distinctive features of this plant, identification is easy.

Habit. Scape erect, often stiffly so, glabrous below, pubescent among flowers above. Pubescence dense, capitate. Basal leaves linear-lanceolate, 12–15 cm long, 10–12 mm wide, acute, withering early, absent at anthesis. Cauline leaves reduced to sheathing bracts with erect, free, distal blades. Sheath-blades often overlapping. Raceme densely flowered, 15–30 mm in diameter, 5–18 cm long, densely flowered with ranks obscured. Floral bracts ovate-attenuate, 10–25 mm long. Flowers white to creamy white, under surface of lip yellow, strongly fragrant of newly mown alfalfa or coumarin, backs of sepals sparsely capitate-pubescent. Dorsal sepal lanceolate, acuminate, 7–12 mm long, 1.5–3 mm wide. Lateral sepals oblique, free, linear-lanceolate, curved, often meeting over the flower behind the somewhat connivent dorsal sepal and petals, 7–11 mm long, 2 mm wide. Petals linear-acuminate, 8–10 mm long, 1–2 mm wide. Lip 7–12 mm long, 4–6 mm wide, oblong-ovate to rhombic-ovate, arcuate, the apical portion sometimes strongly reflexed, especially with age; without a basal dilation or central constriction, but bearing a thickened, cream-yellow central fleshy-firm pad. Basal calli of lip short, conical, about as wide as long, less than 1 mm long. Column about 3 mm long. Seeds reportedly monoembryonic (Luer 1975).

Season. Mid-September to killing frost, in western, prairie portion of the range, often in good bloom into early November. In the eastern, wet-sand prairie and Great Lakes shoreline habitats, often (in Michigan and Ontario, at least) commencing bloom somewhat earlier, from very late August to October. Plants from tight bud to senescing flowers may be found in the same habitat over a long season.

General Distribution. Center of occurrence the prairies and grasslands of the eastern Great Plains region, from Texas north at least to North Dakota (Sheviak 1973), eastward across the "prairie peninsula" of southwestern Minnesota, Iowa, Missouri, southern Wisconsin, and most of Illinois into the Lake Michigan regions of Indiana and extreme southwestern Lower Michigan. In Michigan, locally frequent along Saginaw Bay east of the mouth of the Saginaw River across the shoreline regions of the Thumb to the islands of Lake St. Clair and the adjacent mainland of Ontario. Much rarer inland, locally on dry prairies and fen borders. Also present on the Black Belt soils of Alabama and Mississippi, and reported very locally as far west as Colorado, Utah, and New Mexico. This is one of our most recently described *Spiranthes.* Details of its range, particularly east and north of its Great Plains center of distribution, are incompletely known.

Habitat. Spiranthes magnicamporum blooms concurrently with *S. cernua,* but is largely isolated from it by a requirement for basic soils (*S. cernua* grows on acidic soils). Its moisture tolerances appear broad; it grows on very dry grasslands and borders of interdunal swales, in sand, and in mucky, humus-filled, wet-sand prairie soils, and occasionally in drier areas of marl fens. Overall, it prefers drier sites than those occupied by extensive colonies of *S. cernua.* While natural shoreline cobble, dune ridges,

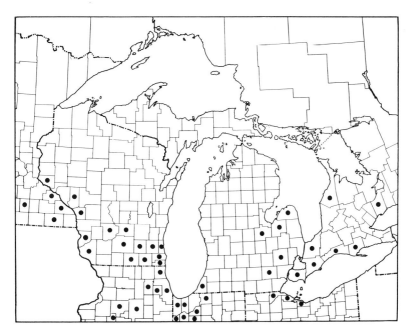

44. *Spiranthes magnicamporum*

and prairies are its ideal habitat, it is able to colonize borrow pits on raw yellow sand, roadsides, fallow fields, and other mildly disturbed habitats. Since it has such a range of occurrence and habitat tolerance, it is difficult to list consistent companion species. On moist prairie cover companion orchids include *Platanthera leucophaea, Cypripedium candidum, Spiranthes cernua* (in nearby swales), and very rarely *Calopogon tuberosus*. Other plant companions include *Liatris spicata, Potentilla fruticosa, Potentilla anserina, Solidago rigida, Lupinus perennis, Carex* spp., and *Juncus torreyi*.

While I have observed the prairie ladies'-tresses in a wide variety of habitats and areas in Michigan and Ontario, I have seldom seen truly large stands of hundreds of plants such as are characteristic of *S. cernua* in ideal habitats. Rather, *S. magnicamporum* occurs as widely scattered individuals, sometimes surprisingly scarce in good cover. Occasionally, one finds dense clumps of flowering stems arising from one mass of roots. These are obviously clonal offsets, and probably arose initially from damage or destruction of the growth bud of the original plant. Unquestionably, the preferred habitat of *S. magnicamporum* near the Great Lakes is the low, moist sand-prairie created by the periodic inundations and recessions of the lakes themselves.

These regions of frequent water table change are particularly abundant in the Thumb of Michigan east of the Saginaw River. Here, where prairie remnants still exist, S. *magnicamporum* is usually present. In Huron County, Michigan, where limestone bedrock lies close to the surface, the plant thrives and grows not only on the prairie remnants, but also on beach cobble, railroad fill, mowed fields, airport runways, and road shoulders.

Spiranthes magnicamporum, closely resembling S. *cernua* and its relatives, can be difficult to identify from herbarium specimens. Fresh plants, however, are singularly distinctive once one learns their characteristics. The strong, pleasant odor, the gaping-arcuate lip (looking like a S. *cernua* flower had been forced apart by a too-large bee), the thickened central lip tissue distinctly yellow when viewed from below, and most distinctive of all, the almost "cow's horn" appearance of the free, curved, and overarching lateral sepals of the mature flowers assure identification. I expect that further exploration by local botanists will reveal the presence of S. *magnicamporum* in those districts of southern Michigan, northern Indiana, Ohio, and southwestern Ontàrio where moist prairie vegetation and alkaline fens commonly occur.

YELLOW LADIES'-TRESSES

Spiranthes ochroleuca (Rydberg) Rydberg   Plate 32B, 34D

In 1901, Rydberg described a new *Spiranthes* (*Gyrostachys ochroleuca*) from Mt. Washington, Massachusetts. Later botanists relegated this taxon to a varietal status under S. *cernua*, or simply ignored it. Those botanists who did recognize the variety usually ascribed to it an occasional occurrence throughout the range of S. *cernua*. Most authorities did, correctly, ascribe to this variety an upland habitat and more yellowish flowers.

In the first edition of this book, I included S. *ochroleuca* as a variety of S. *cernua* because I followed Correll's nomenclature throughout. I have always regarded S. *ochroleuca* as a distinct species for it differs from S. *cernua* and other closely related taxa in flower and leaf structure, flower color, habitat requirements, flowering season, and distribution. When Luer came to my area to see and photograph S. *ochroleuca* for his book (Luer 1975), we examined together a great many specimens and we agreed that the plant seemed distinct. In 1980, C. J. Sheviak and P. M. Catling (*Rhodora* 82: 525–562) published a detailed study of the nature of S. *ochroleuca*. They consider that it is a distinct, although admittedly difficult to identify, species.

Herbarium material of S. *ochroleuca*, however, can be almost impossible to identify, even for experts. Consequently, distribution maps based largely upon herbarium specimens will contain many inaccuracies. Sheviak and Catling (*op. cit.*) produced an excellent distribution map based upon clearly distinct herbarium specimens and personal, fresh collections only. The range of the species is less extensive than given in older works, and very limited within the Great Lakes region.

Habit. Plant relatively tall, sometimes weakly erect, usually with flowers opening up the spike slowly to form a tapered spike of bloom and buds (in contrast to *S. cernua* which tends to open most of its flowers rapidly to form a broad spike). Leaves 3–6, basal and cauline, diminishing gradually to bracts, persistent through flowering, varying from relatively short and broad to elongated, usually elongated, widest beyond the middle, linear-oblanceolate to lanceolate, up to 20 cm long and 2.5 cm wide (usually 1 cm or less wide). Raceme long and slender, densely flowered, usually a single tight spiral (sometimes appearing several-ranked owing to the density of the spiral). Open mouth of flower facing outward or slightly upward in contrast to the somewhat nodding appearance of *S. cernua.* Floral bracts of lowermost flowers 13 mm long, 5 mm wide, the margins very narrowly and regularly hyaline, long-attenuate and evenly tapered. Flowers cream-yellow, fading with age to white. Dorsal sepal 8–10 mm long, 3–4 mm wide, thick textured, greenish cream, not translucent. Lateral sepals 9–10 mm long, 3–3.5 mm wide, opaque due to the arched nature of the flower, somewhat ascending, with little or no curvature when viewed from above. Petals linear-lanceolate, 10 mm long, 2.5 mm wide. Lip ovate-quadrate (when flattened) 9–10 mm long, 5–6 mm wide, widest immediately below calli with a thickened, opaque, creamy yellow, central-grooved pad. Apex of lip slightly expanded, thin, and crenulate. Base of lip with prominent calli, the calli 2 mm long, pubescent, sharply and conspicuously incurved and hornlike (when lip is flattened). Ovary at anthesis not strongly enlarged, 5–10 mm long. Seeds monoembryonic.

Season. In western Great Lakes region, very late August, September, to early October, peaking around mid-September, as local plants of *S. cernua* decline.

General Distribution. Lake Michigan districts of Indiana, southwestern, southeastern, and Saginaw Bay regions of Michigan, southwestern Ontario, central Lake Erie region and Ohio River districts of Ohio, rare and local, becoming more abundant in Pennsylvania, New York, and Vermont, New Hampshire, and southern New England, southern Maine, and southern Nova Scotia (Sheviak and Catling 1980). In the western Great Lakes region

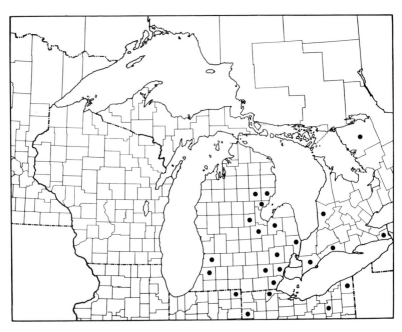

45. *Spiranthes ochroleuca*

local, reported only from the districts listed above. Recently reported from the mountains of North Carolina. Somewhat similar plants reported from Wisconsin are *S. casei.*

Habitat. A plant of openings in pioneer woodland usually of red maple (*Acer rubrum*), aspen (*Populus tremuloides*), and red oak (*Quercus rubra*) on low, damp to dryish, sterile, sandy-acid soils. Although able to tolerate some disturbance, *S. ochroleuca* is much less a plant of recently disturbed sites than *S. cernua,* although in our area it is sometimes abundant on long-drained highbush blueberry cover. Frequent companions are wintergreen (*Gaultheria procumbens*), *Viburnum cassinoides,* witch hazel (*Hamamelis virginiana*), *Aronia melanocarpa,* and *Polytrichum* moss species. Prefers rather open areas within the proper habitat, but is able to tolerate some shading.

In our region, *S. ochroleuca* may be widespread locally, but difficult to detect. It rarely forms large stands in the manner of *S. cernua,* but rather occurs as widely scattered, often solitary plants. Occasionally the plant forms small clumps from asexual offsets. Where old ditched swampland occurs in our region, *S. ochroleuca* may grow on ditchbanks in high and drier sites, while *S. cernua* may grow only a few feet away in wet ditch bottoms.

In such situations, I have occasionally seen colonies of plants which seemed to be intergrades.

OVAL LADIES'-TRESSES

Spiranthes ovalis Lindley   Plate 32C, 35A
    var. *erostellata* Catling

In 1966, R. W. Pippen of Western Michigan University discovered this primarily southern species in Kalamazoo County, Michigan. This colony, another in Lucas County, Ohio (A. Cusick, pers. comm. and specimen, OSU), and the recent discovery of *S. ovalis* on Walpole Island, Lambton County, Ontario, by J. Ross Brown represent the only known occurrences of this species in the western Great Lakes region. Sheviak (1974) reports both an increase in Illinois populations and a trend to appear (or be discovered) farther north in that state than had previously been reported. While the oval ladies'-tresses is still one of the rarest known orchids within our region, it may be expanding its range, or be more widely present than had been suspected. That it is one of our latest *Spiranthes* to commence blooming may also account for few reports in our district. While *S. ovalis*, like most other *Spiranthes*, can thrive on disturbed sites, and may build large populations in such habitats, it is one of the few truly forest dwelling ladies'-tresses. It can not only survive, but also bloom under conditions of fairly dense shade and mature timber.

Habit. Variable in height, rather slender, 1–4 dm tall, basal leaves erect-arching, glabrous, deep green, oblong-elliptic or oblanceolate to linear-lanceolate, usually conspicuously narrowed below the middle (almost petiolate), the base sheathing the stem, 6–15 cm long, 5–17 mm wide, gradually reduced to sheathing bracts above. Spike short and compact for stem height, somewhat oval in outline (hence *ovalis*), composed of extremely uniform and compact ranks of small, white flowers. Floral bracts ovate to lanceolate, often strongly acuminate, 4–11 mm long, 3–4 mm wide. Ovary dark green, stout, about 6 mm long. Flowers very white, small, rarely over 5 mm long. Dorsal sepal lanceolate-acute, the tip slightly recurved, 4–5 mm long, 2–3 mm wide. Lateral sepals similar, to 5 mm long, tips often spreading. Petals adherent to the dorsal sepal, linear-lanceolate, 4–5 mm long, 1–1.5 mm wide, conduplicate-concave, tips often slightly spreading. Lip ovate-oblong to rhombic-ovate, either somewhat constricted or appearing so when flattened because of the strongly arcuate-recurved carriage, basal half broadly ovate-rounded with slender, strongly incurved callosities, distal portion finely undulate-corrugated, crystalline, usually narrowed, 4–5 mm long, 2–4 mm

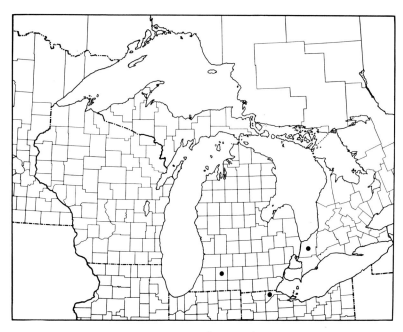

46. *Spiranthes ovalis*

wide at widest point. Column 2 mm or less long; seed capsule ellipsoid, 5–6 mm long. Plants with shorter lateral sepals (3.5–5 mm) and the absence of rostellum and viscidium on the column are var. *erostellata* Catling. Catling has examined the Michigan material and determined that it belongs to this new, autogamous variety (Catling 1983).

Season. Late September and October in the north, into November in the southern portion of its range.

General Distribution. Apparently disjunct in Pennsylvania (Luer 1975), Michigan, northern Ohio, and Ontario. Generally rare and local, but widely distributed from Virginia, West Virginia, and Kentucky southward to central Florida and westward along the Gulf Coast into Texas. Northward into eastern Oklahoma, Arkansas, Missouri north at least to central Illinois and extreme southwestern Indiana. In our area, known at present only from Kalamazoo County, Michigan, Lucas County, Ohio (A. Cusick, pers. comm. and specimen, OSU), and on Walpole Island, Ontario.

Habitat. Oval ladies'-tresses is distinctly a forest species throughout most of its range. In the Michigan station, the plants grew on mossy hummocks or on the floor of a forest of oaks, tulip (*Liriodendron*), and sugar maple. Plants were generally widely scattered, although at times small clusters grew on favorable hummocks. Shade was surprisingly dense. The soil was a very moist, sandy, clayey loam without much humus. Nearby, quite a few seedlings grew in relatively open, more sandy soil on a forest service roadway. While few were mature enough to flower, they appeared more vigorous than those in deep shade. R. W. Pippen states that when this station was discovered in 1966 it was a more open, fieldlike area which has since brushed in. Sheviak also reports that the species grows in old field situations in Illinois. The Ontario plants grew in open, moist prairie soil.

The spike of S. *ovalis* is small for the size of the plant, and the flowers are very white. It is a very fresh, distinctive plant, notable for the recurved tips of all flower segments in most specimens in our area. These, coupled with its late blooming season and rather different habitat, make for easy identification. At present oval ladies'-tresses may be one of the rarest known native orchids in our region. However, its habitat is plentiful and the nature of *Spiranthes* is to appear and proliferate. Further exploration of the moist deciduous forests in October will almost certainly bring more stations for this species to light.

Hooded Ladies'-tresses

Spiranthes romanzoffiana Cham.   Plate 32D, 35C

The only transcontinental *Spiranthes*, this species grows rather commonly in the cooler regions of North America and in Ireland. It lacks the sparkle and crisp appearance of other ladies'-tresses, owing partly to the creamy white color and partly to the softer texture of the corolla. It has a distinctive odor which the late Dr. Edgar T. Wherry (in Correll) compared to coumarin.

Habit. Height variable, 10–30 cm tall, rarely to 50 cm, usually under 30 cm in our region. Leaves basal, linear to oblanceolate 5–20 cm long, 5–13 mm wide, glabrous. Floral bracts thin, ovate-lanceolate, 1–2.5 cm long. Flowers distinctly creamy white, appearing strongly 2-lipped, the "lips" being composed of the labellum below and the connivent sepals and petals above. Sepals oblong-lanceolate, 6–13 mm long, 3–4 mm wide, petals linear, 6–12 mm long, 1–2 mm wide, sepals and petals appearing superficially as one organ and forming a distinct hood over column and lip. Lip strongly fiddle-shaped, the concave basal portion oval, with a constricted isthmus and a dilated, spade-shaped apical region, the distal margin of which is upturned, 9–12 mm long, 5 mm wide at widest point, basal callus obscure. Flowers in several spiral ranks which are sometimes secund, each in a separate axis, giving a curiously angular flat-sidedness to the raceme.

Season. July to October, mainly August or early September; begins to bloom ahead of *S. cernua* where they share the same cover.

General Distribution. Transcontinental in the North, southward in the East to New York, westward through the Lakes states, Iowa, and Nebraska to the Rockies, southward at higher elevations in mountain bogs and meadows to Colorado, Arizona, New Mexico, and California. A variety, var. *porrifolia* (Lindl.) Ames and Correll, recognized in the western United States but unknown from our region, may be a distinct species.

Habitat. Marly, neutral fens, lake shores, streambanks, and wet meadows, sometimes in damp, brushy woods. Often growing in trickles or very shallow water, especially on marl beds and openings in fens. Common companions are various horsetails, tall white bog-orchid, arrow grass, calciphile mosses, and sometimes nodding ladies'-tresses (which, however, is usually found in drier spots). While occasionally found in sphagnum where superficial surface acidity exists, it does not grow in the deep-piled sphagnum of the intensely acid peat bogs. Usually found in very wet situations, it sometimes grows in drier fields and old roadbeds.

Hybrids. Putative hybrids of *S. romanzoffiana* with *S. cernua* have been designated *Spiranthes* ×*steigeri* Correll. Such plants, variable in structure both as individual plants and as blossoms on any one plant, are generally intermediate between the parents. Correll cites known localities for this hybrid in New Hampshire and Nova Scotia. Luer (1975) discusses such putative hybrids from a pasture in Vermont. His accompanying photograph, however, appears to me to be a peloric *S. romanzoffiana* in which the lip structure is repeated on the petals. Such flowers occur in *Cattleya, Phalaenopsis*, and other cultivated orchids with some regularity. Whether the peloria arose through hybridization or simply a genetic error is the question.

Catling (pers. comm.) does not feel that my specimens of *S.* ×*steigeri* from Barry County, Michigan, are examples of the hybrid, but rather abnormal *S. romanzoffiana*. At that time he questioned whether a hybrid of *S. cernua* with *S. romanzoffiana* would occur naturally. Nevertheless, near Cedarville in Chippewa County of Michigan's Upper Peninsula, I have seen a large population of putative *S.* ×*steigeri* growing with both parents in a large borrow pit which had been excavated for fill dirt for roadway construction. The excavation in the damp sand was filled with seeps and springy rivulets—a veritable artificial shore bog richly colonized by bog invaders. In the inch-deep standing water of the lowest areas grew several hundred *S. romanzoffiana*. Higher, and in a typically drier habitat, grew *S. cernua* by the thousands. In an exactly intermediate habitat (the hybrid habitat

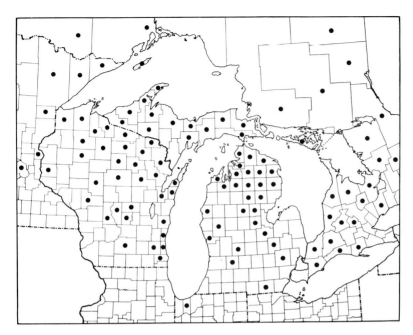

47. *Spiranthes romanzoffiana*

of Anderson) was a zone of unmistakably different, intermediate plants which showed various degrees of apparent intergradation between the two species present. Unfortunately, my herbarium specimens from this population cannot be located. With the newer analytical and chromatographic techniques of today, it might have been possible to make a more positive determination as to whether or not these plants represent hybrids. *S.* ×*steigeri* may or may not occur naturally, but I continue to see occasional plants in mixed populations which appear to me to be intermediate. Don Drife (pers. comm.) reports seeing similar intermediate plants in the eastern end of Michigan's Upper Peninsula. Their real nature remains uncertain. *Spiranthes romanzoffiana* occasionally hybridizes with *S. lacera* var. *lacera* (Simpson and Catling 1978; Catling 1980a). The first report of such a hybrid came from the Parry Sound District, Ontario, within the range of this book.

LITTLE LADIES'-TRESSES

Spiranthes tuberosa Raf.   Plate 33A, 35B

This diminutive species has been known by many epithets in the literature since it was first named by Rafinesque. Specific names formerly applied to this plant include *S. simplex*, *S. grayi*, and *S. beckii*. The first reports of this species from Michigan were based upon unusually small, incomplete specimens of *S. lacera* var. *lacera* (Correll 1950). The plant was actually first collected within the western Great Lakes region in 1969 by B. Stergios in Kalamazoo County, Michigan. Because that specimen was rather incomplete, the species was not admitted to Voss's *Michigan Flora*. The species was next noted in Michigan in 1980 by C. and S. Maisano who found the plants growing in an abandoned core sand pit in Midland County. Case and Catling (1983) visited both the Maisano and the Stergios stations to observe the species, and also found a much more vigorous colony in Calhoun County, Michigan. Apparently this species, although it has been rarely reported, is established at several widely scattered locations in Michigan. Its occurrence elsewhere within the range of this book is not established.

An uncommonly clean-cut, charming species, the plants are, nevertheless, very inconspicuous. Little ladies'-tresses grows in old fields, on dunes, in sandy pine barrens, and in sand pits throughout its range. Such habitats are not likely to attract botanists at bloom time in early August. Very possibly this species is more widely spread in the western Great Lakes region than the record shows. Whether it has always occurred in this region or whether it is a recent immigrant is not known.

Habit. Very slender, plant 10–58 cm tall, usually with a solitary tuberlike root (although 2–3 fleshy roots sometimes occur even in the Michigan plants). Leaves basal, ovate-elliptic, more or less acute, short petioled, 2–6 cm long, 0.5–1.5 cm wide, withering by early anthesis, but produced again late in the season. Scape very slender, with a few minute bracts, flower spike compact, Michigan plants often with a densely coiled spike (contrast with Fernald's statement (1950), "wholly one-sided or with few spiral twists in the glabrous rachis"), 10–30-flowered. Floral bracts tiny, less than 1 mm long, narrow. Ovary at anthesis minute, about 1.5 mm long and 0.5 mm wide. Flowers crystalline white, 2–4 mm long. Sepals narrow, the lateral ones 2–3.5 mm long, 1 mm wide; the dorsal sepal oblong to oblong-lanceolate, obtuse-tipped, to 4 mm long. Petals adherent to dorsal sepal, linear-oblong to spatulate, obtuse at apex, 2.5–4 mm long, 1 mm wide. Lip white, crispcd-undulate at apex, ovate to quadrate-oblong, the apical region decurved and somewhat dilated, 2.3–4 mm long, 1.5–2.5 mm wide, with small slender basal callosities. Column 1.5 mm long, green, the anther dorsal. Seed capsules maturing rapidly, the lower ones often discharging seed while the uppermost flowers are still fresh.

Season. Mainly from late July to early September throughout its range, but Correll (1950) ascribes a season from March to

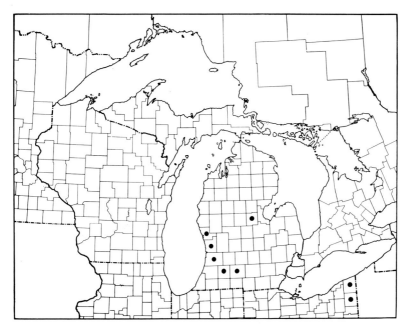

48. *Spiranthes tuberosa*

October for the full range. The Michigan plants are in full bloom about August 10th.

General Distribution. Coastal plain portions of Massachusetts, Rhode Island, and Connecticut south along the Atlantic coastal plain to south-central Florida, westward along the Gulf Coast to eastern Texas, northward through Arkansas, Missouri, southern Illinois (*fide* Luer), and Kentucky (Correll 1950). Also southern and central Michigan (Case and Catling 1983).

Habitat. Sandy soils in old fields, dunes, and ridges, often in areas in which soil had been disturbed 8–12 years previously. The Kalamazoo County and Calhoun County plants in Michigan grow in old fields, along with black cherry (*Prunus serotina*), small scrubby oaks (*Quercus* spp.), and New Jersey teas (*Ceanothus americanus*, *C. ovatus*). Meadow and prairie grasses such as *Leptoloma cognatum*, *Poa compressa*, *Aristida basiramea*, *Danthonia spicata*, and *Andropogon virginicus* commonly grow near the orchid (Case and Catling 1983). Hawkweeds and other adventive weeds abound. Perhaps the most frequent plant companion observed is the moss *Polytrichum*, commonly called pigeon-wheat. The Midland County, Michigan, plants grow in the bottom of an old foundry core sand excavation in almost pure beds of *Polytrichum* moss, either in the open or under young paper birches. Soils tested strongly acid, with a pH of 3.9–4.1 (Case and Catling 1983).

Little ladies'-tresses grows in damp to very dry situations in essentially brightly lighted locations. Although it is a handsome species with its sparkling white flowers, it is not easy to detect in the tall grasses. I feel confident that this species will prove to be widespread in old fields in southern Michigan.

GOODYERA R. Brown

According to Correll (1950), about 25 species of *Goodyera* grow in temperate and tropical regions of the world. Four species occur in North America, and all of them grow in the Great Lakes region. In general, the members of this genus have rosettes of rather attractive, leathery or fleshy leaves, conspicuously marked with white or light silvery green. The snakelike patterns of the leaves, the plantainlike leaf rosette, and the long, slender flower spike combine to give the group their common name—rattlesnake plantains. With the exception of the downy rattlesnake plantain, which is widespread in the eastern United States, the species, boreal or montane, are primarily denizens of coniferous forests, bogs, or swamps.

Rattlesnake plantains develop their rosettes at the terminus of a creeping rhizome which bears a few thick, fleshy, fibrous roots, especially near the active tip. The alternate leaves, arranged in a rosette, are evergreen and last for several seasons. From time to time, lateral buds along the rhizome give rise to branches which form their own rosettes. When a growth tip produces a flower scape, further growth of that axis ceases; the flower-bearing rosette gradually degenerates and dies. Then numerous, small lateral buds develop behind the terminal, degenerating growth, so that many smaller rosettes arise. Consequently these rattlesnake plantains tend to form compact colonies of rosettes, sometimes covering a considerable area. In some dense conifer forests of northern Lakes Huron and Superior, the patches of rattlesnake plantains may be the only plants in evidence.

The rattlesnake plantains hybridize with one another, giving rise to some perplexing material which is difficult to identify. Since most of the hybridization reported comes from our region, local orchid hunters must be prepared for an occasional individual or colony which does not correctly fit the book description of any species.

Goodyera is technically a difficult group, and in many ways similar to the related *Spiranthes*. The flowers are characterized by small size, with petals and dorsal sepals connivent and forming a hood over the column and lip. The sessile lip is conspicuously saccate-concave near the base and prolonged into a boat-shaped beak at the apex. The column is short and beaked. "Pure" specimens of these species may be distinguished by the key.

Key to *Goodyera*

A. Flower spike cylindrical; flowers opening on all sides of spike.

 B. Leaves ovate, dark green, conspicuously veined and reticulate with white lines throughout. Lip globular-saccate. Spike compactly cylindrical.

G. pubescens
page 193

 BB. Leaves lanceovate, bluish green, or with a faint glaucous bloom throughout, marked and reticulated with light green. Lip narrowly saccate. Spike elongate-cylindrical.

G. tesselata
page 197

AA. Flower spike one-sided or loosely spiraled.

 B. Spike rather loosely one-sided or spiraled. Flowers greenish on outside, 6 mm or more long, leaves 2–7 cm long. Plants normally over 15 cm tall.

 C. Leaves green, marked with white mainly along midrib, flowers and pedicellate ovary over 1 cm long.

G. oblongifolia
page 192

 CC. Leaves bluish green, with obscured reticulations throughout, and covered with a faint bloom. Flowers and pedicellate ovary together 1 cm or less long.

G. tesselata
page 197

BB. Spike rather densely one-sided. Flowers white on outside or, if green, on midveins only, less than 5 mm long. Leaves 1–3 cm long, ovate to oblong-elliptic. Plants normally under 15 cm tall.

G. repens var. *ophioides*
page 195

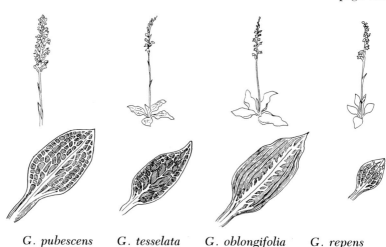

G. *pubescens*   G. *tesselata*   G. *oblongifolia*   G. *repens*

MENZIES' RATTLESNAKE PLANTAIN

Goodyera oblongifolia Raf.   Plate 35D, 36A

A handsome species and largest of the rattlesnake plantains, this orchid occurs only in limited parts of our region. It grows far more abundantly in the northern Rocky Mountains. In the Great Lakes region it usually forms colonies smaller than those of the other species. Owing to its green, nearly mark-free leaves and its barely saccate lip, it was first classed with *Spiranthes*.

Habit. Leaves glabrous, scape densely glandular-pubescent, 10–50 cm tall, quite variable. Scape with appressed sheaths. Leaves more or less basal, forming a rosette, somewhat erect, petiolate, oblong-elliptic, rarely lanceolate, dark green, with a conspicuous white feathered strip along midrib; in a few individuals (possibly hybrid) leaves have obscure white tesselations throughout. Raceme rather laxly flowered, flowers sometimes remote, loosely spiraled to somewhat one-sided. Flowers white on inner surfaces, outer surfaces greenish or green-streaked, overall effect greenish. Sepals puberulent on outer surface. Dorsal sepal lanceolate-deltoid, recurved at apex, concave below, 6–10 mm long, 3.5 mm wide. Lateral sepals ovate-lanceolate, acuminate, 5–8 mm long, 3–4 mm wide. Petals and dorsal sepal form a hood over lip. Petals 6–10

192

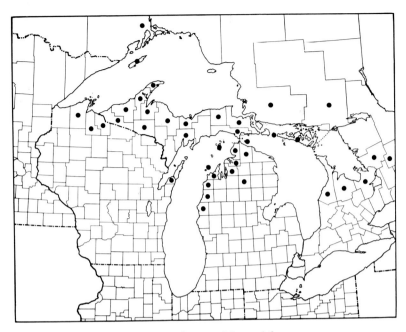

49. *Goodyera oblongifolia*

mm long, 3–4 mm wide, dilated at middle. Lip deeply concave-saccate, prolonged into a long beak, margins inrolled and boat-like, 5–8 mm long or longer.

Season. Late July, August.

General Distribution. Nova Scotia, New Brunswick, and Quebec, across the continent (apparently) to southern Alaska, southward in the West to Colorado, California, and New Mexico. In the East, south to Maine, northern Lower Michigan, and northern Wisconsin.

Habitat. Grows most abundantly in rather dry cedar-spruce woods in immediate vicinity of Upper Great Lakes shores, and occasionally inland in a variety of mixed conifer-deciduous woods or on margins of wooded bogs and swamps. Locally abundant in rather dry coniferous woods in limestone regions; rare and local elsewhere. Common along south shore of Lake Superior, but largely absent from central region of north shore.

DOWNY RATTLESNAKE PLANTAIN

Goodyera pubescens (Willd.) R. Br.   Plate 35D, 36B

This widespread species, less boreal than the rest of its genus, adapts to a greater variety of habitats and may be found in north

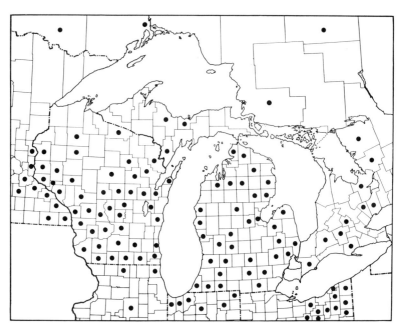

50. *Goodyera pubescens*

or south, either in bogs or dry, rocky woods. The leaves are the most conspicuous and attractive of any in the genus. Frequently used in dish gardens, it is a familiar plant to many who little suspect it to be an orchid.

Habit. Basal rosettes formed at end of creeping-branching rhizome, and giving rise, from the more vigorous rosettes, to a downy-pubescent flower scape 10–40 cm tall. Leaves about 6–8, evergreen, lasting more than one season, 2–9 cm long, 1–4 cm wide, ovate to obovate, with a short, broad petiole; green with a faint bluish bloom, and heavily marked with white veins and reticulations. Raceme densely flowered, cylindrical, wider than in the other species, flowers generally facing out on all sides, or with only a slight tendency to be secund. Floral bracts linear-lanceolate, about 6 mm long. Flowers distinctly globose, small, white, or with greenish outer parts. Upper sepal ovate to oblong-elliptic, concave, with a beaked apex. Lateral sepals ovate, concave, beaked. Sepals 4–5 mm long, 3–4 mm wide. Petals, as in all the group, connivent with dorsal sepal and forming a hood over lip, spatulate-oblong, 5–6 mm long, 3 mm wide. Lip very strongly saccate, the sac bulbous, prolonged into a short beak. Outer surface of flower parts pubescent-glandular. Capsules nearly globular.

Season. Varies considerably with type of environment. In brushy, open, warm woods, July; in cold bogs and swamps, August. It is not unusual to find upland colonies in bloom nearly a full month ahead of neighboring swamp colonies.

General Distribution. Quebec and Ontario southward, especially in the Appalachian uplands to Georgia and Alabama. Frequent in uplands and acid soil regions of eastern Tennessee and Kentucky, and as a disjunct in Arkansas. Westward through the Great Lakes states to Minnesota. Rare in Upper Michigan.

Habitat. Within its range, almost any type of wooded cover with acid surface conditions. Most frequent on sandy, humus-filled soils. Bogs, coniferous swamps, brushland, hemlock groves, dry or wet cedar woods, beech-maple forests, mixed woodlands of aspen, white cedar, balsam fir, and red maple; areas which have formerly been more or less covered by swamp evergreens. In northwestern Wisconsin, grows abundantly in moss and brush on or at the foot of talus slopes of great quartzite outcroppings, in company with purple clematis and common polypody fern. Because it so often grows in rather dry habitats, the most surprising stations are on the wet floors and pathways of densely wooded spruce-cedar-balsam swamps, where it may grow in company with other rattlesnake plantains.

CREEPING RATTLESNAKE PLANTAIN,
LESSER RATTLESNAKE PLANTAIN

Goodyera repens (L.) R. Br.   Plate 35D, 36C
    var. *ophioides* Fernald

A widespread species, this orchid grows around the world in the Northern Hemisphere. Though far from common, it is probably more often overlooked than absent from the cool, coniferous, northern regions. Summerhayes, in *Wild Orchids of Britain* (1951), suggests that the leaf rosettes of this orchid reach flowering age or strength only in the eighth year, but he does not specify the source of this information. In this country, at least, I believe the species requires a shorter period to attain flowering. I have only general field observations as a basis for this statement. To my knowledge, no one has marked individual plants and carried on the required detailed observations for a period of years.

Habit. Rosette forming, with creeping rhizomes. Leaves 4–7, with short, broad petioles; normally ovate, occasionally oblong-elliptic, obtusely acute, dark green with light silvery green veins and numerous similarly colored cross veins having a peculiar crystalline texture; 1–4 cm long, 0.5–2 cm wide. Flower scapes produced sparingly, scape (in our region) seldom over 15 cm tall

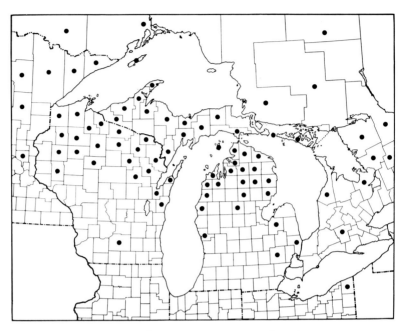

51. *Goodyera repens* var. *ophioides*

(taller plants probably represent hybrid forms with *G. tesselata*). Racemes strongly erect-appressed, lanceolate-acuminate, up to 10 cm long. Flowers white, parts somewhat crystalline-pubescent on outer surface. Sepals about 3–4 mm long, 1–2 mm wide, dorsal sepal concave and with petals forming a hood over column and lip. Petals also 3 mm long, 1–2 mm wide. Lip with basal portion deeply saccate, apical portion prolonged into a rather long-acuminate beak, which is reflexed or recurved. Margins of lip upturned, boatlike. Lip 4–5 mm long, 2 mm wide. The form of *G. repens* found in Eurasia and locally in the American West differs from the var. *ophioides* in lacking the light green to whitish markings of the leaves. Only rarely are colonies of plants lacking these conspicuous markings found in the Great Lakes region.

Season. Late July and August.

General Distribution. Transcontinental in the cool evergreen forests of boreal America, south in the East to New England, New York, Pennsylvania, and at higher elevations, to North Carolina and Tennessee. Westward through the Great Lakes states to Minnesota, but rare or absent from the southern portions of this region. Also along the western mountains to New Mexico. Both the type and this variety occur across Eurasia.

Habitat. A plant of cool, shaded soils, it grows almost entirely in coniferous woods and bogs. Its stoloniferous rhizomes seldom enter the mineral soil layers; instead, they entwine throughout the surface litter of decaying spruce, cedar, or pine needles, and various mosses. A favorite upland site is under hemlocks on the sides of ravines or on north-facing slopes. Densely wooded bogs and bog borders (especially under cedar-balsam thickets) house large colonies in Lower Michigan and northern Wisconsin. North of our region, in a more subarctic type of forest, this species is found more generally on upland sites in almost any type of habitat. In the far North, as elsewhere, it roots in moss and litter with its frequent companions, twinflower, blunt-leaf orchid, large round-leaved orchid, and dwarf bishop's-cap. Since it can survive in very dense shade, it frequently has no companions when it grows in the dark wells at the bases of trees.

Hybrids. At times this orchid grows with all other species of its genus. It often intergrades with the tesselated rattlesnake plantain. The resulting hybrid populations become hopelessly confusing, especially in dried herbarium material. The center of this hybridization is in our region, particularly around northern Lakes Huron and Michigan, and around Lake Superior. The botanist is hard pressed to assign all specimens of this complex to a clear-cut taxonomic position, and some of these specimens cannot be readily taken through an identification key.

TESSELATED RATTLESNAKE PLANTAIN

Goodyera tesselata Lodd.   Plate 35D, 36D

Less common in most districts than its cogenitors, and more restricted in range, this orchid has also been the least understood. For nearly a century it was generally misidentified and assigned to one of the other three species. In the first edition of this book, I suggested that the reason for the confusion surrounding tesselated rattlesnake plantain was the frequent hybridization between this species and *G. repens* or *G. oblongifolia*. Recent studies by J. Kallunki (1976; 1981) not only substantiate my observations, but suggest a hybrid origin for this species.

Habit. Basal rosettes from a creeping rhizome, but less prone to branching and somewhat less clump-forming than the other species. Leaves variable, but in most typical material oblong-lanceolate, at least twice as long as broad; widest below middle, broadly petiolate below, 2–8 cm long, 1–2.5 cm wide, distinctly bluish green and with a faint bloom in most forms; faintly to heavily reticulated and tesselated above, with light greenish white lines along veins and cross veins; tesselations densest near margins. Scape erect, 15–35 cm tall, according to Correll averaging

197

20 cm. Raceme somewhat one-sided, but occasionally spiraled or cylindrical. Floral bracts lanceolate-acuminate, 10–12 mm long. Flowers white to greenish white, sepals pubescent on outer surface. Sepals and petals 5–6 mm long, sepals 2.5–3.5 mm wide. Dorsal sepal recurved at apex. Petals 2–3 mm wide, connivent with dorsal sepal into a hood. Lip saccate, sac about 2 mm deep, prolonged into a short beak curved slightly downward; lip about 5–7 mm long, 3–4 mm wide.

Season. July, early August. In a given locality, generally flowers with or ahead of the first *G. repens* and is usually through flowering before *G. oblongifolia* begins to bloom.

General Distribution. Newfoundland, Nova Scotia, west through Ontario to Minnesota, southward through northern Wisconsin, central Lower Michigan, New York, northern Pennsylvania, and New England. Disjunct stations occur in atypical habitats in Maryland.

Habitat. Prefers dryish, upland coniferous woods, mainly spruce-balsam or dry, white cedar thickets, hemlock groves, or mixed woodland. On the north shore of Lake Superior, may grow in almost any mixed birch-aspen-conifer forest. Also grows occasionally in conifer swamp borders, in bogs on islands of drier soil, or rarely, in sphagnum. In northern Michigan, occasionally grows in moist, acid depressions in predominantly hardwood forests where there may be considerable early spring flooding at the surface, and where superficial beds of sphagnum (especially *S. squarrosum*) lace the leaf mold and litter. Common companion plants are twinflower, lesser rattlesnake plantain, pinesap, *Vaccinium* spp., and pink lady's-slipper.

Hybrids and Origin. There has been a long history of confusion concerning this species. Prior to 1899 authors of floras omitted this taxon and included specimens of it under one of the other species, even though it had been described by Loddiges in 1824 (Kallunki 1976). In 1899 Fernald recognized Loddiges' species.

Fuller (1933a) suggested that *G. tesselata* was nothing more than the hybrid population of crosses between *G. repens* var. *ophioides* and *G. oblongifolia.* Indeed, *G. tesselata* resembles an intermediate between these two species in both growth habit and floral structure. In many colonies where it grows with one or both of the parents, plants which represent direct hybrids, back-crosses, and genetic segregates of varying degrees of intermediacy all occur. Such populations obviously confuse naturalists.

In the 1964 edition of this book, I speculated that *G. tesselata* might have arisen as the fertile tetraploid of the hybrid between *G. repens* and *G. oblongifolia.* Kallunki (1976) studied the situation in the Great Lakes region where the most confusing forms of *Goodyera* are found. She presents strong geographic, mor-

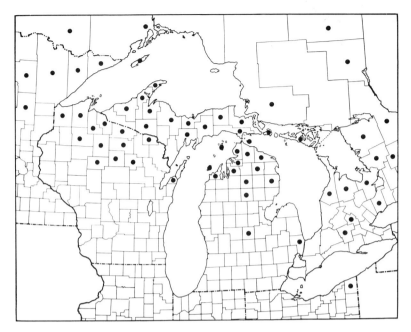

52. *Goodyera tesselata*

phological, cytological, and chromatographic evidence that *G. tesselata*, a tetraploid species (n=60), did arise from the hybridization of the diploid Menzies' and lesser rattlesnake plantains through allotetraploidy of the hybrids. She has also found triploid individuals, which suggest that hybridization between this species and its parental species still occurs.

Almost certainly tesselated rattlesnake plantain is of recent hybrid origin, and has attained species status through chromosomal doubling. It not only grows with its putative parents over much of its range, but has extended its range into regions where neither parent occurs today. *Goodyera tesselata* grows abundantly along the northern shore of Lake Superior, and is particularly common along the "Orchid Trail" up Mt. St. Albert, Gaspesian Provincial Park, Gaspé Peninsula, Quebec, Canada, east of our region.

MALAXIS Soland.

Like the closely related false twayblades, the adder's-mouths are not showy. They do, however, challenge the field botanist because of their small size and relative rarity. *Malaxis* is a genus of terrestrial herbs which rise from a more or less swollen or cormoid base. Except in one of our species, the stem bears only one leaf, near the center. Some species from outside our region have more leaves. The terminal inflorescence, composed of numerous, tiny flowers, may be elongated or headlike. The sepals are small, linear to lanceolate, and spreading. The sessile lip is entire, lobed or toothed at the apex, and more or less thickened. The short column bears a terminal anther with four waxy pollinia. The seed capsules are small and ovoid. This large genus numbers about 250 species, of which the three growing in the Great Lakes region may be distinguished by means of the following key.

Key to *Malaxis*

A. Leaves 2–3 or more, basal, clustered about corm, usually under 2 cm long on flowering plants. Lip less than 2 mm long. Entire plant slender and inconspicuous.

M. paludosa
page 202

AA. Leaves 1 (or 2 in atypical plants), prominent, borne well above corm and appearing attached near middle of flowering stem, but rising lower and clasping stem. Lip 2 mm long or more.

B. Lip 3-lobed, acuminate at tip, flowers in a loose, elongate, spicate raceme, pedicels short.

M. monophylla var. *brachypoda*
page 201

BB. Lip tridentate at apex, flowers in a dense raceme. Pedicels of older flowers elongating to place them with younger blooms and buds in a dense, somewhat flat-topped head.

M. unifolia
page 204

Malaxis monophylla (L.) Sw.   Plate 37A
   var. *brachypoda* (A. Gray) Morris and Eames

The white adder's-mouth has one of the tiniest blossoms found among orchids. The entire plant, small, shiny green, and hidden in moss or among bog vegetation, may be easily overlooked by even the diligent orchid searcher.

Habit. Plant generally small, rising from an ovoid basal corm which is often anchored on the surface of moss or conifer leaf rubble; pale green, glossy, with scape 5–15 cm tall; some much smaller or larger. Corms of previous year often persist. Leaf 1 in our form, occasionally 2 in typical form; broad, ovate to elliptic in older plants, sometimes linear in very young flowering plants, 1.5–10 cm long, 1–5 cm wide. Raceme extremely slender, elongate, many-flowered, flowers often remote. Floral bracts tiny, 1 mm long. Sepals linear-oblong, acuminate, 2 mm long, up to 1 mm wide. Petals linear, acute, 1.5 mm long, threadlike. Lip lowermost in our variety (uppermost in typical forms from Europe or western America), vaguely triangular, 3-lobed to auriculate, the small lateral lobes inrolled, 2–2.5 mm long, 1–2 mm wide. Basal sides of lip rough-thickened.

Season. Mid-June to August; variable even within the same colony.

General Distribution. Newfoundland, Labrador, and Quebec south through New England to New York and Pennsylvania, westward through the Great Lakes region to Minnesota and Manitoba. Correll ascribes this form to California and Japan. Typical *M. monophylla* occurs in Alaska and the Aleutians as well as throughout Europe and Asia.

Habitat. Always local or spotty. Inhabits cold, wet soils, mainly neutral in reaction and usually shaded. Most often found in cedar-balsam-spruce swamps over marly soils, where it grows in moss or among sedges. The simplest way to locate this diminutive plant for the first time is to search in the very wettest deer trails or rabbit runs, or in very wet wells about the roots of old cedars for it thrives in such situations. Plants scattered, seldom in clumps. Occasionally found in hardwood borders of conifer swamps, if margin is sufficiently wet, and along streams or on margins of mossy springs. In the North, dry evergreen woods, wet sandstone ledges, and damp cliff crevices all harbor a few of these orchids.

In essence the plant is small, nonaggressive, and noncompetitive. Within the limits of its soil and temperature requirements, it grows in a variety of habitats. Although it occurs in many

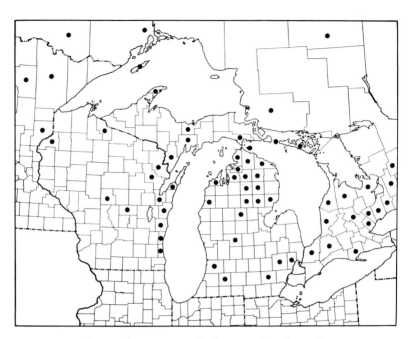

53. *Malaxis monophylla* var. *brachypoda*

sphagnous-acid situations, it does not grow in strongly acid soil, but rather in pockets or "microhabitats" of neutral reaction.

BOG ADDER'S-MOUTH

Malaxis paludosa (L.) Sw.   Plate 37B

Regarded by many botanists as one of the rarest plants in the North American flora, this orchid has recently been found in several places in northern Canada and Minnesota and may prove to be more overlooked than rare. The field botanist exploring bogs in the western Lake Superior region should keep an alert watch for it, since suitable habitat occurs throughout this region. While similarity of habitat or geological history does not ensure the presence of a plant, the orchid hunter should bear in mind that *Malaxis paludosa* does grow in adjacent areas and that it is exceedingly inconspicuous. Some idea of its tiny size is given by the fact that I once found a clump of 14 blooming plants occupying an area smaller than a 25-cent piece! Thus, this orchid offers the field naturalist a real chance of discovery and a chance to further our knowledge of plant geography.

Habit. Very slender, 4–20 cm tall, usually not over 10 cm, from a tiny, oval corm. As with all its group, old corms of the previous

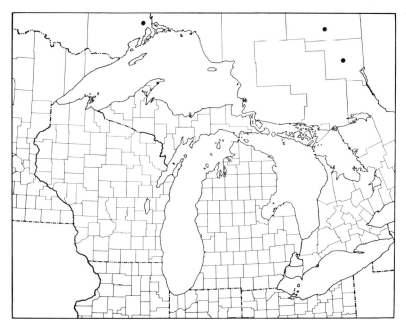

54. *Malaxis paludosa*

season often persist. Leaves several, some rising from below the corm, some from above; lowermost leaves sheathing and sometimes scalelike, most often 2–5 in number, with only 2 large and well-developed. Largest leaves 5–12 mm long, occasionally twice as long; 3–10 mm wide, and producing tiny, bulbil-like excrescences at apex which are said to reproduce the plant vegetatively. Scape very slender, raceme long. Floral bracts tiny, linear, appressed to pedicel and ovary. Flowers 15–30, yellowish green to white, *nonresupinate* (with lip uppermost) by a double twist of ovary and pedicel instead of no twist at all. Sepals ovate-elliptic, 2 mm long, 1 mm wide, spreading. Petals ovate to lanceolate, acute and reflexed, 1–1.5 mm long, less than half as wide. Lip uppermost, triangular, apiculate, somewhat dilated at base, 1–1.5 mm long, up to 1 mm wide.

Season. July, August.

General Distribution. Eurasia, where it is frequent in northern bogs; North America, exceedingly rare; local in Lake Itasca area of Minnesota, Thunder Cape area of Sibley Peninsula, Lake Superior, the northern Ontario clay belt and the Sudbury district, Alberta, and Alaska. I have collected specimens at the Liard Hot Springs along the Alaska Highway, near the British Columbia-Yukon border.

Habitat. Openings in bogs, muskegs, and fens, usually in black spruce-balsam fir-cedar cover. Frequently grows in very wet, turfy spots of moss (rarely sphagnum). It is normally a sun lover, but on the Sibley Peninsula of Lake Superior and in the Minnesota stations it sometimes grows down in dark, mossy wells in deep shade, as well as in open spots.

GREEN ADDER'S-MOUTH, GREEN MALAXIS

Malaxis unifolia Michx.   Plate 37C

Like many of its kin, this orchid is widespread but inconspicuous.

Habit. Variable, 6–20 cm tall, rarely taller, bluish green throughout, smooth, leaves often dull. Stem rising from a basal, oval to spherical corm, which is often at the surface. Leaf sheathing stem for nearly half its length and rising from scalelike tubular sheaths below; abruptly flaring, ovate-cordate to ovate-lanceolate, 2–9 cm long, up to 6 cm wide; veins and cross veins often darker green, so that leaves appear faintly reticulated. Raceme elongate in lower part, congested and restricted above, so that upper part of inflorescence forms an umbel-like head. Floral bracts minute, awl-shaped. Flowers small, rich green; pedicellate ovaries threadlike, relatively long (in marked contrast to the other two species of *Malaxis* in our region), 3–10 mm. Sepals spreading, linear-oblong, 1–3 mm long, 1 mm wide, often somewhat rolled. Petals threadlike, recurved, up to 3 mm long. Lip at first uppermost, becoming lowermost at maturity. Lip variable, triangular to cordate, tridentate at apex, middle tooth smallest, lip 2–4 mm long and wide.

Season. Late June to August.

General Distribution. Forested regions of eastern North America from Newfoundland and Nova Scotia to northern Florida, Texas, Mexico, Guatemala, and Cuba. Frequent but local in the Great Lakes region.

Habitat. Like many other orchids whose main soil requirements are acidity and relative sterility, this orchid can occupy many habitats. In the northern Lakes states it grows most frequently in sphagnous areas of wooded swamps, either in the sphagnum moss itself or in resinous crumble of conifer needles, or on rotting logs. Usually grows alone or in scattered colonies, but may, at times, form clumps. Occasionally found growing in moist, acid, sandy humus of hillsides and pastures, often near rotting pine stumps or under bracken ferns. Southward, this type of habitat seems to be preferred.

Though the green and the white adder's-mouth orchids may occur in the same swamp, they differ in soil requirements. When

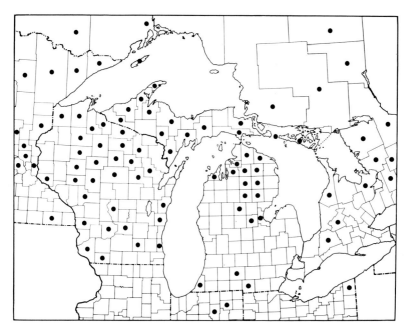

55. *Malaxis unifolia*

growing in proximity, the white adder's-mouth grows in very wet pockets of muck or moss of neutral reaction, while the green adder's-mouth grows elevated in sphagnum or on dryish stumps and logs where the reaction is acid.

LIPARIS L. C. M. Rich.

Liparis, the false twayblades, a large and widely distributed genus, contains about 260 species, three of which grow in North America. The name, from the Greek, means "greasy" or "fat" and alludes to the appearance of the shiny leaves. Members of this genus are usually terrestrial herbs rising from a corm and bearing one to several fleshy or plicate leaves. The inflorescence is a raceme of relatively insignificant flowers composed of oblong-lanceolate sepals and filiform petals. The lip is arcuate-recurved and attached to the base of the column. The strongly incurved, winged column bears a terminal anther having four waxy pollinia. In old plants the corm often lies exposed on the surface of the soil among the remnants of corms of previous seasons. The genus is closely allied to *Malaxis*. Two species growing in the Great Lakes region may be distinguished by the following key.

Key to *Liparis*

A. Flower pedicel and ovary together 3–6 mm long. Lip 4–5 mm long, green or yellowish. Plants of wet meadows, bogs, or ditch banks.

L. loeselii

page 208

AA. Flower pedicel and ovary together 1 cm or more long. Lip large, 10–15 mm long, madder-purple or liver-brown, thin and translucent. Plant of upland thicket and forest.

L. lilifolia

page 206

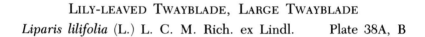

LILY-LEAVED TWAYBLADE, LARGE TWAYBLADE
Liparis lilifolia (L.) L. C. M. Rich. ex Lindl.   Plate 38A, B

A rare plant in parts of the Great Lakes region and absent from the northern portions, this orchid becomes more common southward. While not conspicuous or beautiful, its charm of proportion and habit makes it a favorite with those who know it. There is considerable evidence that it actively invades many areas before the heavy timber develops. It may help in understanding its ecology to cite its behavior in two such instances.

After seeking this orchid in Michigan for many years, my success finally came as a surprise. A casual examination of a moist thicket of willows and seedling cottonwoods on my own property revealed about a dozen large plants growing at the bases of silky cornel and red-osier dogwood. This area had been plowed and planted with crops 15 years earlier, and the orchid was obviously a newcomer.

Dr. J. T. Curtis reported a similar and more spectacular occurrence at the University of Wisconsin Arboretum. For many years a few plants of *L. lilifolia* were known to occur in a mature forest at the arboretum. A few years after a small area was worked and planted to young pines, plants of this species began to appear in the developing pine plantation. The population grew until there were several thousand plants. As the pines grew and dense shade developed, the number of orchids decreased. Dur-

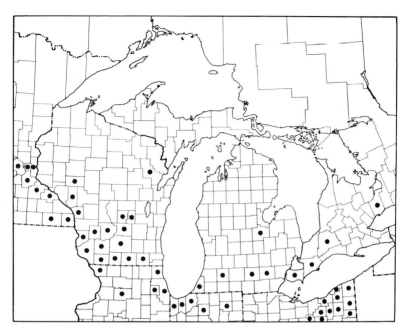

56. *Liparis lilifolia*

ing this time the old colonies in the mature hardwoods showed almost no fluctuation. Thus, it appears that this orchid, which invades a particular habitat at an early stage of development, is sufficiently tolerant of shade to persist long after its active invasion ceases.

Since the first edition of this book, an interesting new pattern of growth for the lily-leaved twayblade has appeared. In several instances in southern Michigan, enormous colonies have developed in plantations of Norway spruce (*Picea abies*) or more rarely in plantings of Scots pine (*Pinus sylvestis*). In all instances the plantations were on a continuously damp, somewhat sandy soil. These large populations frequently prove to be of short duration, primarily because larger, more aggressive plants shade them out. Mice and voles present another hazard to the plants since they frequently eat the fleshy dormant corms.

Habit. Plant rising from a bulbous corm which, in old plants, develops at or upon the surface; corm with a few fleshy-fibrous roots below. Leaves 2, practically basal, sleek, fleshy, ovate-elliptic, subacute, close-sheathing stem below, wide flaring in upper portion, keeled, 4–15 cm long, 2–6 cm wide. Flower scape angled, faintly winged, up to 15 cm tall. Raceme 4–12 cm long, 4- to many-flowered; floral bracts minute, 2 mm long. Pedicellate ovaries 15 mm long, slender. Sepals greenish white to brown, translucent, narrowly lanceolate, 1 cm long. Petals madder-purple to liver-brown, linear to threadlike, 10–12 mm long. Lip by contrast very large and conspicuous, obovate to suborbicular, abruptly mucronate at apex, translucent, madder-purple to liver-brown, often fading with age, 10–13 mm long, 8–10 mm wide. Column club-shaped, incurved, 3 mm long. Capsules ellipsoid, 15 mm long, erect.

Season. Early to late June. Raceme expanding gradually with additional flowers opening in succession over a long period.

General Distribution. Northern New England, New York to upland regions of Georgia and Alabama, west to Arkansas and Missouri. Westward across Central states to Iowa, southern Wisconsin and Minnesota. Recently discovered in southern Ontario and central Michigan.

Habitat. Prefers sandy, subacid humus in mixed deciduous forest or brushy thickets, often growing on banks. Occasionally grows in floodplain woods, but more often in upland areas of maple and oak, if the soil is reasonably moist. In Michigan, at least, large populations occasionally appear in Norway spruce (*Picea abies*) plantations of moist, sandy soils. In the southern United States, this plant occurs in almost any type of upland habitat.

LOESEL'S TWAYBLADE, FEN ORCHID

Liparis loeselii (L.) L. C. M. Rich.   Plate 37D, 38C, D

Though actually rather common, this orchid so often grows inconspicuously among sedges or tangled vegetation that it is frequently overlooked. Its uniform yellow-green color and small size in exposed habitats further serve to conceal the plant.

Habit. Leaves from a bulbous corm, with a very few slender-fleshy roots below; corm of previous season usually persists and appears as a leafless offshoot. Leaves 2, virtually basal, sheathing new-forming corm, oblong to oblong-lanceolate, often widest just above middle, subacute, light yellowish green, keeled below, 2–20 cm long, 1–9 cm wide. Leaf size dependent on age and vigor, plus degree of exposure; plants in very open situations with reduced leaves. Scape 4–25 cm tall, mostly 10–14 cm, raceme 1- to many-flowered, lax to dense. Floral bracts minute, 1–2 mm long. Flowers yellowish green, fading to greenish white. Pedicels and ovaries together, 3–6 mm long. Sepals and petals linear, 5–6 mm long, greenish, 1–2 mm wide, petals narrower and slightly shorter than sepals. Sepals and petals wide-spreading, slightly reflexed. Lip somewhat cuneate-orbicular to obovate, arcuate-recurved; thus lateral margins are in a plane above median portion of lip, apiculate. Floor of lip with 5 prominent veins.

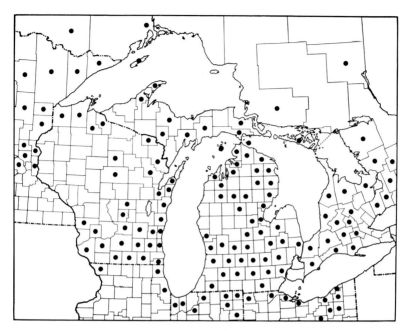

57. *Liparis loeselii*

Column stout, 2 mm long. Capsule ellipsoid, 1 cm long.

Season. June–August. Blooms much later in cold bogs or shade than in meadow or lake shore situations.

General Distribution. Nova Scotia, Quebec, and Ontario to Minnesota and Manitoba, south through Lakes states to mountains of North Carolina and Alabama. Locally reported from Dakotas and Washington. Also found in Europe.

Habitat. Grows in a wide variety of situations, including deep sphagnum bogs, sedge mats on lake bogs, marly lake shores, damp meadows, and ditch banks. Its main requirements seem to be rather sterile, moist situations where there is little competition from other vegetation. In bogs, it grows in pathways and deer trails more frequently than with larger vegetation. Often grows at the edge of open water, sticking out into the sunlight from clumps of grass. It can tolerate considerable shade. It is difficult to give indicator plants for this cosmopolitan orchid.

The most unusual colony I have seen—with dozens of plants—grew in the cracks of upright logs in an old dock piling at a northern Michigan lake. The plant, invasive in wet, sandy meadows, will spread for a time, and then, as sod develops, gradually disappear. In the central Michigan area, old postglacial lake sand bars are excavated for foundry core sand. These old sand pits, often damp or with a trickle of stream, offer fine habitat for Loesel's twayblade, and these plants often line the tiny water courses.

TIPULARIA Nutt.

Named for the crane-flies of the genus *Tipula*, orchids of this genus emulate their namesakes. The asymmetrical, tawny, inconspicuous blooms look for all the world like a small cloud of crane-flies hovering above the forest floor. *Tipularia* is a genus of about three species, one of eastern America, the others of Asia. The description of the American species will serve for the genus.

CRANE-FLY ORCHID

Tipularia discolor (Pursh) Nutt.   Plate 39A, B, C

This orchid has a wide distribution in the deciduous forests of the southern and eastern United States, but it barely enters our region. Even where it is common, it is so inconspicuous and the blooms are so sparse that few detect its presence.

Habit. Leaf solitary, from a whitish corm and a few fleshy roots, produced in the fall, lasting until late spring; ovate-elliptic to cordate, acuminate, strongly ribbed and wrinkled, dark green, often with brownish rust spots above, deep purple below, 5–10 cm long, 3–8 cm wide. Spike produced in midsummer; scape erect, 10–70 cm tall, many-flowered, very slender. Flowers greenish tan to purplish, on pedicellate ovaries about 1 cm long. Sepals oblong, obtuse, 5–8 mm long, 1.5–3 mm wide. Petals narrowly linear-oblong or spatulate, 6 mm long, 1–1.5 mm wide. Lip 3-lobed, prolonged backward into a long, slender spur; 5–8 mm long, up to 3 mm wide; spur 1.5–2 cm long. Central lobe of lip much larger than lateral lobes, tongue-shaped and slightly expanded at tip. Column 3 mm long.

Season. July–September

General Distribution. New York and Massachusetts south to the Gulf of Mexico; north Florida to Texas, abundant locally along the Appalachian Mountains, Piedmont and Cumberland Plateaus, Arkansas, locally northward to central Indiana (Bloomington, *fide* Case) and eastern Ohio. Disjunct colonies in Berrien County, Michigan, known since about 1972. W. J. Beal's *Michigan Flora* cites a J. Macoun report of the species from the "eastern coast of Lake Huron," but no specimens have been reported from Lake Huron by others. Whether Macoun misstated the locality or

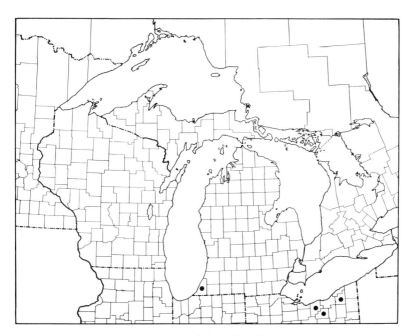

58. *Tipularia discolor*

whether he actually found the plant on the Ontario shore of Lake Huron is not known. Favorable habitat for *Tipularia* is rather extensive near Port Huron, Michigan, and along the Michigan shore of Lake Huron south of the limestone districts of the Thumb, and is present on the Ontario shore. Macoun was a most astute botanist and observer.

Habitat. Mostly in beech groves or rich, mixed deciduous tree cover; occasionally in brushy oak woods. Usually grows at the base of a slope or on flats along a stream. Prefers deep leaf mold. More adaptable southward, it occurs there in a wider variety of wooded cover. At DeSoto Falls State Park, Alabama, I found it growing abundantly on sandstone ledges under rhododendron and laurel.

Tipularia discolor was discovered almost simultaneously in Michigan in two different Berrien County localities by William Schwab and Victor Soukup, respectively. A third colony also grows in Berrien County. I have observed one of these colonies for a period of 10 years. The population has decreased from about 500 plants to about 50. The area is subject to considerable disturbance; foot traffic, motorcycles, and digging for worms. It is not clear whether the orchid colony declined naturally or whether the decline is due to physical damage or habitat deterioration.

CALYPSO Salisbury

Botanists currently recognize only one species in this genus which takes its name from the sea nymph in Homer's *Odyssey*. However, at least one western American form differs from the other American forms in markings, proportion in details of the lip structures, and some features of physiology. Whether these differences constitute a subspecific difference or are inconsequential awaits further study. Regardless of technical differences, all have great beauty. Calypso occurs locally across all boreal North America, Europe, and Asia. Since *Calypso* is monotypic, the species description also serves for the genus.

CALYPSO, FAIRY SLIPPER, DEER'S-HEAD ORCHID

Calypso bulbosa (L.) Oakes   Plate 40A

No other northern orchid has so captured the imagination of flower lovers as calypso! Its intricate and exotic beauty and early blooming date, the cool, mossy enchanted quality of its environs, and its rarity near any populated area add up to romance and adventure for those who search for it.

Habit. Height variable, even at same locality. Leaf solitary, basal, rising from summit of a globose corm, distinctly free from flower scape; 1–6 cm long, 2–5 cm wide; cordate, ovate or semi-orbicular, prominently ribbed, somewhat plicate, dark green, produced in fall, withering after anthesis. Scape 6–20 cm tall, averaging 10–12 cm, produced from a bud on corm of previous summer, sheathed below by 2–3 semitransparent, tubular sheaths, purplish, with a faint bloom. Floral bract lanceolate, 7–20 mm long. Flowers solitary, showy, somewhat pendent; pedicellate ovary 1.5–2 cm long. Sepals and petals much alike, lanceolate to linear-oblong, 1–2 cm long, 3–5 mm wide, spreading, pinkish purple to white, turning to salmon-coffee colored about one day before withering. Lip slipper-shaped, 1.5–2.5 cm long, 7–12 mm wide; lip-sac expanded and folded forward into a white apron, with margins slightly uprolled. Base of apron bearded with yellow or brown spotted hairs. Lip below apron prolonged into a 2-toed apex, lavender or yellowish, strongly marked with rust-red to golden-brown lines and spots. Column lavender, large and spreading, semiorbicular, convex, and filling lip orifice; 7–10 mm long and wide. Capsule becoming erect, cylindrical and strongly ribbed, 2 cm long. Capsules rarely produced in Great Lakes region, much more commonly in western mountains.

Season. Early May to early July. In northern Lower Michigan, blooms in last week of May or earlier. Later dates cited are for islandic stations and promontories of Lake Superior. One of the first plants to bloom in some of its habitats, it has even been seen in flower near old, dwindling snowbanks.

General Distribution. In spruce and other cold, coniferous forests in entire Northern Hemisphere, but local everywhere. Southward in higher elevations of Rocky Mountains and Sierras, it reaches California and Arizona. In the East, occurs southward to northern portions of Minnesota, Wisconsin, Michigan, and Ontario, and in northern New England.

Habitat. Found in cool soils only. Grows in old, undisturbed, heavily wooded spruce-balsam-cedar swamps, or in evergreen woods along Great Lakes shores. In bogs, it may be found on small "islands" of drier soil, or up around the bases or sides of stumps. It does not grow in soggy soils or in sphagnum moss, though such conditions may occur only a few feet away. Commonly grows with twinflower, lesser rattlesnake plantain, and striped coral-root. Prefers shade, but does not choose the darkest areas of old cedar swamps.

In our region the largest colonies of calypso grow in rather dry cedar and fir thickets along the shores of the Upper Great Lakes, especially in limestone areas. Here, among mosses, mats of twin-flower, or old cedar and balsam needles, scattered plants and sometimes large clumps may be found. It is not a plant of open situations in our region, although it may be in the far North.

Truly a beautiful plant when robust, calypso is quite variable, and some plants are not impressive. The eastern plant seems less aggressive than its western counterpart, for it grows mostly as scattered individual plants, with few seedlings in evidence. Those who have attempted the culture of the eastern form have met with complete failure under garden conditions. The western form— aggressive, often carpeting fir glades, pine woods, and even aspen woods on mountain slopes—is more tractable, and survives for several years under the care of expert gardeners.

A distressing situation has developed in Michigan in relation to calypso. So many photographers, all nature lovers, visit known stations in our state parks to observe and photograph the species that the plant colonies have suffered. Not only do the plants get trampled, but competitive photographers are reported to destroy especially fine clumps after they have photographed them, so that no other photographer can picture the same clump. Roberta Case and I observed one photographer carefully cutting out the discolored, salmon-coffee tinted flowers from his clump. These happened to be the pollinated flowers so vital to the continuance of

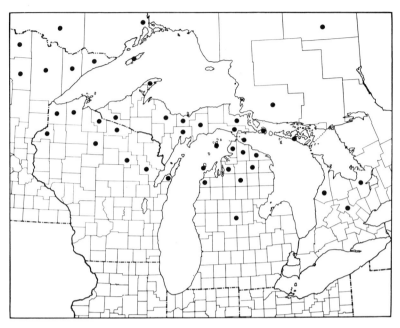

59. *Calypso bulbosa*

calypso in a given locale. For calypso, although perennial, grows in our region mainly on rotting logs and in litter which is, itself, of short duration. Given plants do not persist long owing to the transitory nature of their growing sites. Continual reseeding is vital to the continuation of a station.

This was clearly shown in one of the few remaining inland stations for *Calypso* in northern Lower Michigan, a large cedar swamp along a trout stream. Here, we had the chance to observe a colony of these orchids for about 20 years. Numbers of flowering calypsos have varied from over 75 to as few as 23. Most of the plants grew on logs or cradled in beds of cedar-leaf crumble on raised stumps and roots. At the time of our discovery of the station, we carefully marked all of the blooming plants we found. Marked individuals have appeared and bloomed for up to five seasons, although this was the exception. Two or three vigorous seasons followed by a decline was the more typical pattern. The deterioration of a given plant or clump seemed to coincide directly with the decay and deterioration of its substrate log or stump, or with an overgrowth of mosses, herbs, or seedling balsam-fir (*Abies*).

APLECTRUM Nuttall

The genus *Aplectrum* has only one species in America, and thus the species description will serve for the genus. This orchid grows almost throughout the eastern deciduous forests.

PUTTY-ROOT, ADAM-AND-EVE

Aplectrum hyemale Torr.   Plate 41A, B, C

Frequent in the southern part of our region, this orchid is neither large nor conspicuous. Thus, it is probably more frequent than botanical records show, but is often overlooked.

Habit. Smooth, scapose, 20–50 cm tall, lower part of scape enclosed in 2–3 scarious, membranous sheaths. Scape terminated by a loose raceme of 3–20 flowers. Flowers each subtended by a small (3–6 mm) awl-shaped bract. Sepals and petals yellowish green, often madder-streaked. Lip white to yellowish, 3-crested, cuneate, 3-lobed, central lobe much the largest, 1–1.2 cm long. Sepals oblong to oblong-spatulate, 1–1.5 cm long, 3–4 mm wide. Petals obtuse-spatulate, 1–1.2 cm long, 2–3.5 mm wide. Capsules prominent, spindle-shaped, 2 cm long, prominently ribbed, pendent. Leaf solitary, basal, developing in autumn, disappearing at flowering, strongly white-ribbed above, dark greenish purple below, 10–20 cm long, 4–8 cm wide or wider. Entire plant produced from a globular, underground corm, with fleshy-fibrous roots below. A new corm is produced by means of a stolon each year; old corms persist for several years, hence a series of corms will be present.

Season. May, early June, over most of its range.

General Distribution. Southern Quebec and southern Ontario through central Michigan to Minnesota, south throughout deciduous forest belt to Georgia, Alabama, and Arkansas.

Habitat. In rich deciduous forests, especially those of beech and sugar maple. Its favorite site is a pocket of deep humus on the edge of a "cradle hole" created by the uprooting of some ancient tree, or the edge of the crumbling remains of an old log pile. It often grows under spicebush in flat, moist areas not far above the level of temporary ponds. When growing in the mellow mold of rotten log piles, it often produces coralloid rather than cormose roots, suggesting a strong tendency to a saprophytic habit.

It produces only a few flower spikes per colony in any season. This habit, in addition to the withering of the leaves in late spring, renders it uncommonly difficult to detect. It is easiest to locate

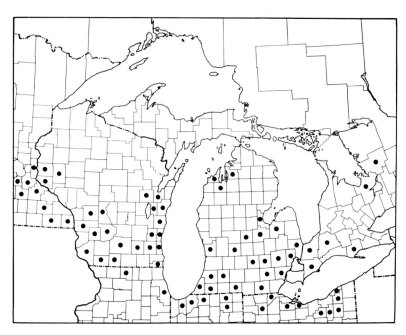

60. *Aplectrum hyemale*

in late autumn, or during a snowless period in late winter, when the solitary, wrinkled green leaves are more conspicuous in contrast to the dead leaves of the forest floor.

An "albino" form with clear apple green sepals and petals dominates one large southwestern Michigan colony (see Plate 41D). This color variant has been named forma *pallidum* House.

Putty-root is one of the easier orchids to cultivate, and may be grown in a shaded bed of woods soil or sandy leaf mold. It is often damaged by slugs and snails, both in the wild and in the garden.

CORALLORHIZA [Haller] Chatelain

Corallorhiza, according to Correll a small genus of about 12 species, is almost exclusively American. Only *C. trifida*, the early coral-root, grows in Eurasia. Plants of this genus are saprophytic in nature. They derive their nourishment either from dead organic matter in the soil or through indirect nourishment from living plants with the aid of an intermediate soil fungus. Their food relationships are poorly understood and are just now being untangled. While these plants do not produce significant amounts of chlorophyll, some species are rich in other coloring matter. Few native orchids are more attractive than the striped coral-root.

Coral-roots are scapose, with the leaves reduced to thin, tubular sheaths. The flowers, borne in a raceme, may be small and inconspicuous or relatively large and showy. Structurally the group is distinguished by the joined bases of the lateral sepals, by the drawing of the base of the lip into a spurlike process slightly attached to the base of the column, and by their saprophytic habit. Coral-roots are essentially rootless. The root function is carried out by many-branched, underground rhizomes which give the group their common and scientific names. Four species, one with a complex of rather distinctive taxa, grow in the Great Lakes region. They may be distinguished by the following key.

Key to *Corallorhiza*

A. Lip with distinct lobes or teeth at sides.

B. Lateral sepals 3-nerved, plants large, 1.5 dm or more tall, blooming late spring to fall, mostly in upland woods or coniferous forest.

C. Sepals and petals brownish or madder-purple, lip white, purple spotted. Stem reddish purple to brown.

C. maculata
complex and its varieties
f. *intermedia*
f. *punicea*
page 219

late type

CC. Stem, sepals, and petals yellowish or light greenish yellow, lip white, immaculate.

C. maculata
f. *flavida*
page 219

early type

BB. Lateral sepals 1-nerved, plants usually small, 1.5 dm tall or less; blooming early spring to early summer, mostly in bogs or swamps, or boreal coniferous forests.

C. trifida
page 225

217

AA. Lip without teeth or lobes, or with only obscure, vestigial, poorly developed teeth or lobes present on occasional specimens.

  B. Flowers cleistogamous or autogamous, with floral segments underdeveloped, failing to expand. Ovaries well developed by time plant reaches full size.

C. odontorhiza
page 222

  BB. Flowers of normal type (chasmogamous), segments developed and flowers expanding normally, ovaries small and undeveloped until pollinated.

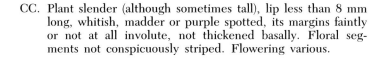

    C. Plant stout, lip 8–16 mm long, sharply down-curved or pendent, its margins involute (boat-shaped), and basally thickened, heavily striped or solid red-purple; sepals and petals striped, widely spreading. Flowering spring to early summer.

C. striata
page 224

    CC. Plant slender (although sometimes tall), lip less than 8 mm long, whitish, madder or purple spotted, its margins faintly or not at all involute, not thickened basally. Floral segments not conspicuously striped. Flowering various.

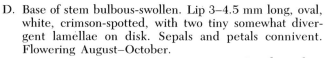

      D. Base of stem bulbous-swollen. Lip 3–4.5 mm long, oval, white, crimson-spotted, with two tiny somewhat divergent lamellae on disk. Sepals and petals connivent. Flowering August–October.

C. odontorhiza
page 222

      DD. Base of stem only slightly thickened. Lip 4–6 mm long, ovate, weakly cupped, its margins raised or very weakly involute, erose-denticulate or undulate; disk with a pair of conspicuous linear lamellae; lip arcuate-curved beyond the claw giving the flower a raised, gaping quality. Flowering early spring to early summer.

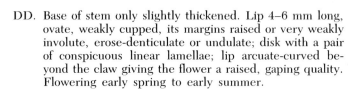

C. wisteriana
page 227

SPOTTED CORAL-ROOT, LARGE CORAL-ROOT

Corallorhiza maculata (Raf.) Raf.   Plate 42A, B, D

This widespread coral-root "species" has long been regarded as confusing and variable. Botanists have named many variants and many of these occur within our area. Several years ago, Don Henson brought to my attention some striking floral differences between populations in Michigan's Upper Peninsula. Ultimately, study of this puzzling complex was undertaken by John V. Freudenstein, then a student at the University of Michigan. In his senior honors thesis submitted to the Department of Botany faculty in April 1985, Freudenstein demonstrates that there are two distinct taxa currently treated as one species. Both have been named previously, indeed, several names in the botanical literature have been applied to the "early flowering taxon." Exactly which of these names carries botanical priority and must be applied to this taxon is the question currently under study. Until Freudenstein completes his studies for all of North America and the questions of nomenclature and taxonomic level have been resolved, I choose to treat both of his taxa as a single species complex within our region, while recognizing that the "species" represents two distinct taxa and a number of variants within one of them. The distribution map does not distinguish between the two taxa or their variations.

Following a general description which will serve for either taxon, I present in tabular form the distinguishing features of the "early flowering" and the "late flowering" spotted coral-roots as outlined by Freudenstein.

Habit. Stout to slender, erect; with leaves reduced to tubular sheaths, brownish, madder-purple or yellowish throughout, 10–80 cm tall. Raceme laxly to densely flowered, with floral bracts obscure. Flowers spreading, on rather stout pedicels in typical form. Sepals and petals purple-brown to clear yellow, spotted or unspotted, linear, 6–8 mm long, 1–2 mm wide, petals slightly smaller than sepals. Lip 3-lobed, central lobe much the largest, 5–8 mm long, 4–5 mm wide, central portion of lip with 2 narrow, longitudinal ridges (lamellae) in basal half, lateral lobes slightly inrolled and directed forward. Lip white, spotted with crimson in typical form. Capsules pendent, large, 1–2 cm long.

The two taxa commonly referred to as *C. maculata* or as the *C. maculata* complex consist of an early flowering taxon and a late flowering taxon. The type of *C. maculata* is presumed to be the late flowering form, hence this taxon correctly may be referred to as *C. maculata* (Raf.) Raf. Freudenstein found the following differences:

"Early Flowering" C. maculata	"Late Flowering" C. maculata
Lip, [particularly apex of middle lobe] dilated	Lip parallel-sided
Pedicellate ovary long, 8.6–13.0 mm	Pedicellate ovary relatively short, 7.2–9.4 mm long
Lip long	Lip short
Dorsal sepal long	Dorsal sepal short
Column 3.8–5.6 mm long	Column short, 3.0–4.6 mm long
Bracts 1 mm or longer, furcate	Bracts 1 mm or less, rounded
Mentum protrusion prominent	Mentum protrusion slight
Mentum sinus narrow, deep	Mentum sinus broad, shallow
Plants 18–40-flowered	Plants 10–20-flowered

The "early flowering" *C. maculata*, the most frequent form northward in our region, has a robust manner of growth, with stout, rather erect pedicels at anthesis, brownish overall coloring (or yellow in forma *flavida*), a rather dense inflorescence, a tendency to grow in clumps, and a preference for coniferous or mixed deciduous-coniferous forests.

The "late flowering" *C. maculata*, the only taxon known at the southern edge of our area (but occurring in the north as well), tends to a tall but slender manner of growth, a brownish tan coloring, fewer flowers displayed in a rather open inflorescence, groupings of one or two stems, or single stems, and occurs frequently in mature deciduous forests and woodlots southward. In the north of our region, it grows with the "early flowering" variety in a diversity of habitats, mostly dominated by conifers.

All of the named varieties described by various authors for our region belong (according to Freudenstein) to the "early flowering" *C. maculata* taxon. They are described in the section of this treatment designated "Forms."

Season. June, July, or August; variable.

General Distribution. Forested regions of eastern North America, from Newfoundland south to North Carolina, mainly in mountains southward. Locally common and widespread in various forms, through Lakes states and westward to Washington, Oregon, and thence southward in mountains and wooded canyons to Arizona and Mexico.

Habitat. Almost any type of mature mesophytic or coniferous woods, usually in dry soils of subacid reaction. The various forms and taxa show little preference for any particular vegetative cover.

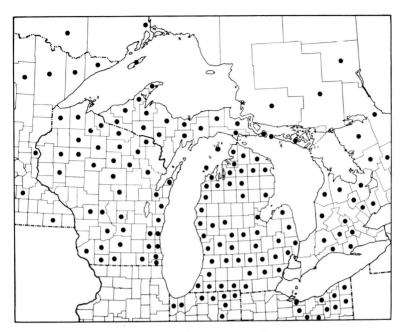

61. *Corallorhiza maculata*

Especially frequent in beech-sugar maple forests at the south of our region and in coniferous forests and lakeshore forests northward.

Forms. C. maculata f. *flavida* (Peck) Farwell (Plate 42C) differs little structurally from the typical form, but has clear yellow coloring throughout, except for the lip which is white and immaculate. Though not physically distinct, this form has peculiarities worth noting. It seems to be confined to sites only a few miles from the Great Lakes shores; it is rarely reported from inland stations. If this is an "albino", that is, an anthocyanin-free mutant, the color seems to confer an evolutionary advantage. In areas where this form occurs it often becomes one of the conspicuous plants of the understory, far outnumbering the typical form. Large colonies exist in the Lake Superior areas of Michigan and Minnesota. North of Duluth the plant is so abundant and forms such large clumps that it can readily be seen at a distance from a moving automobile, a feature few native orchids can claim.

The f. *intermedia* (Farw.) Farw. is an uncertain entity, mainly distinguished from other forms by its intermediate brownish color. It possibly represents only older specimens of other varieties.

The f. *punicea* (H. H. Bartlett) Weatherby and Adams shows some structural, color, and seasonal differences. It has pale sheaths and intensely dark reddish purple stems, sepals, and petals; the colors fade somewhat with age. There are fewer flowers, and they are more remotely spaced than in the typical form. The lip is white, crimson-spotted, and narrower than in the typical form. The entire plant is slender, with flowers at anthesis borne on an ascending, spreading, but not erect pedicel. It grows in hemlock groves and spruce-fir forests, and on drier islands in bogs, usually in very deep humus, and in situations tending to be more acid than where the typical form is found. It occurs in both the northern and central portions of our region. Detailed field studies, especially regarding changes in structure, color, or size occurring in individual plants as the season progresses, could throw light on the validity of the various forms.

In summary, *C. maculata* is a species complex represented in our area by two rather distinct taxa. One taxon is early flowering and occurs primarily in our northern, coniferous districts, while the other is late flowering and occurs throughout our area and to the south. Studies currently under way will surely illuminate the situation further.

AUTUMN CORAL-ROOT, FALL CORAL-ROOT

Corallorhiza odontorhiza (Willd.) Nutt.   Plate 43A, B

This species is rather rare and local in our region, and is also one of the least conspicuous of our orchids. Primarily a southern and Appalachian species, it is seldom seen in our region even when present, partly because it has little beauty or color to attract attention, and partly because few students of native plants visit in autumn the dense hardwoods it inhabits.

Two forms of this orchid occur. One is apparently self-fertilizing and cleistogamous. The ovaries are not only well developed at flowering, but each capsule also matures seed regularly, and wild populations are entirely uniform. The second form, far less common in our area in my experience, appears to be a normal, insect-pollinated plant. Its sepals and petals spread normally, its ovaries are not well developed at anthesis, and the lip is fully expanded. Although very inconspicuous, it is by far the most attractive of the two types.

Habit. Slender, 10–40 cm tall, usually under 20 cm; stems with characteristic tubular sheaths of the genus, brownish purple, *bulbously enlarged* at the base. Raceme rather lax, floral bracts minute, flowers small. Pedicels threadlike, ovaries inflated and well developed at anthesis. Sepals and petals are dark purple-brown, dorsal sepal linear-lanceolate, obtuse, 3–4 mm long, 1–

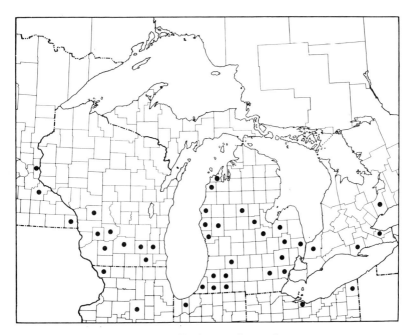

62. *Corallorhiza odontorhiza*

1.5 mm wide in larger flowers of raceme; lateral sepals linear, 3–5 mm long, 1 mm wide. Petals 3–4 mm long, 1 mm wide, clawed at base. Lip clawed, rounded to oval, erose along margins, white, magenta-streaked and -spotted, 3–4 mm long, 3–5 mm wide. Floor of lip with 2 divergent ridges or lamellae near base. All flower parts connivent (grouped together and not opening in typical fashion) in most plants of our region. Seed capsule ovoid.

Season. August and September.

General Distribution. Maine and Vermont south to Georgia, especially in mountains, westward to Mississippi in the South and through Ohio and Michigan to Wisconsin, Iowa, and Missouri. Rare or local in our region. A Central American plant may be this or a similar appearing species.

Habitat. Rich deciduous woods, mostly beech-sugar maple or mixed hardwood forests under oaks, where it grows in either dry or damp situations; occasionally in pine plantations in sandy soils. Distinctly a southern and eastern element in our flora; not reported to grow in northern Lakes areas, but has recently been found in northwestern Lower Michigan.

Corallorhiza striata Lindl.   Plate 43C, D

By far the most striking and attractive of the coral-roots, because of its rather large flowers and particularly its rich, red-madder coloring. The lip, when struck by sunlight, has been likened to the "glowing color of a fine ruby."

Habit. Somewhat stout, erect, 10–50 cm tall, reddish to madder-purple throughout when fresh, occasionally brownish when older, leafless. Stem with 3–4 slightly inflated sheaths of lighter color than stem. Raceme lax, few- to many-flowered. Floral bracts triangular, about 2 cm long. Sepals elliptic-oblong to lanceolate, obtuse at apex, conspicuously 3–5-nerved; nerves of a dark red-purple to madder, sepals 7–15 mm long, 3–5 mm wide. Petals linear-oblong to obovate-elliptic, rounded at apex, nerved like sepals, and slightly smaller. Lip entire, boat-shaped, pendent, 6–12 mm long, 8 mm wide, margins somewhat inrolled, and base with a bilobed callus. Lip base color whitish, but with dark, rich madder-purple veins, so broad and colored that they are confluent or cause lip to appear solid madder colored.

Season. Late May through June; occasional plants, but not whole populations, flower later.

General Distribution. Infrequent and local in Quebec, New Brunswick, and New York, westward through Ontario, northern Michigan, Wisconsin, Minnesota, Saskatchewan, Alberta, and British Columbia. Locally in western mountains of Wyoming, Colorado, Arizona, New Mexico, California, Washington, and Oregon. Known also, according to Correll, from Oklahoma and Mexico. Locally abundant in the Upper Great Lakes region, Oregon, and California.

Correll speculates that, since striped coral-root and also the Alaskan orchid (*Piperia unalascensis*) have somewhat the same distribution—widespread on the West Coast but in our region local and often occurring near water—they may owe their eastern distribution to accidental seed transport by waterfowl. While both species do grow near water, neither one grows in habitats regularly visited by waterfowl. Their chosen environment is rather dry brushlands or woods over limestone pavements. Both are rare away from distinctly calcareous soils, whether or not water is nearby. I suspect that the key to their distribution in our region lies in the geological history of the area concerned and their relationship to limestone soil.

Habitat. Most commonly in dry white cedar woods along Great Lakes shorelines, especially in limestone areas of the Niagara series. Very common in the Bruce Peninsula of Ontario, limestone islands of Georgian Bay, the tip of Lower Michigan, and the

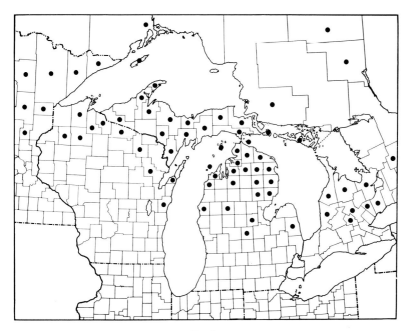

63. *Corallorhiza striata*

eastern parts of Upper Michigan. On limestone soils it shows little habitat preference, except that it does not grow in soggy situations. May be found in open woods, brushlands, and even along roadbeds. Very colorful, large clumps form regularly.

Outside the limestone areas in its Great Lakes range, it is local or rare. It grows in beech-sugar maple forests on clay or sand soils, in hemlock groves, and occasionally in marly wells in balsam-spruce swamps. A cool soil species, it is not found in the warmer, more southern parts of our region.

Since this orchid is a saprophyte, it cannot be expected to survive transplanting to a garden. Until more is known of saprophyte-environment relationships, the only avenue open to growing such a species is to distribute seed in suitable spots and hope that plants will develop.

EARLY CORAL-ROOT, NORTHERN CORAL-ROOT

Corallorhiza trifida Chat.   Plate 44A, B

Although primarily northern in our region and mostly small, this orchid is so common locally that it is likely to be the most frequently met of the coral-root species. It begins to bloom early, and the bright greenish yellow stems and seed pods are a fa-

225

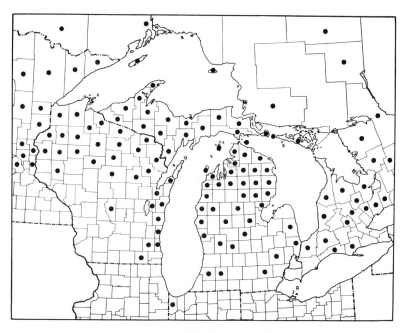

64. *Corallorhiza trifida*

miliar sight to those who prowl wooded swamps and bogs in search of orchids.

Some authors place the yellow-green flowered, unspotted-lip form of the species in the var. *verna* (Nutt.) Fernald. This form is the one common in our region. The more northern and European form is more brownish in color, and has a madder-spotted lip, but many intermediate forms occur. Yellow-green, white-lipped forms with a few tiny madder-purple spots near the base of the lip are frequent along the northern Lake Superior shoreline.

Habit. Small, stiffly erect, 5–30 cm tall, averaging 15 cm. Stem slender, with 2–3 tubular sheaths, pale yellow-green, becoming somewhat greener in fruit. Raceme laxly few–20-flowered; rarely more. Floral bracts minute, acute, 1–2 mm long. Floral parts spreading, usually yellowish white, though other color forms occur. Sepals linear-oblong, blunt-tipped and concave, 4–7 mm long, 1–2 mm wide. Lateral sepals spreading. Petals and dorsal sepal connivent and forming a hood over column, 4–5 mm long, 1–2 mm wide. Lip white or spotted with dark purple, oblong-quadrate, narrowed and nearly clawed at base, with 2 triangular, small lateral lobes or teeth near base. Floor of lip has a pair of flattened ridges; tip abrupt, truncate. Seed capsules obovoid, with shallow ribs, becoming pendent in maturity.

Season. Early May to July.

General Distribution. Arctic America from Greenland to Alaska, southward through New England to New York and Pennsylvania (reported from much farther south, but apparently without substantiating specimens). Through central and northern Lakes states to South Dakota. In western mountains grows south to New Mexico, Colorado, and Oregon. Also found in Eurasia and Great Britain. Though common in northern half of the Lakes states, it is rare or absent in the southern parts.

Habitat. Has a wide range of habitats, especially northward. At the south edge of its range, in the central portion of the Lakes states, it occurs most frequently in the mucky, brushy borders of cedar-balsam-spruce swamps and in cedar thickets so dark and dense that often little other flowering plant life is in evidence. Northward, grows also in drier and more upland habitats, in alder thickets, birch-aspen woodlands, spruce headlands of Lake Superior, and beech-maple forests. Ubiquitous across America in the subarctic spruce-aspen forests.

In dense cedar-balsam fir thickets, quite commonly forms very large clumps, densely packed with flowering stems, with 30–40 stems per clump not unusual. At other points few clumps can be found. Thus the plant has rather different aspects in various locations of an area. These differences may confuse the orchid hunter, but checking the structural details of the blooms will confirm the identity of the orchid.

WISTER'S CORAL-ROOT, SPRING CORAL-ROOT

Corallorhiza wisteriana Conrad   Plate 44C, D

The inclusion of Wister's coral-root in this edition of this book rests upon two herbarium records, one from La Salle County, Illinois (1961) in the herbarium of Illinois State Natural History Survey (ILLS), and the other, previously annotated by myself and others as *C. maculata*, from St. Joseph County, "Ind." This specimen was collected by Mottier and Picket and is deposited in the herbarium of the University of Indiana (IND 2855). I have examined the Illinois specimen, and have carefully reexamined the St. Joseph County specimen. In my opinion, both clearly represent *C. wisteriana*. The Illinois record, within our area, while disjunct from the more southerly material in that state, is carefully documented and discussed by Sheviak (1974). In Illinois, at least, *C. wisteriana* clearly occurs within the area covered by this book.

I have some doubts, however, concerning the accuracy of the Indiana record. The specimen (Mottier and Picket 1473) lists "St.

Joseph County, June 1914" as the place and date of collection. The abbreviation "Ind." appears in pencil in a different hand, as if added at a later date. Curators at the University of Indiana Herbarium inform me that Mottier did botanize in St. Joseph County, Indiana, but the nature of the labeling leaves open the possibility of locality error.

It is well known, however, that many orchids occur in disjunct colonies sometimes at some distance from their usual range. *C. wisteriana* grows in southern Indiana, Illinois, and Ohio, its range extending to within two or three counties of our region. Its occurrence within our range, therefore, would be less surprising than some well documented occurrences which presently exist, i.e. *Isotria medeoloides* in Illinois, Michigan, and Ontario; *Triphora* in northern Lower Michigan; *Galearis spectabilis* in western Upper Michigan; or *Spiranthes tuberosa* at diverse points in Michigan.

Habit. Slender to moderately stout, often quite tall for stem thickness, 1–4 dm tall, the base slightly thickened. Leaves reduced to tubular sheaths, reddish brown to madder-purple. Raceme densely to laxly few-flowered, 2–15 cm long. Floral bracts 1–2 mm long, inconspicuous. Flowers, before pollination, held somewhat horizontal-erect, gaping, due to the arcuate-recurved lip. Sepals and petals approximate, yellowish brown to purplish with 1–3 darker nerves. Dorsal sepal linear, obtuse to acute at apex, 6–9 mm long, 1.5–2 mm wide on lowermost flowers. Lateral sepals linear to lanceolate, to 9 mm long, 1–2 mm wide. Petals linear to oblong, acute to apiculate at tip, margins faintly erose, 5–7 mm long, 2 mm wide. Lip short-clawed, strongly arcuate-recurved beyond the claw, elliptic to suborbicular, the margins weakly involute and erose-toothed, very rarely with an obscure tooth or lobe on each side, 5–7 mm long, 4–6 mm wide, white, purple spotted, with two linear lamellae on disk near base of lip. Column 4 mm or less long, arched over the lamellae of the lip. Capsules ovoid, 8–11 mm long, to 6 mm wide.

Season. Early spring, March or April in deep South, to June in Indiana.

General Distribution. Widespread in the eastern deciduous forests, mostly south of areas of Pleistocene glaciation, from Delaware and Pennsylvania westward across southern Ohio, Indiana, and Illinois (occurring north to La Salle County, Illinois and St. Joseph County (?), Indiana), southward to Kansas, Arkansas, and eastern Texas. Present in all states south and east of these limits but absent from subtropical Florida (Luer 1975). Occurs also along the Rocky Mountains from extreme southern Montana and eastern Idaho and Wyoming to southern Mexico, with disjunct stations in the Black Hills (Correll 1950).

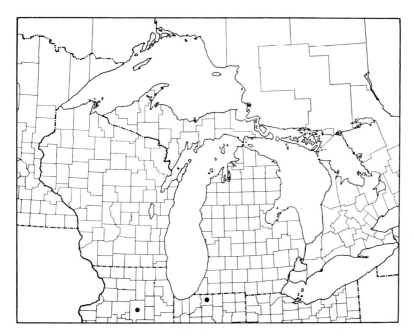

65. *Corallorhiza wisteriana*

Habitat. Often in circumneutral soils (*fide* Wherry, in Correll 1950) of rich deciduous forests. Sheviak (1974) reports Illinois habitat as rich mesic woodlands and dry-mesic sites with oaks and hickories. The plant companions he cites are those of the typical eastern springtime deciduous forest flora: toothworts (*Dentaria* spp.), Jack-in-the-pulpit (*Arisaema triphyllum*), showy orchis (*Galearis spectabilis*), mayapple (*Podophyllum peltatum*), and bloodroot (*Sanguinaria canadensis*). Morris and Eames (1926) aver that it associates with spicebush thickets near Washington, D. C. I have seen it in Tennessee, growing with poison ivy (*Rhus toxicodendron*) in rather trashy, disturbed, wooded bluffs along streams. In northern Alabama, I have found it in dry oak woods on bluffs.

This species should be looked for in the southern portions of our region, especially in northern Indiana and Illinois. Here, at the southern tip of Lake Michigan, many remarkable occurrences of southern species have been documented.

SELECTED BIBLIOGRAPHY

Some of them will saye, seeing that I graunte that I have gathered this booke of so many writers, that I offer unto you an heape of others mennis laboures, and nothing of mine owne. . . . To whom I answere that if the honye that the bees gather out of so many floure of herbes, shrubbes and trees, that are growing in other mennis meadowes, feldes and closes may justelye be called the bee's honye . . . so maye I call that I have learned and gathered of so many good autores . . . my booke. —William Turner, 1551. (Quoted from Jones and Fuller 1955.)

Since the literature on orchids is exceedingly diverse and much of it difficult to access, I have not attempted to list all the works I have consulted, or even all those dealing with the orchids of our region. Instead, I have selected a number of representative works that deal with the material of this book. The often extensive bibliographies in the works cited will enable the student of orchids to pursue the subject further.

ACHERMAN, J. D.
  1977   Biosystematics of the Genus *Piperia* Rydb. (Orchidaceae). Bot. Jr. of the Linnaean Soc. 75: 245–270.
AMES, OAKES
  1905   A Synopsis of the Genus *Spiranthes* North of Mexico. Orchidaceae. Fasc. 1, 145 pp. Boston.
  1906   *Habenaria orbiculata* and *H. macrophylla*. Rhodora 4: 1–5.
  1921   Notes on New England Orchids. 1. *Spiranthes*. Rhodora 23: 73–85.
  1922   Notes on New England Orchids. 2. The Mycorrhiza of *Goodyera pubescens*. Rhodora 24: 37–46.
  1924   An Enumeration of the Orchids of the United States and Canada. Boston. 120 pp.
ANDERSON, A. B. AND J. P. GOLTZ
  1982   Common Twayblade, *Listera ovata* (Orchidaceae) in Wellington County, Ontario: A Second North American Record. Can. Field-Nat. 96: 351–352.
ANDREWS, H.
  1961   Two New Orchid Records for Ontario. Rhodora 63: 175–176.
AUCLAIR, A. N.
  1972   Comparative Ecology of the Orchids *Aplectrum hymale* and *Orchis spectabilis*. Bull. Torrey Bot. Club 99 (1): 1–10.

AYENSU, E. S. AND R. A. DEFILIPPS
1978 Endangered and Threatened Plants of the United States. Smithsonian Institution and World Wildlife Fund, Inc. Washington, D. C. 403 pp.

BALDWIN, HENRY
1884 The Orchids of New England. Wiley, New York. 158 pp.

BARTLETT, HARLEY H.
1922 Color Types of *Corallorhiza maculata* Raf. Rhodora 24: 145–158.

BINGHAM, MARJORIE T.
1939 Orchids of Michigan. Cranbrook Inst. Sci. Bull. 15. 87 pp.

BLAIR, K. R.
1909 The Orchids of Ohio. Ohio Nat. 10: 24–35.

BRACKLEY, F. E.
1985 The Orchids of New Hampshire. Rhodora 87: 1–117.

BRAUN, E. LUCY
1950 Deciduous Forests of Eastern North America. Blakiston, Philadelphia. 596 pp.

BROWN, J. R. AND PAUL M. CATLING
1981 The Status and Distribution of Yellow Lady's-tresses Orchid (*Spiranthes ochroleuca* (Rydb.) Rydb.) in Ontario. Ontario Field Biol. 35 (1): 7–12.

BURGEFF, H.
1936 Die Samenkeimung der Orchideen. G. Fischer, Jena. 312 pp.

CAIN, STANLEY A.
1944 Foundations of Plant Geography. Harper, New York. 556 pp.

CAMPBELL, E. O.
1970 Morphology of the Fungal Association in Three Species of *Corallorhiza* in Michigan. Mich. Bot. 9: 108–113.

CASE, F. W. JR.
1962 Growing Native Orchids of the Great Lakes Region. Am. Orchid Soc. Bull. 31: 437–445.

1964 A Hybrid Twayblade and Its Rarer Parent, *Listera auriculata*, in Northern Michigan. Mich. Bot. 3: 67–70.

1964a Orchids of the Western Great Lakes Region. Cranbrook Inst. Sci. Bull. 48. 147 pp.

1965 Discovery of the Northern Twayblade, *Listera borealis*, in the Lake Superior Region of Ontario. Mich. Bot. 4: 118–121.

1965a Growing Native Orchids. Orchidata 9 (2). New.York.

1967 Growing Native Orchids. In *Handbook on Orchids*. Plants and Gardens 23 (2): 66–72.

1983 "Notes Concerning Changes in Great Lakes Populations Since 1964." In *Proceedings from Symposium II and Lectures—North American Terrestrial Orchids*, pp. 133–141. Michigan Orchid Society, Southfield, Mich.

1983a *Platanthera* ×*vossii*, A New Natural Hybrid Orchid from Northern Lower Michigan. Mich. Bot. 22: 141–144.

CASE, F. W. JR. AND P. M. CATLING
1983 The Genus *Spiranthes* (Orchidaceae) in Michigan. Mich. Bot. 22: 79–92.

CASE, F. W. JR. WITH WILLIAM SCHWAB
1971 *Isotria medeoloides*, the Smaller Whorled Pogonia, in Michigan. Mich. Bot. 10: 39–43.

CATLING, PAUL M.
1976 On the Geographic Distribution, Ecology, and Distinctive Features of *Listera* ×*veltmanii* Case. Rhodora 78: 261–269.

1976a *Spiranthes magnicamporum* Sheviak, an Addition to the Orchids of Canada. Can. Field-Nat. 90: 467–470.

1980 Autogamy in Northeastern North American Orchids. Publ. of Abstracts, Can. Bot. Assoc., Bot. Soc. of Am., Misc. Series Publ. 158: 20.

1980a Systematics of *Spiranthes* L. C. Richard in Northeastern North America. Ph.D. Thesis, University of Toronto. 551 pp.

1983 Autogamy in Eastern Canadian Orchidaceae; A Review of Current Knowledge and Some New Observations. Naturaliste Canadien 110: 37–53.

CATLING, PAUL M. AND J. E. CRUISE
1974 *Spiranthes casei*, a New Species from Northeastern North America. Rhodora 77: 526–536.

CHAMPLIN, R. L.
1976 Scotch Pine as an Associate of the Tesselated Rattlesnake Plantain. Rhodora 78: 788–789.

CORRELL, DONOVAN S.
1950 Native Orchids of North America North of Mexico. Chronica Botanica, Waltham, Mass. 399 pp.

CUNNINGHAM, A. M.
1896 Distribution of the Orchidaceae in Indiana. Proc. Ind. Acad. Sci.: 239–242.

CURTIS, J. T.
1932 A New *Cypripedium* Hybrid. Rhodora 34: 239–242
1937 Non-specificity of Orchid Mycorrhizal Fungi. Proc. Soc. Exp. Bio. and Med. 36: 43–44.

1939 The Relation of the Specificity of Orchid Mycorrhizal Fungi to the Problem of Symbiosis. Am. Jr. Bot. 26: 390–399.

1943 Germination and Seedling Development in Five Species of *Cypripedium* L. Am. Jr. Bot. 30: 199–205.

1959 The Vegetation of Wisconsin. University of Wisconsin Press, Madison. 657 pp.

DARLINGTON, H. T.
1919 Distribution of the Orchidaceae in Michigan. 21st Rept. Mich. Acad. Sci: 239–261.

DARWIN, CHARLES R.
1862 On the Various Contrivances by Which British and Foreign Orchids Are Fertilised by Insects. Murray, London. 300 pp.

DEAM, CHARLES
1940 Flora of Indiana. Indiana State Dept. of Conservation, Indianapolis. 1236 pp. (see p. 335–351)

DENSLOW, H. M.
1924 *Isotria verticillata*. Addisonia 9: 33–34.
1927 Native Orchids in and near New York. Torreya 27: 61–63.

DODSON, C. H.
1961 Natural Pollination of Orchids. Bull. Missouri Bot. Gar. 49: 133–152.

DOWNIE, D. G.
1940 On the Germination and Growth of *Goodyera repens*. Trans. Bot. Soc. Edinburgh 33: 36–51.

DRESSLER, R. L.
1981 The Orchids, Natural History and Classification. Harvard University Press, Cambridge. 332 pp.

DRESSLER, R. L. AND CALAWAY DODSON
1960 Classification and Phylogeny in the Orchidaceae. Ann. Missouri Bot. Gar. 47: 25–68.

DUPRERREX, A.
1961 Orchids of Europe. Blandford Press, London. 235 pp.

ELLIOTT, H. V.
1969 A Possible New Orchid for North America. Ontario Nat. 69: 15.

ELLIOTT, H. V. AND F. S. COOK
1970 *Listera ovata* (L.) R. Br. in the Bruce Peninsula, Ontario. Rhodora 72: 274–275.

FASSETT, N. C.
1931 Spring Flora of Wisconsin. University of Wisconsin, Madison. 178 pp. (see p. 36–42)

FERNALD, M. L.
1899 The Rattlesnake Plantains of New England. Rhodora 1: 2–7.

1950 Gray's Manual of Botany. 8th rev. ed. American Book, New York. 1632 pp.

FREUDENSTEIN, J. V.
1985 Variation in the *Corallorhiza maculata* (Raf.) Raf. Complex in North America (excluding Mexico) with Special Reference to Michigan. Senior Honors Thesis, Department of Botany, University of Michigan, Ann Arbor.

FULLER, ALBERT M.
1933 A Natural *Cypripedium* Hybrid from Wisconsin. Rhodora 34: 97–101.

1933a Studies on the Flora of Wisconsin, Pt. I, The Orchids; Orchidaceae. Milwaukee Pub. Mus. Bull. 14: 1–284.

GARAY, LESLIE A.
1960 On the Origin of the Orchidaceae. Bot. Mus. Harvard 19: 57–96.

1972 On the Origin of the Orchidaceae, II. Jr. Arnold Arb. 53: 202–215.

GIBSON, WILLIAM H.
1905 Our Native Orchids. Doubleday, New York. 158 pp.

GLEASON, HENRY A.
1952 Illustrated Flora of the Northeastern United States and Adjacent Canada, 1: pp. 455–476. New York Botanical Garden, New York.

GREENWOOD, E. W.
1962 Occurrences of the Orchid *Listera australis* in the Vicinity of

Quebec City. Can. Field-Nat. 76: 199–202.

1974   Broad-leaved Helleborine Now Present in Manitoulin District,
       Ontario. Can. Field-Nat. 88: 87–88.

HANES, CLARENCE AND FLORENCE H. HANES

1947   Flora of Kalamazoo County, Michigan. Clarence R. Hanes,
       Schoolcraft, Mich. 295 pp. (see p. 74–80)

HARVAIS, G.

1980   Scientific Notes on *Cypripedium reginae* of Northeastern Ontario,
       Canada. Am. Orchid Soc. Bull. 49: 237–244.

HENRY, L. K. AND W. E. BECKER

1955   Orchids of Western Pennsylvania. Ann. Carnegie Mus. 33: 299–
       346.

HIGLEY, W. K. AND C. S. RADDIN

1891   The Flora of Cook County, Illinois and a Part of Lake County,
       Indiana. Bull. Chicago Acad. Sci. 2: 1–168.

HOLM, T.

1904   The Root Structure of the North American Terrestrial Orchideae.
       Am. Jr. Sci. 18: 197–212.

HOMOYA, M.

1977   Some Aspects of the Life History of *Isotria medeoloides*, an
       Endangered Orchid Species. Trans. Ill. State Acad. Sci. 70:
       196.

HOUSE, H. D.

1918   Wildflowers of New York. N. Y. State Mus. Mem. 15, Pt. 1:
       64–67.

JONES, G. N. AND G. D. FULLER

1955   Vascular Plants of Illinois. University of Illinois Press, Urbana.
       593 pp. (see p. 142–150)

KALLUNKI, J. A.

1976   Population Studies in *Goodyera* (Orchidaceae) With Emphasis
       on the Hybrid Origin of *G. tesselata*. Brittonia 28: 53–75.

1981   Reproductive Biology of Mixed-species Populations of *Goodyera*
       (Orchidaceae) in Northern Michigan. Brittonia 33: 137–155.

KNUDSEN, LEWIS C.

1922   Non-symbiotic Germination of Orchid Seeds. Bot. Gaz. 73: 1–
       25.

1924   Further Observations on Non-symbiotic Germination of Orchid
       Seeds. Bot. Gaz. 77: 212–219.

1925   Physiological Study of the Symbiotic Germination of Orchid
       Seeds. Bot. Gaz. 79: 345–379.

LAKELA, O.

1965   A Flora of Northeastern Minnesota. University of Minnesota
       Press, Minneapolis. (see p. 127–140)

LOWNES, A. E.

1926   *Triphora trianthophora*. Addisonia 11: 61–62.

LUER, C. A.

1975   The Native Orchids of the United States and Canada Excluding
       Florida. New York Botanical Garden, Bronx, N. Y. 361 pp.

MACDOUGAL, D. T.

1895   Poisonous Influences of Various Species of *Cypripedium*. Minn.
       Bot. Studies (Minneapolis) Bull. 9: 450–451.

MEHRHOFF, L. A.
1980   Reproductive Systems in the Genus *Isotria* (Orchidaceae). Bot. Soc. Am. Misc. Ser. Pub. 158: 72.
MORRIS, F. AND E. A. EAMES
1929   Our Wild Orchids. Scribners, New York. 464 pp.
MORTON, J. K. AND JOAN M. VENN
1984   Flora of Manitoulin Island. 2nd ed. University of Waterloo Dept. of Biology, Waterloo, Ont. 181 pp.
MOSQUIN, T.
1970   The Reproductive Biology of *Calypso bulbosa*. Can. Field-Nat. 84: 291–296.
MOUSLEY, H.
1940   *Listera australis* Lindl. in the Province of Quebec. Can. Field-Nat. 54: 95–96.
1941   A Distinctive New Variety of *Orchis rotundifolia* from Canada. Can. Field-Nat. 55: 64–65.
NILES, G. G.
1904   Bog-trotting for Orchids. Putnam, New York. 310 pp.
PRINGLE, J. S.
1980   An Introduction to Wetland Classification in the Great Lakes Region. Royal Bot. Gar. Tech. Bull. 10, Hamilton, Ontario. 11 pp.
RAVEN, P. H., RAY F. EVERT AND HELENA CURTIS
1981   Biology of Plants. 3rd ed. Worth, New York. 686 pp.
RYDBERG, P. A.
1901   The American Species of *Limnorchis* and *Piperia*, North of Mexico. Bull. Torrey Bot. Club 28: 605–643.
SADOVSKY, O.
1968   Orchideen im Eigenen Garten. Bayerisher Landwirtschaftsverlag GmbH., Munich. 160 pp.
SANDFORD, W. W.
1974   The Ecology of Orchids. In *The Orchids: Scientific Studies*, edited by C. L. Withner. Wiley, New York. 624 pp.
SHEVIAK, C. J.
1973   A New *Spiranthes* from the Grasslands of Central North America. Bot. Mus. Leaflet (Harvard Univ.) 23: 285–297.
1974   An Introduction to the Ecology of the Illinois Orchidaceae. Ill. State Mus. Sci. Papers XIV. 89 pp.
1982   Biosystematic Study of the *Spiranthes cernua* Complex. N. Y. State Mus. Bull. 448. 73 pp.
1983   "United States Terrestrial Orchids . . . Patterns and Problems." *Proceedings from Symposium II and Lectures—North American Terrestrial Orchids*, pp. 49–60. Michigan Orchid Society, Southfield, Michigan.
SHEVIAK, C. J. AND M. L. BOWLES
1986   The Prairie Fringed Orchids: A Pollinator-Isolated Species Pair. Rhodora 88: 267–290.
SHEVIAK, C. J. AND P. M. CATLING
1980   The Identity and Status of *Spiranthes ochroleuca* (Rydberg) Rydberg. Rhodora 82: 525–562.

SIMPSON, R. C. AND P. M. CATLING
1978 *Spiranthes lacera* var. *lacera* × *S. romanzoffiana*, A New Natural Orchid Hybrid from Ontario. Can. Field-Nat. 92: 350–358.
SMITH, HELEN V.
1961 Michigan Wildflowers. Cranbrook Inst. Sci. Bull. 42. 465 pp. (see p. 65–95)
SPOONER, D. M. AND J. S. SHELLY
1983 The National Historical Distribution of *Platanthera peramoena* (A. Gray) A. Gray (Orchidaceae) and its Status in Ohio. Rhodora 85: 55–64.
STOUTAMIRE, W. P.
1964 Seeds and Seedlings of Native Orchids. Mich. Bot. 3: 107–119.
1967 Flower Biology of the Lady's-slippers (Orchidaceae, *Cypripedium*). Mich. Bot. 6: 159–173.
1974 Relationships of the Purple Fringed-orchids *Platanthera psycodes* and *P. grandiflora*. Brittonia 26: 42–58.
STUCKEY, I.
1967 Environmental Factors and the Growth of Native Orchids. Am. Jr. Bot. 54: 232–241.
SUMMERHAYES, V. S.
1951 Wild Orchids of Britain. Collins, London. 366 pp.
SWAMY, B. G. L.
1948 Vascular Anatomy of Orchid Flowers. Bot. Mus. Leaflet (Harvard Univ.) 13: 61–95.
SWINK, F. A.
1966 Orchids of the Indiana Dune Regions. Am. Orchid Soc. Bull. 35: 706–710.
VAN DER PIJL, L. AND C. H. DODSON
1966 Orchid Flowers, Their Pollination and Evolution. University of Miami Press, Coral Gables, Fla. 214 pp.
VOSS, E. G.
1966 Nomenclatural Notes on Monocots. Rhodora 68: 435–463.
1972 Michigan Flora, Part I: Gymnosperms and Monocots. Cranbrook Inst. of Sci. Bull. 55. 488 pp. (see p. 433–463)
WAGNER, W. H., E. G. VOSS, J. H. BEAMAN, E. A. BOURDO, F. W. CASE, JR., J. A. CHURCHILL, AND P. W. THOMPSON
1977 Michigan's Endangered and Threatened Species Program. Mich. Bot. 16: 99–102.
WATERMAN, W. G.
1949 *Cypripedium reginae* Walt. in North Central Michigan. Am. Orchid Soc. Bull. 18: 90–97.
1950 Habitats of *Cypripedium reginae* in North Central Michigan. Am. Orchid Soc. Bull. 19: 588–594.
WHERRY, E. T.
1918 The Reactions of the Soils Supporting the Growth of Certain Orchids. Jr. Wash. Acad. Sci. 8: 589–598.
WHITING, R. E. AND R. S. W. BOBBETTE
1974 The Orchid *Listera auriculata* Rediscovered in Ontario. Can. Field-Nat. 88: 345–347.
WHITING, R. E. AND P. M. CATLING
1977 Distribution of the Auricled Twayblade Orchid (*Listera auri-*

culata) in Canada and Description of New Station in Southern Ontario. Can. Field-Nat. 91: 403–406.

WHITING, R. E. AND P. M. CATLING
1986 Orchids of Ontario. CanaColl Foundation, Ottawa, Ont. 169 pp.

WIEGAND, K. M.
1899 A Revision of the Genus *Listera*. Bull. Torrey Bot. Club 26: 157–171.

WILLIAMS, L. O.
1937 The Orchidaceae of the Rocky Mountains. Am. Midl. Nat. 18: 830–841.

WINTERRINGER, G. S.
1967 Wild Orchids of Illinois. Ill. State Mus. Pop. Sci. Ser. 7. 130 pp.

WITHNER, C. L.
1948 The Genus *Cypripedium*. Am. Orchid Soc. Bull. 17: 143–151.
1959 The Orchids, A Scientific Survey. Ronald Press, New York. 648 pp.

GLOSSARY

Acid. A compound which, in aqueous solution, undergoes dissociation with the formation of hydrogen ions, creating in water or moist soil an environment acceptable to certain plant species, but not to others. *Acidity.* The condition of being in an acid state.

Acuminate. Tapered gradually to a point.

Acute. Ending in a point, or having a sharp angle.

Adherent. Having parts united or attached to one another.

Adnate. United to another organ of a different sort or origin.

Agamospermy. Production of a viable seed from an unfertilized ovule.

Albino. A color-free individual plant. Usually, in photosynthetic plants, true albinism is impossible, for such plants, lacking chlorophyll, cannot manufacture foods. In extremely rare instances, certain orchid plant albinos may exist if the plant is nourished and sustained by its mycorrhizal associate. Such a condition has been reported in our area for occasional plants of *Epipactis helleborine.* The term is often, but incorrectly, applied to forms with white flowers.

Alkali. A compound which forms soluble carbonates with fatty acids, creating in water or moist soil an environment acceptable to certain plant species but not to others. *Alkalinity.* The condition of being in an alkaline state.

Alluvial soil. Soil deposited by running water.

Anther. The pollen-bearing portion of the stamen.

Anthesis. The time of full expansion of the flower; often considered the start of blooming.

Apex. The tip of an organ.

Apiculate. Ending abruptly in a short point.

Apomixy. A phenomenon of reproduction in which flowering plants produce offspring without normal sexual reproduction.

Arcuate. Moderately curved.

Auricle. An ear-shaped lobe or appendage, usually much smaller than the organ on which it appears.

Auriculate. Bearing auricles.

Autogamous. Self-fertilizing without the aid of a living pollinator.

Axil. The angle formed between an organ and the stem or rachis to which it is attached.

Bifid. Cleft into two approximately equal segments.

Bifurcate. Two-forked.

Blade. Expanded portion of a leaf.

Bog. An essentially undrained, peat-filled wetland, with strongly acid, mineral-poor soil, supporting on its surface a specialized flora dominated, on the soil surface at least, by species of sphagnum moss. Many bogs develop in glacial "kettles," basins which contain ponds or small lakes. In many bogs, the original lake has been completely filled by accumulations of the peat-forming plant remains; in others there still remains a portion of the former lake, often with a floating marginal shelf (bog mat) of peat and living vegetation. In the strictest sense, true bogs are not forested. Some ecologists include "treed bogs" in their definition.

Bract. A reduced, leaflike or scalelike structure usually subtending a flower.

Bracteate. Having bracts.

Bulb. A subterranean, modified bud bearing fleshy, scale-leaves.

Bulbous. Having a bulblike appearance.

Calcareous. Limy. A term usually applied to soils containing large amounts of calcium compounds. In the Great Lakes region calcareous deposits in lakes and fens, mixed with clay and peat, are frequently called marls.

Calceolate. Shaped like a slipper or pouch.

Calciphile. Lime-loving species.

Calciphobe. Lime-shunning species.

Callose. Bearing a hard protuberance or thickening.

Callus (or *callosity*). A hardened, thickened structure.

Calyx. All the sepals of one blossom.

Capsule. A dry, dehiscent fruit derived from more than one carpel; the type of fruit in orchids.

Carpel. A single seed-forming unit, one or more forming a pistil.

Caudate. Tail-like.

Cauline. Borne on a stem; associated with a stem.

Cellular. Composed of cells, or with a texture like the surface of a group of cells.

Centimeter (cm). 10 millimeters, or 0.3937 inch.

Chasmogamous. Flower open, potentially out-crossing, although not precluding self-pollination.

Chlorophyll. The green coloring matter in plants which absorbs light energy and is involved in photosynthesis.

Ciliate. Bearing cilia; that is, having a hairlike fringe.

Circumboreal. Occurring around the world in northern regions.

Circumneutral. A chemical condition of the soil which is neither excessively acid nor alkaline.

Clavellate. Club-shaped.

Claw. A narrowed area of a floral segment; usually applied to the narrowed base of a petal.

Clay. A very fine-grained mineral soil, usually a hydrous aluminum silicate.

Cleistogamous. Self-fertilizing, with the flower not opening.

Clone. The aggregate of individual plants derived asexually from a single sexually produced plant (organism); hence, all plants of the clone are genetically identical.

Column. An organ formed through the union of the stamens and pistil in orchids.

Conduplicate. Folded lengthwise.

Coniferous. Cone-bearing; usually referring to evergreen gymnosperms.

Connivent. Converging but not actually uniting; in orchids, referring to the converging of sepals and petals to form a hood.

Convex. Having an outward-rounded surface.

Coralloid. Coral-like, many and irregularly branched.

Cordate. Heart-shaped.

Corm. A short, solid, fleshy, underground stem with a few thin, sheathing membranes or scale leaves, and bearing buds at the summit.

Corolla. All the petals of one flower.

Crested. Having raised ridges or protuberances.

Cuneate. Wedge-shaped, with the narrowed portion closest to the plant.

Deciduous. Falling at the end of the growing period, as leaves, fruits, etc., or after anthesis, as petals of many flowers.

Decimeter (dm). 10 centimeters, or 3.937 inches.

Dehisce. To split or burst, i.e., the bursting open of a capsule at maturity; the opening of an anther for the discharge of pollen by longitudinal slits, pores, etc.

Dentate. Toothed.

Disk. The dorsal surface of the lip in orchids.

Distal. Referring to a position remote from the point of attachment or origin of a structure.

Dorsal. Referring to a position on the outer surface or back of a structure.

Ecology. The study of the mutual relations between species and their environment.

Elliptic. Oblong, with regularly rounded ends.

Elongated. Drawn out in length.

Endemic. Confined to, or indigenous to, a certain area or region.

Entire. Having no marginal features; opposed to *dentate* and *erose*.

Erose. Slightly eroded, gnawed, or ragged.

Excrescences. Small outgrowths; warty.

Falcate. Sickle-shaped.

Family. A group of related genera of plants or animals.

Fen. A wetland with impeded drainage having calcareous-neutral to alkaline soils and dominated by herbs, mostly smaller grasses and sedges. In fens, water flows into the area but its flow is obstructed. Peats, if present, are mineral-rich. A fen in the strictest sense is without shrubs or trees. If numerous shrubs develop, the fen is frequently called a "shrub carr," if trees develop in numbers (as is common northward), the community is called a "treed fen."

Fertilization. In seed plants, the process of union of pollen sperm nucleus with the egg within the ovule sac. The zygote resulting from the union forms the embryo plant within the developing seed. In some orchids, especially the tropical species, fertilization may occur days, or even months, after pollination.

Filament. A threadlike appendage; the anther-bearing stalk of a stamen.

Fimbriate. Fringed.

Fruit. Any ripened ovary and its associated parts.

Fugacious. Withering or falling early.
Furcate. Forked.

Galea. A hood.
Genus. A group of similar species forming a unit distinct from other groups of species.
Glabrous. Smooth; hairless.
Glandular. Glandlike, or bearing glands.
Glaucous. Covered with a pale waxy covering or bloom.
Globose. Spherical; globe-shaped.

Habit. The general appearance of a plant; its characteristic form and constitution.
Habitat. The type of locality or environment in which a particular species occurs.
Hardwoods. Forests dominated by broad-leaved, deciduous trees as distinguished from coniferous trees.
Heath. An open, more or less level area with shrubby growth, especially of members of the heath family, Ericaceae.
Herb. A nonwoody plant.
Herbarium. A collection or repository of dried, pressed plants, preserved for the purpose of verifying records and for comparative botanical studies.
Hirsute. Having stiff hairs.
Humus. Decomposing leaf mold or other organic matter in the soil.
Hyaline. Thin, translucent.
Hybrid. The offspring of dissimilar parents, especially parents of two different species.

Inflorescence. Flower-bearing branch of a plant.

Keel. A central ridge.

Labellum. A lip; a modified petal of an orchid, distinct from the other petals.
Lamellae. Thin, flat plates.
Lanceolate. A structure longer than wide, tapered, broadest below the middle; lance-shaped.
Lateral. Pertaining to the side of an organ or of the axis; opposed to *terminal, median,* and *basal.*
Limb. The expanded part of a leaf or petal which also has a narrowed claw.
Linear. A long, narrow shape, like a blade of grass.
Lip. The labellum of orchids; a modified petal usually quite different in shape from the others.
Lobe. Any rounded division or projection of an organ, especially a leaf.

Maculate. Having spots.
Marginal. Pertaining to the edge.
Marl. A limy soil; in the northern regions, a deposit of white, clayey

lime forming in lakes, streams, fens, and sometimes in bogs.

Marsh. A wet area with slow but definite drainage, usually with standing water and cattail or rushlike emergent vegetation, and with few or no trees.

Meadow. An essentially treeless or shrubless tract of moist land, bearing grasses, wildflowers, and similar vegetation; an area that normally does not flood.

Mediacid. Having a hydrogen-ion value of 4.5–5.0; said of certain moderately acid soils.

Mentum. A chinlike projection formed by the sepals and the foot of the column.

Millimeter (mm). A measure; 1/10 centimeter, or 0.03937 inch.

Minimacid. Having minimum acidity (see *mediacid*).

Monocarpic. Blooming only once after maturity, then dying; a condition not as yet reported in orchids, though some may be monocarpic.

Monocotyledon. A member of a class of the *Anthophyta* having only one seed leaf and other morphological distinctions.

Monotypic. A taxonomic unit of plants comprised of a single species.

Mucronate. Ending in a small, abrupt tip.

Muskeg. A boreal sphagnum bog, usually rather open.

Mycorrhiza. A fungus–flowering plant root tissue association or structure, in which certain fungi are associated with the roots of a seed plant, as in orchids.

Neutral. Having an exact balance between acidity and alkalinity, i.e., in soils.

Oblanceolate. Lanceolate, but broadest toward the apex.

Oblong. Longer than broad, usually with the sides parallel.

Obtuse. Blunt or rounded.

Orbicular. Nearly circular or spherical.

Organic. A compound containing carbon and usually associated with life.

Orifice. An opening, e.g., the opening of the lady's-slipper pouch.

Oval. Elliptic; egg-shaped.

Ovary. A part of the pistil or female organ of the flower which bears the ovules or young seeds.

Ovate. Egg-shaped.

Ovoid. Egg-shaped.

Pandurate. Fiddle-shaped.

Panicle. A loose or irregular branched inflorescence with pedicellate flowers, i.e. a branched raceme.

Papillae. Minute, nipplelike outgrowths.

Papillose. Bearing papillae.

Parasite. An organism that derives all or part of its food from another living organism at the expense of the latter.

Peat. Dead plant material, especially the remains of sphagnum mosses and associated vegetation, partially decomposing and accumulating under water.

Pedicel. The stalk of a single flower, especially in a compound inflorescence.

Pedicellate. On or like a pedicel.

Peduncle. The stalk of an inflorescence or of a solitary flower.

Pedunculate. Borne on a peduncle.

Perianth. The floral parts, in one or more ranks, that surround the stamens and pistil(s); in orchids, calyx and corolla.

Petal. A division of the corolla; one segment of the inner whorl or floral envelope.

Petaloid. Like a petal; e.g., the floral bract in *Calypso*.

Petiole. The stalk of a leaf.

Photosynthesis. The production of carbohydrates, usually sugars, in living plants in the presence of chlorophyll and light, utilizing molecules of water and carbon dioxide.

Pistil. The female or seed-bearing organ of a plant, generally with three recognizable parts: the ovary, style (often modified), and the stigma. May consist of one or several fused carpels.

Plicate. Folded or plaited, with prominent ribs.

Pollen. The grains or microspores borne in the anther and possessing the ability to fertilize an ovule.

Pollinate. To apply pollen to the stigma.

Pollinium, pollinia. A specialized mass or masses of pollen grains found in certain plant families, including the Orchidaceae.

Polymorphic. Having more than one form; variable in structure.

Porrect. Extended outward and forward.

Puberulent. Covered with very short hairs.

Pubescent. Hairy, with soft hairs.

Quadrate. Four-sided.

Raceme. A simple inflorescence of pedicellate flowers borne on an elongated axis.

Rachis. The axis of an inflorescence.

Ranks. An arrangement of flowers into rows along an axis, especially in orchids, as in *Spiranthes.*

Reaction. The condition and degree of acidity or alkalinity of soils.

Receptacle. The end of the floral stem in which the floral organs are inserted.

Recurved. Curved downward or backward.

Reflexed. Bent abruptly downward.

Regular. Uniform in structure; radially symmetrical.

Remote. Separated by intervals greater than usual.

Reniform. Kidney-shaped.

Repent. Creeping, prostrate.

Resupinate. Having the lip lowermost in relation to the position of the flower, owing to a twisting of the pedicel which brings the lip to that position; the normal lip position in most orchids.

Reticulate. Having a network of veins, etc.

Rhizome. An underground, creeping stem bearing numerous adventitious roots at the nodes, and terminating each season with an erect, leafy stem.

Ribbed. Having prominent veins.

Rosette. A cluster of leaves, usually basal, and consisting of a spiral of leaves borne on a much-shortened stem—appearing as a circular cluster.

Rostellum. Literally, "a little beak"; in orchids, a slender growth forward from the upper edge of the stigma.

Saccate. Pouch-shaped; sac-shaped.

Saprophyte. A plant deriving its nourishment mainly from the digestion directly or indirectly of dead organic matter. Flowering plant saprophytes usually lack chlorophyll.

Scape. A peduncle rising from the ground and devoid of leaves, or with bracts only.

Scapose. Resembling a scape.

Scarious. Dry and membranous in texture, generally translucent.

Secund. Borne along one side of an axis.

Segment. Any division or part of an organ.

Sepal. One division of a calyx.

Serrate. Having sawlike teeth.

Sessile. Attached without a stalk.

Sheath. A tubular covering; *sheathing*, forming such a covering, to clasp and surround all or part of an organ or segment.

Simple. Having one piece; not divided into several parts.

Sinus. A space, cleft, or recess between two lobes.

Species. A discrete breeding population of similarly constructed plants, distinguishable from other such discrete breeding populations.

Spicate. Spikelike.

Spike. An elongate inflorescence axis with attached and essentially sessile flowers.

Spur. A hollow, saclike, or tubular extension of an organ; in orchids, the base of the lip, usually bearing nectar in its distal end.

Stalk. A supporting, stemlike organ.

Stamen. The pollen-bearing organ.

Staminode. The sterile stamen in orchids.

Stigma. The tissue of a pistil which receives and collects the pollen.

Stolon. A basal trailing branch or runner.

Stoloniferous. Bearing stolons.

Striate. Striped with fine longitudinal lines.

Style. The narrow portion of a pistil, connecting the ovary with the stigma.

Subacid. Having a hydrogen-ion concentration of 5.5–6.0; said of certain slightly acid soils.

Subalkaline. Having a hydrogen-ion concentration of 8.0–8.5; said of certain soils of moderate alkalinity.

Swale. A small, grassy or sedgy, open, marshy spot which becomes dry seasonally.

Swamp. Any wooded, wet area, with water at or near the surface most of the year, but with slow drainage usually preventing stagnation; the soils may or may not be heavily organic. Trees and shrubs dominate the swamp, but many herbaceous species grow here as well.

Symbiosis. Individuals of two different species living together for mutual benefit.

Taxonomy. The science of classification of organisms.

Translucent. Allowing light to pass through, but not transparent.

Truncate. Ending abruptly; cut off.

Tuber. A thickened, subterranean, branch-bearing buds.

Tubercle. A small tuber; or, an enlarged process, body, or appendage on an organ, as the raised appendage on the upper lip surface of *Platanthera flava* var. *herbiola.*

Tuberoid. Resembling a tuber, as some fleshy roots.

Undulate. Having a wavy margin.

Variety. A structural variant within a species; a recognizable unit of a population below the rank of species having minor differences in character which separate it from the typical members of that species.

Vegetative. Any feature of a plant not concerned with sexual reproduction.

Vein. A strand of vascular tissue within a plant structure.

Ventral. Pertaining to the under or inner side of an organ.

Vernal. Pertaining to the spring season.

Verticillate. Whorled.

Viscid. Glutinous; sticky.

Whorl. A group of organs, e.g., leaves, arranged spokelike around a given point on an axis.

INDEX OF LATIN NAMES

INDEX OF COMMON NAMES

Backispiece: Eastern Prairie Fringed-orchid (*Platanthera leucophaea*), possibly our region's most severely endangered orchid, blooming on a moist prairie.